MARTIAL

II

LCL 95

MARTIAL

EPIGRAMS

WITH AN ENGLISH TRANSLATION BY

D. R. SHACKLETON BAILEY

VOLUME II

HARVARD UNIVERSITY PRESS
CAMBRIDGE, MASSACHUSETTS
LONDON, ENGLAND

First published 1993
Reprinted 2006

Library of Congress Catalog Card Number 92-8234
CIP data available from the Library of Congress

ISBN 0-674-99556-2

Printed on acid-free paper and bound by
Edwards Brothers, Ann Arbor, Michigan

CONTENTS

EPIGRAMS
BOOKS VI–X

LIBER VI

1

Sextus mittitur hic tibi libellus,
in primis mihi care Martialis:
quem si terseris aure diligenti,
audebit minus anxius tremensque
5   magnas Caesaris in manus venire.

2

Lusus erat sacrae conubia fallere taedae,
    lusus et immeritos execuisse mares.
utraque tu prohibes, Caesar, populisque futuris
    succurris, nasci quos sine fraude iubes.
5 nec spado iam nec moechus erit te praeside quisquam
    at prius — o mores! — et spado moechus erat.

3

Nascere Dardanio promissum nomen Iulo,
    vera deum suboles; nascere, magne puer,

---

[a] Cf. 5.75n and 2.60n.
[b] An echo of Virg. *Aen.* 1.288 *Iulius, a magno demissum*

2

BOOK VI

1

This, my sixth little book, is sent to you, Martialis, dear to me above all men. If you tidy it with attentive ear, it will dare with less fear and trembling to come into Caesar's mighty hands.

2

It used to be a game to betray the sacred marriage torch and a game to castrate innocent males. You forbid both,[a] Caesar, and come to the aid of future generations; for by your order their birth is made safe. Under your rule no man shall be either eunuch or adulterer. Formerly (alas for our morals!) even a eunuch was an adulterer.

3

Be born, name promised to Dardanian Julus,[b] true child of gods; be born, great boy, so that ages hence

nomen Iulo, but the significance of *nomen* is not clear. Had Domitian declared an intention to call the expected child Julius or Julia (*SB*[3])?

cui pater aeternas post saecula tradat habenas,
quique regas orbem cum seniore senex.
5 ipsa tibi niveo trahet aurea pollice fila
et totam Phrixi Iulia nebit ovem.

4

Censor maxime principumque princeps,
cum tot iam tibi debeat triumphos,
tot nascentia templa, tot renata,
tot spectacula, tot deos, tot urbes,
5   plus debet tibi Roma quod pudica est.

5

Rustica mercatus multis sum praedia nummis:
mutua des centum, Caeciliane, rogo.
nil mihi respondes? tacitum te dicere credo
'non reddes.' ideo, Caeciliane, rogo.

6

Comoedi tres sunt, sed amat tua Paula, Luperce,
quattuor: et κωφὸν Paula πρόσωπον amat.

your father may hand you the everlasting reins and you may rule the world, an old man with an older. Julia[a] herself with snowy finger will draw golden threads for you and spin Phrixus' entire sheep.

4

Greatest of censors, prince of princes, though Rome already owes you so many triumphs, so many temples coming to birth, so many reborn, so many spectacles, so many gods, so many cities, she owes you more because she is chaste.

5

I have bought a country property for a large sum and I ask you, Caecilianus, to lend me a hundred thousand. Don't you answer me? I think you say to yourself: "You won't pay it back." That is why I ask, Caecilianus.[b]

6

There are three actors in a comedy, but your Paula, Lupercus, loves four. Paula loves a *muta persona*[c] too.

[a] Niece of Domitian, deified after her death. She shall watch over the destiny of Domitian's expected child instead of the Fates, and spin his life's threads in gold.

[b] I.e. if I could raise enough money to repay a loan, I should not be asking for one.

[c] A "walker-on."

7

Iulia lex populis ex quo, Faustine, renata est
    atque intrare domos iussa Pudicitia est,
aut minus aut certe non plus tricesima lux est,
    et nubit decimo iam Telesilla viro.
5 quae nubit totiens, non nubit: adultera lege est.
    offendor moecha simpliciore minus.

8

Praetores duo, quattuor tribuni,
septem causidici, decem poetae
cuiusdam modo nuptias petebant
a quodam sene. non moratus ille
5 praeconi dedit Eulogo puellam.
dic, numquid fatue, Severe, fecit?

9

In Pompeiano dormis, Laevine, theatro:
    et quereris si te suscitat Oceanus?

10

Pauca Iovem nuper cum milia forte rogarem,
    'ille dabit' dixit 'qui mihi templa dedit.'
templa quidem dedit ille Iovi, sed milia nobis
    nulla dedit: pudet, ah, pauca rogasse Iovem.

7

It is less than thirty days or certainly not more since the Julian law was reborn for the peoples and Chastity bidden enter our homes; and Telesilla is already marrying her tenth husband. A woman who marries that often doesn't marry; she is a legalized adulteress. I am less put off by a more honest slut.

8

Two praetors, four tribunes, seven barristers, and ten poets asked a certain old man for the hand of a certain lady. He without hesitation gave the girl to Eulogus the auctioneer.[a] Say, Severus, did he act foolishly?

9

Laevinus, you sleep in Pompey's theater; and do you complain if Oceanus rouses you?[b]

10

When lately I happened to be praying to Jupiter for a few thousand, he said: "*He* will give it who gave me temples." Temples indeed he gave to Jupiter, but no thousands did he give me. I am ashamed, ah

[a] A lucrative calling (cf. 5.56.11), but low in the social scale.
[b] See second note to 5.23. "Rouses" is intentionally ambiguous.

5   at quam non tetricus, quam nulla nubilus ira,
      quam placido nostras legerat ore preces!
talis supplicibus tribuit diademata Dacis
      et Capitolinas itque reditque vias.
dic, precor, o nostri dic conscia virgo Tonantis,
10   si negat hoc vultu, quo solet ergo dare?
sic ego: sic breviter posita mihi Gorgone Pallas:
      'quae nondum data sunt, stulte, negata putas?'

11

Quod non sit Pylades hoc tempore, non sit Orestes
      miraris? Pylades, Marce, bibebat idem,
nec melior panis turdusve dabatur Orestae,
      sed par atque eadem cena duobus erat.
5   tu Lucrina voras, me pascit aquosa peloris:
      non minus ingenua est et mihi, Marce, gula.
te Cadmea Tyros, me pinguis Gallia vestit:
      vis te purpureum, Marce, sagatus amem?
ut praestem Pyladen, aliquis mihi praestet Oresten.
10   hoc non fit verbis, Marce: ut ameris, ama.

me, to have asked Jupiter[a] for so few. But how far from stern, how unclouded by any touch of anger, with how benign a countenance did he read my petition! So he looks when he bestows diadems on suppliant Dacians and goes and returns along the road to the Capitol![b] Say, I beg, oh say, Maiden, our Thunderer's confidante, if that is how he looks when he says no, how does he look when he says yes? So said I, and so briefly to me said Pallas, laying aside her Gorgon: "You silly man, what has not yet been granted, do you think it has been refused?"

11

Do you wonder that there is no Pylades today, no Orestes? Pylades, Marcus, drank the same wine, nor was Orestes given better bread or thrush; dinner was equal and identical for the pair. You devour Lucrine oysters, I am fed with watery mussels;[c] my palate, Marcus, is as gentlemanly as yours. Cadmean Tyre clothes you, greasy Gaul clothes me; wearing soldiers' wool, am I to love you in your purple? If I am to play Pylades, somebody must play Orestes to me. Words don't do it, Marcus. To be loved, love.

[a] Domitian. M. regrets having asked so little of one so great: cf. 11.68.

[b] In triumph.

[c] Peloris, supposed to be a sort of large mussel (called from Cape Pelorus in northeast Sicily).

9

12

Iurat capillos esse, quos emit, suos
Fabulla: †numquid, Paule, peierat†?

13

Quis te Phidiaco formatam, Iulia, caelo,
    vel quis Palladiae non putet artis opus?
candida non tacita respondet imagine lygdos
    et placido fulget vivus in ore decor.
5 ludit Acidalio, sed non manus aspera, nodo,
    quem rapuit collo, parve Cupido, tuo.
ut Martis revocetur amor summique Tonantis,
    a te Iuno petat ceston et ipsa Venus.

14

Versus scribere posse te disertos
affirmas, Laberi: quid ergo non vis?
versus scribere qui potest disertos,
non scribat, Laberi, virum putabo.

12.2 Paule] *fort. interpolatum* (*Heraeus*) 13.7 reuocetur
γ : renoue- β

12

Fabulla swears that the hair she buys is her own. Is that perjury, Paulus?

13

Julia, who would not think you molded by Phidias' chisel or a work of Pallas' artistry? The white lygdus[a] matches[b] with a speaking likeness, and living beauty shines in your face. Your hand plays, but not roughly, with the Acidalian knot[c] that it snatched from little Cupid's neck. To win back Mars' love and the supreme Thunderer's,[d] let Juno and Venus herself ask you for the girdle.

14

You declare you can write good verses, Laberius. Why won't you then? Let somebody capable of writing good verses not write them, Laberius, and I'll think him a stout fellow.[e]

[a] Parian marble from the Cyclades.

[b] *respondet* = "corresponds to the original"; usually understood as "answers" (the questions in vv. 1–2; but these are rhetorical, not calling for any reply).

[c] The girdle (*cestus*) of Venus, which inspired love.

[d] In the *Iliad* (14.214ff) Hera (Juno) borrows Aphrodite's (Venus') girdle before consorting with Zeus (Jupiter). For Mars' vagaries cf. 6.21.5.

[e] I.e. I don't believe such a persons exists (*SB*[3]).

15

Dum Phaethontea formica vagatur in umbra,
    implicuit tenuem sucina gutta feram.
sic modo quae fuerat vita contempta manente,
    funeribus facta est nunc pretiosa suis.

16

Tu qui falce viros terres et pene cinaedos,
    iugera sepositi pauca tuere soli.
sic tua non intrent vetuli pomaria fures,
    sed puer aut longis pulchra puella comis.

17

Cinnam, Cinname, te iubes vocari.
non est hic, rogo, Cinna, barbarismus?
tu si Furius ante dictus esses,
Fur ista ratione dicereris.

18

Sancta Salonini terris requiescit Hiberis,
    qua melior Stygias non videt umbra domos.
sed lugere nefas: nam qui te, Prisce, reliquit,
    vivit qua voluit vivere parte magis.

16.1   falce ... pene *Gronovius* (*cf. SB*^{2}) : p- ... f-
αβγ   16.2 soli α : loci βγ

---

[a] I.e. in the shade of a poplar.
[b] Priapus.

15

As an ant was wandering in Phaethontic shade,[a] a drop of amber enfolded the tiny creature. So she that was despised but lately while life remained has now been made precious by her death.

16

You[b] that terrify men with your sickle and queens with your cock, protect these few acres of secluded soil. So may no elderly thieves enter your orchard, but a boy or a lovely long-tressed girl.

17

Cinnamus,[c] you bid us call you Cinna. I ask you, Cinna, is that not a barbarism? By that token, if your name had formerly been Furius, it would now be Fur.[d]

18

In Iberian ground the hallowed shade of Saloninus rests, than which none better sees the Stygian halls. But it is a sin to mourn. He has left you behind, Priscus, and so he lives with that part of him with which he more wished to live.[e]

[c] A freedman who wished to take a Roman name in place of his Greek one.
[d] Thief.
[e] In his alter ego. M. may be thinking of Hor. *Od.* 2.17.5.

19

Non de vi neque caede nec veneno,
sed lis est mihi de tribus capellis:
vicini queror has abesse furto.
hoc iudex sibi postulat probari:
5   tu Carrhas Mithridaticumque bellum
et periuria Punici furoris
et Sullas Mariosque Muciosque
magna voce sonas manuque tota.
iam dic, Postume, de tribus capellis.

20

Mutua te centum sestertia, Phoebe, rogavi,
   cum mihi dixisses 'exigis ergo nihil?'
inquiris, dubitas, cunctaris meque diebus
   teque decem crucias: iam rogo, Phoebe, nega.

19.5 Carrhas *L. Müller* : cannas Tβγ

19

I have gone to law, not about assault or killing with a weapon or poisoning, but about three nanny goats. I claim that they are missing because a neighbor has stolen them. The judge requires proof. In loud tones, using your whole stock of gestures,[a] you boom about Carrhae and the Mithridatic War and the perjuries of Punic rage and Sullas and Mariuses and Muciuses.[b] Postumus, it's time you got to my three goats.[c]

20

Phoebus, I asked you for a loan of a hundred thousand sesterces after you had said to me: "Is there nothing you require then?" You question, hesitate, procrastinate, keep me and yourself on tenterhooks for ten days. Now please, Phoebus, say no.

[a] Or perhaps "stretching out your hand as far as it will go"; cf. Quint. 11.3.118.

[b] Not, surely, the legendary Mucius Scaevola (cf. 1.21, etc.) but Q. Mucius Scaevola (the Pontifex), consul in 95 and a celebrated jurist, who fell victim to the Marians in 82. But he seems to be thrown in mainly for the sake of assonance.

[c] Copied from a Greek epigram of the age of Nero: *Anth. Pal.* 11.141.

21

Perpetuam Stellae dum iungit Ianthida vati
    laeta Venus, dixit 'plus dare non potui.'
haec coram domina; sed nequius illud in aurem:
    'tu ne quid pecces, exitiose, vide.
5 saepe ego lascivum Martem furibunda cecidi,
    legitimos esset cum vagus ante toros,
sed postquam meus est, nulla me paelice laesit:
    tam frugi Iuno vellet habere virum.'
dixit et arcano percussit pectora loro.
10   plaga iuvat: sed tu iam, dea, parce tuo.

22

    Quod nubis, Proculina, concubino
    et, moechum modo, nunc facis maritum,
    ne lex Iulia te notare possit:
    non nubis, Proculina, sed fateris.

23

    Stare iubes semper nostrum tibi, Lesbia, penem:
        crede mihi, non est mentula quod digitus.
    tu licet et manibus blandis et vocibus instes,
        te contra facies imperiosa tua est.

21.3 aurem βγ : aure T   21.4 luxuriose *Heinsius*
21.8 uirum β : iouem γ   21.10 parce (ς) tuo *Heinsius* :
pare deo γ : caede duos β   23.4 te contra *Schneidewin* :
e c- T : c- te βγ

21

As joyous Venus was uniting Ianthis for ever to Stella the poet, she said: "I could not give you more." Thus before the lady, but a naughtier word in his ear: "See you don't misbehave, you villain(?). I often beat wanton Mars in a rage when he played the gadabout before we were formally married. But since he has been mine, he has never betrayed me with another woman. Juno would have wished to have so well-conducted a husband."[a] She spoke and struck his breast with a secret thong. He is the better for the blow. But now, goddess, spare your servant.

22

You are marrying your lover, Proculina, and making the adulterer of yesterday your husband so that the Julian law can't put a mark against you. That's not a marriage, Proculina, it's a confession.

23

You are always telling my cock to stand for you, Lesbia. Believe me, a cock is not a finger. For all your urging with seductive hands and words, your face[b] is in authority against you.

[a] Izaac remarks that Venus' marriage to Mars seems to be M.'s contribution to mythology.
[b] I.e. your ugliness; cf. 9.37.10.

24

Nil lascivius est Carisiano:
Saturnalibus ambulat togatus.

25

Marcelline, boni suboles sincera parentis,
　　horrida Parrhasio quem tegit ursa iugo,
ille vetus pro te patriusque quid optet amicus
　　accipe et haec memori pectore vota tene:
5　cauta sit ut virtus, nec te temerarius ardor
　　in medios enses saevaque tela ferat.
bella velint Martemque ferum rationis egentes;
　　tu potes et patris miles et esse ducis.

26

Periclitatur capite Sotades noster.
reum putatis esse Sotaden? non est.
arrigere desît posse Sotades: lingit.

24.1 Carisiano] *vide* SB^3　　　25.8 patris . . . ducis Tγ :
patriae . . . d- β : patriae . . . patris SB^3

24

Carisianus[a] is the drollest of beings: he walks about in a gown during the Saturnalia.[b]

25

Marcellinus, true son of a good father, whom the shivering Bear covers with her Parrhasian[c] wagon, hear what an old friend and your father's friend wishes for you, and keep these prayers in a mindful heart: that your courage be cautious and rash ardor not carry you into the thick of swords and cruel spears. Let crazy folk crave war and savage Mars. You can be both your father's soldier and your Leader's.[d]

26

Our friend Sotades' head is in danger.[e] You think Sotades is on trial? Not so. Sotades can no longer erect: he licks.

[a] Cf. 11.88.2. Charis- and Caris- have about equal support in the manuscripts, for what little that is worth on such a point, but see SB^3.

[b] He wears formal clothes when informal are in order.

[c] I.e. Arcadian. Callisto of that region was changed into a bear and became the constellation Ursa Major.

[d] Or "your country's soldier and your father's"; see critical note.

[e] Play on words. The phrase would normally mean "is facing a capital charge."

27

Bis vicine Nepos — nam tu quoque proxima Florae
  incolis et veteres tu quoque Ficelias —
est tibi, quae patria signatur imagine vultus,
  testis maternae nata pudicitiae.
5 tu tamen annoso nimium ne parce Falerno,
  et potius plenos aere relinque cados.
sit pia, sit locuples, sed potet filia mustum:
  amphora cum domina nunc nova fiet anus.
Caecuba non solos vindemia nutriat orbos:
10   possunt et patres vivere, crede mihi.

28

    Libertus Melioris ille notus,
    tota qui cecidit dolente Roma,
    cari deliciae breves patroni,
    hoc sub marmore Glaucias humatus
  5 iuncto Flaminiae iacet sepulchro:
    castus moribus, integer pudore,
    velox ingenio, decore felix.
    bis senis modo messibus peractis
    vix unum puer applicabat annum.
  10 qui fles talia, nil fleas, viator.

28.9 adplicarat *Postgate*

27

Nepos,[a] my neighbor twice over (for you too live
close to Flora[b] and you too near old Ficeliae[c]), you
have a daughter whose face is stamped with her
father's likeness, witness to her mother's virtue.
However, don't be too sparing of your aged Faler-
nian; rather leave behind you jars full of cash. Let
your girl be dutiful, let her be rich, but let her drink
the new wine;[d] the flagon that is new now will grow
old with its mistress. Let not Caecuban vintage
nourish only the childless. Fathers too can enjoy
life, take my word.

28

Melior's well-known freedman, at whose passing all
Rome sorrowed, brief darling of his dear patron,
Glaucias lies buried beneath this marble sepulchre
beside the Flaminian Way; pure in manners, un-
blemished in modesty, nimble of wit, fortunate in
good looks. The boy was scarce adding a single year
to twelve harvests just completed. Passer-by who
weep for such a tale, may you have nothing to weep
for.

[a] Cf. 13.124, which suggests that he was a well-known
connoisseur of wine.

[b] The temple of Flora on the Quirinal, not far from the
Capitolium Vetus: cf. 5.22.4.

[c] Close to M.'s villa near Nomentum.

[d] When she grows up; see *SB* [3].

29

Non de plebe domus nec avarae verna catastae,
    sed domini sancto dignus amore puer,
munera cum posset nondum sentire patroni,
    Glaucia libertus iam Melioris erat.
5 moribus hoc formaeque datum: quis blandior illo,
    aut quis Apollineo pulchrior ore fuit?
immodicis brevis est aetas et rara senectus.
    quidquid ames, cupias non placuisse nimis.

30

Sex sestertia si statim dedisses,
cum dixti mihi 'sume, tolle, dono',
deberem tibi, Paete, pro ducentis.
at nunc cum dederis diu moratus,
5 post septem, puto, vel novem Kalendas,
vis dicam tibi veriora veris?
sex sestertia, Paete, perdidisti.

31

Uxorem, Charideme, tuam scis ipse sinisque
    a medico futui. vis sine febre mori?

30.4 moratus γ : roga- β   31.2 mori *interrog. feci*

29

A boy, not of the common household run, no slave-mart's nursling, but worthy of his master's pure affection, Glaucia was already Melior's freedman before he could appreciate his patron's bounty. This was accorded to his manners and person. Who more winsome than he, who fairer with face like Apollo's? For the unduly blessed life is brief and old age comes rarely. Whatever you love, pray that it not please too much.

30

If you had given six thousand sesterces at once when you told me "take it, pocket it, it's yours," I should feel I owed you for two hundred thousand, Paetus. But as it is, you have made the gift after a long delay, after seven, or is it nine, Kalends. Shall I tell you truer than truth? Paetus, you have wasted six thousand sesterces.

31

You yourself know, Charidemus, that your wife is fucked by your doctor, and you permit it. Do you want to die without a fever?[a]

a I.e. by poison.

32

Cum dubitaret adhuc belli civilis Enyo
  forsitan et posset vincere mollis Otho,
damnavit multo staturum sanguine Martem
  et fodit certa pectora tota manu.
5 sit Cato, dum vivit, sane vel Caesare maior:
  dum moritur, numquid maior Othone fuit?

33

Nil miserabilius, Matho, pedicone Sabello
  vidisti, quo nil laetius ante fuit.
furta, fugae, mortes servorum, incendia, luctus
  affligunt hominem; iam miser et futuit.

34

Basia da nobis, Diadumene, pressa. 'quot' inquis?
  Oceani fluctus me numerare iubes
et maris Aegaei sparsas per litora conchas
  et quae Cecropio monte vagantur apes
5 quaeque sonant pleno vocesque manusque theatro,
  cum populus subiti Caesaris ora videt.

32.4 tota T : nuda $\beta\gamma$

32

Although the goddess of civil warfare was still in doubt, and soft Otho had perhaps still a chance of winning, he renounced fighting that would have cost much blood[a] and with sure hand pierced right through his breast. By all means let Cato in his life be greater than Caesar himself; in his death was he greater than Otho?[b]

33

You have never seen anything more pitiable, Matho, than sodomite Sabellus, once the happiest of mankind. Thefts, flights, deaths of slaves, fires, bereavements afflict him. Poor soul, he has even taken to fornicating.

34

Give me kisses, Diadumenus, tight-pressed. "How many?" you say. You bid me count the ocean waves, the shells scattered on the beaches of the Aegean sea, and the bees that wander over the Cecropian mountain,[c] and the voices and hands that sound in the crowded theater when the people suddenly see Caesar's face. I don't want the number that Lesbia

[a] See his dying speech in Plut. *Otho* 15, Tac. *Hist.* 2.47.
[b] Cato died when his cause was clearly lost: not so Otho, after his defeat by Vitellius at Bedriacum, A.D. 69.
[c] Hymettus.

nolo quot arguto dedit exorata Catullo
    Lesbia: pauca cupit qui numerare potest.

35

Septem clepsydras magna tibi voce petenti
    arbiter invitus, Caeciliane, dedit.
at tu multa diu dicis vitreisque tepentem
    ampullis potas semisupinus aquam.
5   ut tandem saties vocemque sitimque, rogamus
    iam de clepsydra, Caeciliane, bibas.

36

Mentula tam magna est, tantus tibi, Papyle, nasus,
    ut possis, quotiens arrigis, olfacere.

37

Secti podicis usque ad umbilicum
nullas reliquias habet Charinus,
et prurit tamen usque ad umbilicum.
o quanta scabie miser laborat!
5   culum non habet, est tamen cinaedus.

36.1 tantus γ : qua- αβ

gave in answer to clear-voiced Catullus' prayer.[a] He wants but few who can count them.

35

Seven water clocks[b] you loudly demanded, and the judge reluctantly granted them, Caecilianus. You for your part speak much and long, and drink warm water from glass flagons with your head thrown back. To satisfy at last your voice and your thirst, we request you, Caecilianus, to start drinking from the water clock.

36

So large is your cock, Papylus, and so long your nose, that you can sniff it whenever you erect.

37

Charinus' anus is cut right up to his navel; nothing left. And yet he itches up to his navel. Poor devil, how his scabies plagues him! He doesn't have a ring, yet he's a queen.

[a] Cf. Catull. 5 and 7. So (not "tuneful") *arguti Tibulli* in 8.73.6. But in 1.1.3 "witty" or "pointed" comes closer.
[b] The length of speeches was regulated by the dropping of water from *clepsydrae*, shaped like hourglasses.

38

Aspicis ut parvus nec adhuc trieteride plena
    Regulus auditum laudet et ipse patrem,
maternosque sinus viso genitore relinquat
    et patrias laudes sentiat esse suas?
5   iam clamor centumque viri densumque corona
    vulgus et infanti Iulia tecta placent.
acris equi suboles magno sic pulvere gaudet,
    sic vitulus molli proelia fronte cupit.
di, servate, precor, matri sua vota patrique,
10   audiat ut natum Regulus, illa duos.

39

Pater ex Marulla, Cinna, factus es septem
non liberorum: namque nec tuus quisquam
nec est amici filiusve vicini,
    sed in grabatis tegetibusque concepti
5   materna produnt capitibus suis furta.
hic qui retorto crine Maurus incedit
subolem fatetur esse se coci Santrae.
at ille sima nare, turgidis labris
    ipsa est imago Pannychi palaestritae.
10   pistoris esse tertium quis ignorat,
    quicumque lippum novit et videt Damam?

39.7 coci Santrae *Scriverius* : cogis antr(a)e $\beta\gamma$

38

Do you see how little Regulus, not yet three years
old, harkens to his father and joins in the applause?
How he leaves his mother's lap when he sees his sire
and feels his father's glory as his own? Already the
hubbub and the Hundred Men[a] and the dense encir-
cling crowd and the Julian Hall please the infant.
So the offspring of a keen horse rejoices in a cloud of
dust, so a soft-browed calf craves battle. Ye gods, I
pray, grant his mother's prayer and his father's; let
Regulus hear his son, and let her hear them both.[b]

39

By Marulla, Cinna, you have become the father of
seven — not children, for not one of them is yours,
nor yet a friend's, or a neighbor's son; but conceived
on truckle beds and mats, they reveal their mother's
escapades by their heads. This one, that stalks like
a Moor with curly hair, confesses himself the offspr-
ing of Santra the cook. But that one, with flat nos-
trils and blubber lips, is the very image of Pan-
nychus the wrestling coach. Who but knows that
the third is the baker's, if he knows and sees blear-
eyed Dama? The fourth, with catamite's brow and

[a] The court of the *centumviri*, which settled various civil
cases.

[b] The prayer was not granted; the boy died young: Pliny
Ep. 2.4.

quartus cinaeda fronte, candido vultu
ex concubino natus est tibi Lygdo:
percide, si vis, filium: nefas non est.
15 hunc vero acuto capite et auribus longis,
quae sic moventur ut solent asellorum,
quis morionis filium negat Cyrtae?
duae sorores, illa nigra et haec rufa,
Croti choraulae vilicique sunt Carpi.
20 iam Niobidarum grex tibi foret plenus
si spado Coresus Dindymusque non esset.

40

Femina praeferri potuit tibi nulla, Lycori:
    praeferri Glycerae femina nulla potest.
haec erit hoc quod tu: tu non potes esse quod haec est.
    tempora quid faciunt! hanc volo, te volui.

41

Qui recitat lana fauces et colla revinctus,
    hic se posse loqui, posse tacere negat.

39.20 iam niobidarum β : iamni ubida pruit γ : iamque
hybridarum ς

pale complexion, was born to you from your favorite Lygdus. Sodomize your son, if you like; no sin in that. Ah, but this one with the pointed head and long ears that move like donkeys' are wont to do, who denies that he is the son of Cyrta the natural?[a] Two sisters, one black, the other red, are Crotus the flautist's and Carpus the bailiff's. You would now have a troop as numerous as Niobe's, if Coresus and Dindymus had not been eunuchs.[b]

40

No woman *could* be preferred to you, Lycoris; no woman *can* be preferred to Glycera. She will be what you are. You cannot be what she is. Such is the power of time. I want her, I wanted you.

41

A man who recites with his throat and neck wrapped in wool tells us that he can't speak and can't hold his tongue.

[a] Cretins were kept domestically for amusement.
[b] According to one version, Niobe had nine sons and nine daughters; M. converts this, seemingly by inadvertence, into nine children of both sexes.

42

Etrusci nisi thermulis lavaris,
illotus morieris, Oppiane.
nullae sic tibi blandientur undae,
non fontes Aponi rudes puellis,
5   non mollis Sinuessa fervidique
fluctus Passeris aut superbus Anxur,
non Phoebi vada principesque Baiae.
nusquam tam nitidum vacat serenum:
lux ipsa est ibi longior, diesque
10   nullo tardius a loco recedit.
illic Taygeti virent metalla
et certant vario decore saxa
quae Phryx et Libys altius cecidit,
siccos pinguis onyx anhelat aestus
15   et flamma tenui calent ophitae.
ritus si placeant tibi Laconum,
contentus potes arido vapore
cruda Virgine Marciave mergi;
quae tam candida, tam serena lucet
20   ut nullas ibi suspiceris undas
et credas vacuam nitere lygdon.
non attendis et aure me supina
iam dudum quasi neglegenter audis.
illotus morieris, Oppiane.

42.8 uacat γ : micat β

---

[a] Why so is uncertain.

[b] The Aquae Passerianae in Etruria, where were also
the Aquae Apollinares, now Bagni di Vicarello.

42

If you don't bathe in the warm baths of Etruscus, you will die unbathed, Oppianus. No waters will so charm you, not the springs of Aponus by women untried,[a] nor soft Sinuessa and the hot waves of Passer[b] or proud Anxur, nor the shallows of Phoebus or Baiae the paramount. Nowhere is the clear, open sky so bright. The very light stays longer there, from no place does the day depart more slowly. There the quarries of Taygetus[c] are green and stones which the Phrygian and the Libyan[d] have deeply hewn contend in varied beauty. Sleek alabaster breathes arid heat and snakestones are warm with slender flame. If you like the Laconian style,[e] having satisfied yourself with dry warmth, you can plunge into native Virgin or Marcia,[f] so bright, so clear and transparent that you would not suspect any water there, you would think the shining lygdus[g] was empty.

You pay no attention and hear me this while with languid ear, seeming not to care. You will die unbathed, Oppianus.

[c] The green Laconian marble; cf. 9.75.9.

[d] Synnadic and Numidian marble, one streaked with purple, the other yellow.

[e] A hot-air bath followed by a cold plunge. There was a special apartment called *Laconicum*.

[f] Roman aqueducts.

[g] Cf. 6.13.3.

43

Dum tibi felices indulgent, Castrice, Baiae
    canaque sulphureis nympha natatur aquis,
me Nomentani confirmant otia ruris
    et casa iugeribus non onerosa suis.
5 hoc mihi Baiani soles mollisque Lucrinus,
    hoc mihi sunt vestrae, Castrice, divitiae.
quondam laudatas quocumque libebat ad undas
    currere nec longas pertimuisse vias;
nunc urbis vicina iuvant facilesque recessus,
10   et satis est pigro si licet esse mihi.

44

Festive credis te, Calliodore, iocari
    et solum multo permaduisse sale.
omnis irrides, dicteria dicis in omnis;
    sic te convivam posse placere putas.
5 at si ego non belle, sed vere dixero quiddam,
    nemo propinabit, Calliodore, tibi.

45

Lusistis, satis est: lascivi nubite cunni:
    permissa est vobis non nisi casta Venus.
haec est casta Venus? nubit Laetoria Lygdo:
    turpius uxor erit quam modo moecha fuit.

43.2 nympha $\beta\gamma$: unda T
44.3 omnis irrides SB^1 : -ibus adrides (arr-) T$\beta\gamma$
45.4 turpius $\beta\gamma$: -ior α

43

While happy Baiae indulges you, Castricus, and you swim in water white with sulphur springs, the ease of my Nomentan farm and a cottage not oppressive to its acres[a] restores me. This is for me the sunshine of Baiae and soft Lucrine, this is for me, Castricus, your rich men's resorts. Time was when I would gladly run anywhere I fancied to fashionable waters, had no fear of long journeys. But nowadays I like places near the city, retreats within easy reach; it's enough if I can be lazy.

44

You fancy yourself a capital jester, Calliodorus, unrivalled as a fount of abundant wit.[b] You laugh at everyone, crack your jokes against everybody; so you think to please as a dinner guest. But if *I* am to say something not pretty but true, nobody, Calliodorus, will pledge you.

45

You have had your fun, it's enough. Marry, you wanton cunts. Only virtuous love is permitted you.[c] Is this virtuous love? Laetoria marries Lygdus. As a wife she will be more disreputable than she lately was as an adulteress.

[a] Not too big to be supported by the land that went with it (7.31.8 et sim. notwithstanding).

[b] Lit. "that you only have been soaked in much salt."

[c] Cf. 6.4 and 7.

46

Vapulat assidue veneti quadriga flagello
    nec currit: magnam rem, Catiane, facit.

47

Nympha, mei Stellae quae fonte domestica puro
    laberis et domini gemmea tecta subis,
sive Numae coniunx Triviae te misit ab antris
    sive Camenarum de grege nona, veni:
5   exolvit votis hac se tibi virgine porca
        Marcus, furtivam quod bibit aeger aquam.
tu contenta meo iam crimine gaudia fontis
    da secura tui: sit mihi sana sitis.

48

Quod tam grande sophos clamat tibi turba togata,
    non tu, Pomponi, cena diserta tua est.

47.4 veni SB^1 : -s T$\beta\gamma$

---

[a] Lit. "a great thing." The words might also be taken to
mean "making a lot of money," but that does not seem
relevant. Birt was probably right to explain that the
horses are defecating.

46

The team of the Blues is lashed and lashed, but doesn't run. It's doing a big job, Catianus.[a]

47

Nymph, gliding with pure fount in my Stella's home and entering beneath its master's jewelled roof, whether Numa's wife[b] sent you from Trivia's grot or one of the nine Camenae,[c] come hither. With this virgin porker does Marcus absolve himself to you of his vow, because in sickness he furtively drank your water.[d] Be content with my offense[e] and grant me safe joy of your stream; let my thirst be healthy.

48

The gowned throng shouts a mighty "bravo" for you, but it's not you that are eloquent, Pomponius; it's your dinner.

[b] The Nymph Egeria, who was honored in Diana's grove at Aricia as well as in Rome.

[c] Originally Italian water deities, equated with the Muses. Lit. "ninth of the group of Camenae," but no particular Muse seems to be intended (cf. 8.3.9). Stella wrote elegy.

[d] M., contrary to doctor's orders (see 6.86), had drunk cold water from the spring, and had made a vow to the Nymph if the water did him no harm.

[e] I.e. with the sacrifice that resulted.

49

Non sum de fragili dolatus ulmo,
nec quae stat rigida supina vena
de ligno mihi quolibet columna est,
sed viva generata de cupressu:
  5 quae nec saecula centiens peracta
nec longae cariem timet senectae.
hanc tu, quisquis es o malus, timeto.
nam si vel minimos manu rapaci
hoc de palmite laeseris racemos,
10 nascetur, licet hoc velis negare,
inserta tibi ficus a cupressu.

50

Cum coleret puros pauper Telesinus amicos,
  errabat gelida sordidus in togula:
obscenos ex quo coepit curare cinaedos,
  argentum, mensas, praedia solus emit.
5 vis fieri dives, Bithynice? conscius esto.
  nil tibi vel minimum basia pura dabunt.

51

Quod convivaris sine me tam saepe, Luperce,
  inveni noceam qua ratione tibi.
irascor: licet usque voces mittasque rogesque —
  'quid facies?' inquis. quid faciam? veniam.

49

I[a] was not hewn from fragile elm, nor does the column that stands backward so stiff, my member, come from just any wood; it was born of living[b] cypress, which fears not the passage of a hundred generations nor the decay of protracted age. Villain, whoever you be, beware thereof. For if your rapacious hand harms the least cluster on this vine, the cypress will thrust into you (though you would fain refuse) and there will come to birth a fig.[c]

50

When Telesinus, a poor man, cultivated clean-living friends, he went about shabby in a chilly gown. But ever since he began to care for filthy queens, there's nobody like him for buying up plate, tables, estates. Do you wish to get rich, Bithynicus? Share a secret. Chaste kisses will get you nothing, or very little.[d]

51

Since you dine without me so often, Lupercus, I've found a way to spite you. I'm angry. You may invite me all you please, send, beg—"What will you do?" you say. What shall I do? I'll come.

[a] The epigram is on a statue of Priapus.
[b] I.e. cut down specially. Some take *viva* as = *vivaci*, long-lived, which suits the context but not the word.
[c] Cf. 1.65.
[d] As generally understood, "nothing, not a penny." But can *vel minimum = ne minimum quidem*?

39

52

Hoc iacet in tumulo raptus puerilibus annis
    Pantagathus, domini cura dolorque sui,
vix tangente vagos ferro resecare capillos
    doctus et hirsutas excoluisse genas.
5 sis licet, ut debes, tellus, placata levisque,
    artificis levior non potes esse manu.

53

Lotus nobiscum est, hilaris cenavit, et idem
    inventus mane est mortuus Andragoras.
tam subitae mortis causam, Faustine, requiris?
    in somnis medicum viderat Hermocraten.

54

Tantos et tantas si dicere Sextilianum,
    Aule, vetes, iunget vix tria verba miser.
'quid sibi vult?' inquis. dicam quid suspicer esse:
    tantos et tantas Sextilianus amat.

52.6 artifici *Heinsius*

52

In this tomb lies Pantagathus, snatched away in his boyhood years, his master's care and grief, skilled to cut straying locks and shave hairy cheeks with steel that barely touched them. Though you be kind and light, earth, as you should be, you cannot be lighter than the artist's hand.

53

Andragoras bathed with us, ate a cheerful dinner; the same man was found dead in the morning. Do you enquire the cause of so sudden a demise, Faustinus? In his dreams he had seen Doctor Hermocrates.[a]

54

Aulus, if you were to forbid Sextilianus to say "tantos" and "tantas," the poor fellow would hardly put three words together. "What does he mean by it?" you say. I'll tell you what I suspect. Sextilianus loves "tantos" and "tantas."[b]

[a] An expansion of *Anth. Pal.* 11.257.

[b] Masculine and feminine accusative plurals from *tantus*, "so big." "Sextilianus" ran the word to death. *Tantos* in 4 refers to catamites (cf. 2.48.5; 7.62.1; 11.43.4; 12.49.13). With *tantas* understand *mentulas*.

55

Quod semper casiaque cinnamoque
et nido niger alitis superbae
fragras plumbea Nicerotiana,
rides nos, Coracine, nil olentis:
5   malo quam bene olere nil olere.

56

Quod tibi crura rigent saetis et pectora villis,
   verba putas famae te, Charideme, dare?
extirpa, mihi crede, pilos de corpore toto
   teque pilare tuas testificare natis.
5   'quae ratio est?' inquis. scis multos dicere multa:
   fac pedicari te, Charideme, putent.

57

Mentiris fictos unguento, Phoebe, capillos
   et tegitur pictis sordida calva comis.
tonsorem capiti non est adhibere necesse:
   radere te melius spongea, Phoebe, potest.

55

Always smelling of Niceros' leaden boxes and blackened by cassia and cinnamon and the nest of the haughty bird,[a] you laugh at us, Coracinus, who smell of nothing. Rather than smell good I prefer not to smell at all.

56

Do you think you cheat gossip, Charidemus, because your shanks are stiff with bristles and your chest with hair? Be advised by me, extirpate the hairs from your whole body, take your oath that you depilate your buttocks. "What for?" you say. You know that many folk say many things. Make them think you are sodomized,[b] Charidemus.

57

You fabricate false hair with ointment, Phoebus, and your dirty[c] bald pate is covered with painted locks. No need to call in a barber for your head. A sponge can shave you better, Phoebus.

[a] Casia and cinnamon were said to found in the nest of the phoenix: Pliny *N.H.* 12.85.
[b] And not something worse.
[c] From the unguent.

58

Cernere Parrhasios dum te iuvat, Aule, triones
    comminus et Getici sidera ferre poli,
o quam paene tibi Stygias ego raptus ad undas
    Elysiae vidi nubila fusca plagae!
5 quamvis lassa tuos quaerebant lumina vultus
    atque erat in gelido plurimus ore Pudens.
si mihi lanificae ducunt non pulla sorores
    stamina nec surdos vox habet ista deos,
sospite me sospes Latias reveheris ad urbes
10   et referes pili praemia clarus eques.

59

Et dolet et queritur sibi non contingere frigus
    propter sescentas Baccara gausapinas,
optat et obscuras luces ventosque nivesque
    odit et hibernos, si tepuere, dies.
5 quid fecere mali nostrae tibi, saeve, lacernae,
    tollere de scapulis quas levis aura potest?
quanto simplicius, quanto est humanius illud,
    mense vel Augusto sumere gausapinas!

58.2 ferre γ : pigra β

58

While it is your pleasure, Aulus,[a] to gaze at the Parrhasian Bears from close at hand and to endure the lazy stars of a Getic sky, how nearly was I reft from you to the waters of Styx and beheld the dim mists of the Elysian plain! My eyes, though weary, sought your face, and Pudens' name was constantly on my cold lips. If the spinning sisters draw me not dark threads and this voice finds the gods not deaf, I shall live to see you return safely to the cities of Latium and you will bring back the rank of Chief Centurion,[b] a notable knight.

59

Baccara grieves and grumbles because he gets no cold weather; it's on account of his numberless frieze cloaks. He prays for fog, wind, and snow, and hates winter days if they are mild. What harm, cruel fellow, has my cloak done you that a light breeze can lift from my shoulder blades? How much more straightforward, how much kinder to wear your frieze cloaks even in August!

[a] Aulus Pudens was campaigning against the Dacians.
[b] As in 1.31.3, *pili* = *primi pili*.

60 (61)

Laudat, amat, cantat nostros mea Roma libellos,
  meque sinus omnes, me manus omnis habet.
ecce rubet quidam, pallet, stupet, oscitat, odit.
  hoc volo: nunc nobis carmina nostra placent.

61 (60)

Rem factam Pompullus habet, Faustine: legetur
  et nomen toto sparget in orbe suum.
'sic leve flavorum valeat genus Usiporum,
  quisquis et Ausonium non amat imperium.'
5 ingeniosa tamen Pompulli scripta feruntur:
  'sed famae non est hoc, mihi crede, satis:
quam multi tineas pascunt blattasque diserti,
  et redimunt soli carmina docta coci!
nescioquid plus est, quod donat saecula chartis:
10 victurus genium debet habere liber.'

62

Amisit pater unicum Salanus:
cessas munera mittere, Oppiane?
heu crudele nefas malaeque Parcae!
cuius vulturis hoc erit cadaver?

60

My Rome praises my little books, loves them, recites them; I am in every pocket, every hand. Look, somebody turns red, turns pale,[a] is dazed, yawns, is disgusted. This I want. Now my poems please me.

61

Pompullus has it made, Faustinus. He will be read and scatter his name all over the world. "So may the faithless race of the yellow-haired Usipi prosper, and whosoever loves not Ausonia's empire!"[b] And yet Pompullus' work is said to have talent. "But believe me, that is not enough to make him famous. How many good poets are food for moths and bookworms, and only cooks buy their accomplished verses! There is something more that gives centuries to paper. A book that is to live must have a Genius."[c]

62

Father Salanus has lost his only son. Send presents, Oppianus, what are you waiting for? Ah, cruel wrong, evil Fates! Which vulture shall have this carcase?

[a] With anger. Cf. Stat. *Theb.* 11.336.
[b] I.e. may they perish as the works of "Pompullus" will.
[c] Guardian spirit.

63

Scis te captari, scis hunc qui captat, avarum,
  et scis qui captat quid, Mariane, velit.
tu tamen hunc tabulis heredem, stulte, supremis
  scribis et esse tuo vis, furiose, loco.
5 'munera magna tamen misit.' sed misit in hamo;
  et piscatorem piscis amare potest?
hicine deflebit vero tua fata dolore?
  si cupis ut ploret, des, Mariane, nihil.

64

Cum sis nec rigida Fabiorum gente creatus
nec qualem Curio, dum prandia portat aranti,
hirsuto peperit deprensa sub ilice coniunx,
sed patris ad speculum tonsi matrisque togatae
5 filius et possit sponsam te sponsa vocare:
emendare meos, quos novit fama, libellos
et tibi permittis felicis carpere nugas —
has, inquam, nugas, quibus aurem advertere totam
non aspernantur proceres urbisque forique,
10 quas et perpetui dignantur scrinia Sili
et repetit totiens facundo Regulus ore,
quique videt propius magni certamina Circi
laudat Aventinae vicinus Sura Dianae,

63.6 et] sic ς : dic *SB*[1]   64.3 hirsuto *A. Ker* : -ta Tβγ
    deprensa T : rubicunda βγ   64.8 lotam *Heinsius*

48

63

You know you are being angled for, you know the angler is after money, and you know, Marianus, what that angler wants. Yet you write him heir in your last testament, you fool, and would have him step into your shoes, you imbecile. "However, he sent me valuable presents." But he sent them on a hook. And can the fish love the fisherman? Will *he* lament your death with genuine sorrow? If you want him to weep, Marianus, leave him nothing.

64

Although you were not born of the austere Fabian clan nor such a one as his wife bore to hirsute Curius under an oak tree, caught by surprise as she was carrying his lunch to him at the plough, but the son of a father who had his hair cut at a mirror and of a mother who wore the gown,[a] and although your bride to be could call you *her* bride to be, you allow yourself to correct my famous little books and to criticize my happy trifles — yes, these trifles to which the leading lights of city and Forum do not disdain to lend an attentive ear, which the bookcases of immortal Silius deem worthy and Regulus' eloquent lips so often repeat, which Sura, neighbor to Diana of the Aventine, he who sees the contests of the

[a] Cf. 2.39.2n.

ipse etiam tanto dominus sub pondere rerum
15 non dedignatur bis terque revolvere Caesar.
sed tibi plus mentis, tibi cor limante Minerva
acrius, et tenues finxerunt pectus Athenae.
ne valeam, si non multo sapit altius illud,
quod cum panticibus laxis et cum pede grandi
20 et rubro pulmone vetus nasisque timendum
omnia crudelis lanius per compita portat.
audes praeterea, quos nullus noverit, in me
scribere versiculos miseras et perdere chartas.
at si quid nostrae tibi bilis inusserit ardor,
25 vivet et haerebit totaque legetur in orbe,
stigmata nec vafra delebit Cinnamus arte.
sed miserere tui rabido nec perditus ore
fumantem vivi nasum temptaveris ursi.
sit placidus licet et lambat digitosque manusque,
30 si dolor et bilis, si iusta coegerit ira,
ursus erit: vacua dentes in pelle fatiges
et tacitam quaeras, quam possis rodere, carnem.

64.28 uiui nasum β : n- u- Tγ

great Circus from hard by,[a] commends, which even Lord Caesar himself with all his load of business does not scorn to unroll twice and again. But yours is a superior mind, your wits are sharpened by Minerva's file, and subtle Athens molded your intellect. Hang me if that old and malodorous organ, which along with loose guts and a big hoof and a red lung the cruel butcher carries through every crossroad, has not a far *higher* understanding.[b] Furthermore, you dare to write scraps of verse against me, which nobody will know of, and waste the wretched sheets. But if the heat of *my* anger put a brand on you, it will live and stick and be read all over the world, nor shall Cinnamus'[c] cunning skill delete the marks. But take pity on yourself and do not in your desperation tempt with rabid mouth the smoking snout of a live bear. Gentle he may be and lick your fingers and hands, but if hurt and bile and righteous wrath drive him, he will be a bear. Exhaust your fangs on an empty hide, and seek meat that cannot speak to gnaw.

[a] The Circus was in the hollow between the Aventine and Palatine hills.

[b] This passage contains untranslatable puns. *Cor* in v. 16 means intelligence, but *illud* (*cor*) in v. 18 is the heart of an ox (cf. 14.219). *Sapit altius* = "has a loftier wisdom" or "is more highly flavored," though *altus* in this sense (cf. "high") does not seem to occur elsewhere.

[c] A doctor; cf. 10.56.6.

65

'Hexametris epigramma facis' scio dicere Tuccam.
　　Tucca, solet fieri, denique, Tucca, licet.
'sed tamen hoc longum est.' solet hoc quoque, Tucca,
　　　　　　　　　　　　　　　　　　　licetque:
　　si breviora probas, disticha sola legas.
5　conveniat nobis ut fas epigrammata longa
　　sit transire tibi, scribere, Tucca, mihi.

66

　　Famae non nimium bonae puellam,
　　quales in media sedent Subura,
　　vendebat modo praeco Gellianus.
　　parvo cum pretio diu liceret,
5　dum puram cupit approbare cunctis,
　　attraxit prope se manu negantem
　　et bis terque quaterque basiavit.
　　quid profecerit osculo requiris?
　　sescentos modo qui dabat, negavit.

67

Cur tantum eunuchos habeat tua Caelia quaeris,
　　Pannyche? vult futui Caelia nec parere.

66.4 licerent *Gronovius*

65

I know Tucca says: "You make an epigram in hex-
ameters." Tucca, that is quite usual, in fine, Tucca,
it's allowed. "But this is a long one." This too,
Tucca, is usual and allowable. If you like shorter
ones, read only the couplets. Let us make a bargain:
it shall be your privilege to skip long epigrams and
mine, Tucca, to write them.

66

The other day Gellianus the auctioneer was selling
a girl of none too good a reputation, such a one as
those that sit in the middle of Subura. Wishing to
prove to all that she was clean, since for a long time
the bids were low, he drew her close to him against
her will and kissed her twice and thrice and again.
You ask what that kissing accomplished? Somebody
who was bidding six hundred sesterces withdrew.

67

Do you ask why your Caelia has only eunuchs, Pan-
nychus? Caelia wants to be fucked, but not to have
children.

68

Flete nefas vestrum, sed toto flete Lucrino,
    Naides, et luctus sentiat ipsa Thetis.
inter Baianas raptus puer occidit undas,
    Eutychos ille, tuum, Castrice, dulce latus.
5 hic tibi curarum socius blandumque levamen,
    hic amor, hic nostri vatis Alexis erat.
numquid te vitreis nudum lasciva sub undis
    vidit et Alcidae Nympha remisit Hylan?
an dea femineum iam neglegit Hermaphroditum
10   amplexu teneri sollicitata viri?
quidquid id est, subitae quaecumque est causa rapinæ
    sit, precor, et tellus mitis et unda tibi.

69

Non miror quod potat aquam tua Bassa, Catulle:
    miror quod Bassae filia potat aquam.

70

Sexagesima, Marcinae, messis
acta est et, puto, iam secunda Cottae
nec se taedia lectuli calentis
expertum meminit die vel uno.

69.2 basse β : -si γ

---

[a] The goddess of the sea.
[b] The boy.

68

Naiads, weep for your crime, yes, weep all over
Lucrine Lake, and let Thetis[a] herself hear your
wails. A boy has been snatched to his death in
Baiae's waters, Eutychos, your sweet companion,
Castricus. He was the partner of your cares, your
beguiling solace, the love, the Alexis of our poet.
Did a wanton Nymph see you[b] naked under the
glassy water and send Hylas back to Alcides? Or
does the goddess now neglect womanish Herma-
phroditus, stirred to passion by the embrace of a
youthful *man*? Be that as it may, whatever the
cause of the sudden rape, may both earth, I pray,
and water be kind to you.

69

I am not surprised, Catullus, that your Bassa drinks
water. I *am* surprised that Bassa's daughter drinks
water.[c]

70

A sixtieth harvest has passed, Marcianus, and I
think two more, for Cotta, and he does not
remember feeling the discomfort of a fevered bed for
a single day. He points a finger, an indecent one,[d] at

[c] I.e. *fellat*; cf. 2.50. "Bassa" was presumably "Catul-
lus'" wife and her daughter his daughter or stepdaughter
(*SB*[3]).
[d] Cf. 2.28.2.

5   ostendit digitum, sed impudicum,
      Alconti Dasioque Symmachoque.
      at nostri bene computentur anni
      et quantum tetricae tulere febres
      aut languor gravis aut mali dolores
10   a vita meliore separetur:
      infantes sumus et senes videmur.
      aetatem Priamique Nestorisque
      longam qui putat esse, Marciane,
      multum decipiturque falliturque.
15   non est vivere, sed valere vita est.

71

Edere lascivos ad Baetica crusmata gestus
    et Gaditanis ludere docta modis,
tendere quae tremulum Pelian Hecubaeque maritum
    posset ad Hectoreos sollicitare rogos,
5 urit et excruciat dominum Telethusa priorem:
    vendidit ancillam, nunc redimit dominam.

72

Fur notae nimium rapacitatis
compilare Cilix volebat hortum,
ingenti sed erat, Fabulle, in horto
praeter marmoreum nihil Priapum.
5 dum non vult vacua manu redire,
ipsum surripuit Cilix Priapum.

70.6 Alconi *Heinsius*   70.10 separetur *Duff* : -rentur
$\beta\gamma$ 71.6 redimit ς : redemit β : redimet γ

Alcon and Dasius and Symmachus.[a] But let our years be carefully computed and let the time consumed by grim fevers or heavy lassitude or cruel pains be separated from better life: we are children, and we seem old men. He who thinks the span of a Priam or a Nestor long, Marcianus, is much deceived and mistaken. Life is not being alive, but being well.

71

Skilled to match wanton gestures to Baetic airs and dance to the measures of Gades, able to stretch doddering Pelias and stir Hecuba's husband[b] at Hector's pyre, Telethusa burns and torments her former master. He sold a slave girl; now he buys her back as mistress of his house.

72

Cilix,[c] a thief of all too well-known rapacity, wanted to rob a garden, but in that huge garden, Fabullus, was nothing but a marble Priapus. Not choosing to return empty-handed, Cilix made off with Priapus himself.

[a] Doctors.

[b] Priam.

[c] A personal name (cf. Cic. *Fam.* 3.1.2) rather than "a Cilician."

73

Non rudis indocta fecit me falce colonus:
    dispensatoris nobile cernis opus.
nam Caeretani cultor ditissimus agri
    hos Hilarus colles et iuga laeta tenet.
5 aspice quam certo videar non ligneus ore
    nec devota focis inguinis arma geram,
sed mihi perpetua numquam moritura cupresso
    Phidiaca rigeat mentula digna manu.
vicini, moneo, sanctum celebrate Priapum
10   et bis septenis parcite iugeribus.

74

Medio recumbit imus ille qui lecto,
calvam trifilem semitatus unguento,
foditque tonsis ora laxa lentiscis,
mentitur, Aefulane: non habet dentes.

75

Cum mittis turdumve mihi quadramve placentae,
    sive femur leporis sive quid his simile est,
buccellas misisse tuas te, Pontia, dicis.
    has ego non mittam, Pontia, sed nec edam.

73.3 ditissimus β : not- γ

73

No rude farmer made me[a] with unschooled sickle;
you see the steward's noble work. For Hilarus,
wealthiest cultivator of Caere's land, owns these
fields and fertile slopes. See how my face's clear out-
line seems made not of wood, and in my groin I bear
no weapon destined for the fireplace; my rigid cock,
carved immortal from everlasting cypress, is worthy
of Phidias' hand. Neighbors, take heed: honor holy
Priapus and spare the fourteen acres.

74

That person who lies lowest on the middle couch,[b]
he of the bald pate with its three strands of hair and
its trails of pomade, who picks his loose mouth with
smoothed sticks of mastic, is a liar, Aefulanus: he
has no teeth.

75

When you send me a thrush or a slice of cake or a
hare's thigh, or anything resembling these, you say
you have sent me your little mouthfuls, Pontia. I
shall not send them elsewhere,[c] Pontia,[d] but I shan't
eat them either.

[a] A statue of Priapus.

[b] The place of honor.

[c] As would normally be done with an unwanted present
(cf. 4.88).

[d] A notorious poisoner: cf. 2.34. See Appendix B.

76

Ille sacri lateris custos Martisque togati,
    credita cui summi castra fuere ducis,
hic situs est Fuscus. licet hoc, Fortuna, fateri:
    non timet hostilis iam lapis iste minas.
5 grande iugum domita Dacus cervice recepit
    et famulum victrix possidet umbra nemus.

77

Cum sis tam pauper quam nec miserabilis Irus,
    tam iuvenis quam nec Parthenopaeus erat,
tam fortis quam nec cum vinceret Artemidorus,
    quid te Cappadocum sex onus esse iuvat?
5 rideris multoque magis traduceris, Afer,
    quam nudus medio si spatiere foro.
non aliter monstratur Atlans cum compare ginno
    quaeque vehit similem belua nigra Libyn.
invidiosa tibi quam sit lectica requiris?
10   non debes ferri mortuus hexaphoro.

77.7 ginno *Scriverius* : gybbo *vel* gibbo γ : mulo β

---

[a] As Prefect of the Praetorian guard Fuscus had protected the warrior Emperor in civil life.

[b] "Here lies Fuscus."

[c] The epigram is supposed to be an inscription on the tomb, in Dacia, of Cornelius Fuscus, who was defeated and

BOOK VI

76

Here lies Fuscus, guard of the sacred person, of Mars in gown,[a] to whom an army of our supreme Leader was committed. This,[b] Fortune, may be avowed; this stone fears enemy threats no longer. The Dacian has bowed his neck and received the mighty yoke. A victorious shade possesses the captive grove.[c]

77

Since you are poorer than wretched Irus and younger than Parthenopaeus and stronger than Artemidorus in his conquering days,[d] why do you like to be carried by six Cappadocians? You're a laughingstock, Afer, and much more ridiculed than if you were to walk naked in the middle of the Forum. You are pointed at like Atlas[e] with his little mule or a black elephant carrying a Libyan like himself. Do you want to know how invidious is your conveyance? You shouldn't be carried dead in a litter and six.[f]

killed there in 87. The Dacians were later subdued. Cf. Juv. 4.111.

[d] Winner in the Capitoline athletic contest in 86. Apparently he was less successful later on.

[e] A dwarf (cf. Juv. 8.32), named after the giant.

[f] From this it would seem that a bourgeois bier normally had six bearers (cf. 2.81); the paupers' bier in 8.75 had four.

78

Potor nobilis, Aule, lumine uno
luscus Phryx erat alteroque lippus.
huic Heras medicus 'bibas caveto:
vinum si biberis, nihil videbis.'
5   ridens Phryx oculo 'valebis' inquit.
misceri sibi protinus deunces,
sed crebros iubet. exitum requiris?
vinum Phryx, oculus bibit venenum.

79

Tristis es et felix. sciat hoc Fortuna caveto:
ingratum dicet te, Lupe, si scierit.

80

Ut nova dona tibi, Caesar, Nilotica tellus
miserat hibernas ambitiosa rosas.
navita derisit Pharios Memphiticus hortos,
urbis ut intravit limina prima tuae:
5   tantus veris honos et odorae gratia Florae
tantaque Paestani gloria ruris erat;
sic, quacumque vagos gressusque oculosque ferebat,
tonsilibus sertis omne rubebat iter.

80.7 uagos T : vagus R $\beta\gamma$ gressus *scripsi, duce
Heraeo* : -um R $\beta\gamma$ 80.8 tonsilibus $\alpha\beta$: textil- γ : sutil-
Scriverius : pensil- *commentus sum* (SB^3)

---

[a] Nearly three times the usual quantity, eleven *cyathi*
instead of four (*triens*, cf. 6.86.1; 1.106.8). *Deunx* = eleven

78

Phryx, a famous toper, Aulus, was blind of one eye and bleary of the other. Heras, his doctor, told him: "Don't drink. If you drink wine, you'll lose your sight altogether." Phryx laughs, and says to his eye "Good-bye," then forthwith orders trebles[a] mixed for him and plenty of them. You want to know the outcome? Phryx drank wine and his eye drank poison.

79

You are sad and lucky. Mind you don't let Fortune know. She will call you ungrateful, Lupus, if she gets to know.

80

The land of Nile, Caesar, anxious to win favor, had sent you winter roses as a novel gift. But the sailor from Memphis mocked at Pharian gardens when he trod the first threshold of your city. Such was the beauty of spring and the charm of fragrant Flora, so splendid the glory of the Paestan[b] countryside. Wherever he took his wandering steps and eyes, every path blushed with clipped wreaths.[c] But do

twelfths (of a *sextarius*).

[b] Like that of Paestum, which was celebrated for its roses.

[c] Perhaps with reference to wreaths mounted on wooden supports along the roadsides rather than to roses displayed for sale in shops (SB^1).

at tu Romanae iussus iam cedere brumae,
10   mitte tuas messes, accipe, Nile, rosas.

81

Iratus tamquam populo, Charideme, lavaris:
    inguina sic toto subluis in solio.
nec caput hic vellem sic te, Charideme, lavare.
    et caput ecce lavas: inguina malo laves.

82

Quidam me modo, Rufe, diligenter
inspectum, velut emptor aut lanista,
cum vultu digitoque subnotasset,
'tune es, tune' ait 'ille Martialis,
5   cuius nequitias iocosque novit
aurem qui modo non habet Batavam?'
subrisi modice, levique nutu
me quem dixerat esse non negavi.
'cur ergo' inquis 'habes malas lacernas?'
10 respondi: 'quia sum malus poeta.'
hoc ne saepius accidat poetae,
mittas, Rufe, mihi bonas lacernas.

you, Nile, bidden now to yield to Roman winter, send us your harvests and take roses in return.

81

You bathe as though you were angry with the public, Charidemus, washing your groin all over the bathtub. I wouldn't have you wash your head here like that, Charidemus. There now, you're washing your head. I'd sooner you washed your groin.

82

The other day an individual looked me over carefully, like a buyer or a trainer, and after marking me down with eye and pointed finger, says he: "Are you really that Martial whose naughty jests everybody knows that doesn't have the ear of a Batavian?"[a] I smiled a little and with a slight nod allowed that I was the person in question. "Then why do you wear a bad cloak?" he asked. I answered: "Because I'm a bad poet." So that this doesn't happen too often to a poet, Rufus, please send me a good cloak.

[a] I.e. barbarous.

83

Quantum sollicito fortuna parentis Etrusco,
    tantum, summe ducum, debet uterque tibi.
nam tu missa tua revocasti fulmina dextra.
    hos cuperem mores ignibus esse Iovis.
5 si tua sit summo, Caesar, natura Tonanti,
    utetur toto fulmine rara manus.
muneris hoc utrumque tui testatur Etruscus,
    esse quod et comiti contigit et reduci.

84

Octaphoro sanus portatur, Avite, Philippus.
    hunc tu si sanum credis, Avite, furis.

85

Editur en sextus sine te mihi, Rufe Camoni,
    nec te lectorem sperat, amice, liber:
impia Cappadocum tellus et numine laevo
    visa tibi cineres reddit et ossa patri.
5 funde tuo lacrimas orbata Bononia Rufo,
    et resonet tota planctus in Aemilia.
heu qualis pietas, heu quam brevis occidit aetas!
    viderat Alphei praemia quinta modo.

85.8 quinta T : quinque γ : quanta β : quarta *Gruter*

---

[a] He had accompanied his father into exile. As to the father's death, see 7.40.

83

As much as his father's fortunes owe to Etruscus'
solicitude,[a] so much, most exalted of leaders, do
both owe you. For you recalled the bolts that your
hand discharged; I would that Jove's fires behaved
so. If the supreme Thunderer were of your disposi-
tion, Caesar, seldom would his arm use a bolt entire.
Etruscus acknowledges a double bounty of your bes-
towing: he was able both to go with his father and to
bring him back.

84

Philippus, who is sound of body, is carried in a litter
and eight, Avitus. If you think him sound of mind,[b]
you are crazy, Avitus.

85

See, a sixth book of mine is published without you,
Rufus Camonius, and does not hope, my friend, to
have you as its reader. The unholy land of the Cap-
padocians, seen by you under an evil star, returns
your ashes and bones to your father. Pour tears,
Bononia, bereaved of your Rufus, and let lamenta-
tion sound all along the Aemilian Way.[c] Alas, what
filial love, alas, how brief a life has perished! He
had but lately seen Alpheus' prizes for the fifth

[b] Play on two senses of *sanus*, "healthy" and "sane."
[c] Or "throughout Aemilia," the district; cf. 3.4.2.

pectore tu memori nostros evolvere lusus,
10   tu solitus totos, Rufe, tenere iocos,
accipe cum fletu maesti breve carmen amici
atque haec absentis tura fuisse puta.

86

Setinum domitaeque nives densique trientes,
quando ego vos medico non prohibente bibam?
stultus et ingratus nec tanto munere dignus
qui mavult heres divitis esse Midae.
5 possideat Libycas messis Hermumque Tagumque,
et potet caldam, qui mihi livet, aquam.

87

Di tibi dent et tu, Caesar, quaecumque mereris:
di mihi dent et tu quae volo, si merui.

88

Mane salutavi vero te nomine casu
nec dixi dominum, Caeciliane, meum.
quanti libertas constet mihi tanta requiris?
centum quadrantes abstulit illa mihi.

86.1 domitae *Heinsius* : -in(a)e Tβγ

---

[a] If, as usual in M., an Olympiad is reckoned as a five-year period, instead of four, Camonius, if he was twenty when he died (but see on 9.76.3), must have "seen" his first festival in his birth year.

time.[a] You used to reel off my jests from memory, Rufus, and have by heart whole epigrams; so take a sorrowful friend's brief poem along with his tears, and think of it as incense from the absent.

86

Setine wine, and melted snow, and cup hard on cup: when shall I drink you without a doctor's ban? Foolish he and ungrateful and unworthy of so great a boon, who would rather be heir to wealthy Midas. Let one that wishes me ill own Libyan harvests and Hermus and Tagus, and drink warm water.

87

May the gods and you, Caesar, give you all you deserve. May the gods and you give *me* what I wish, if I have deserved it.

88

By chance I greeted you this morning by your real name, Caecilianus, instead of calling you "my lord." Do you want to know how much such freedom costs me? It robbed me of a hundred farthings.[b]

[b] The normal client's dole. M. implies that the dinner which went with it (cf. 4.68; 10.27.3; 13.123 *al.*) would not have been worth eating; cf. 4.26.

89

Cum peteret seram media iam nocte matellam
 arguto madidus pollice Panaretus,
Spoletina data est sed quam siccaverat ipse,
 nec fuerat soli tota lagona satis.
5 ille fide summa testae sua vina remensus
 reddidit oenophori pondera plena sui.
miraris, quantum biberat, cepisse lagonam?
 desine mirari, Rufe: merum biberat.

90

Moechum Gellia non habet nisi unum.
turpe est hoc magis: uxor est duorum.

91

Sancta ducis summi prohibet censura vetatque
 moechari. gaude, Zoile; non futuis.

92

Caelatus tibi cum sit, Anniane,
serpens in patera Myronos arte,
Vaticana bibis: bibis venenum.

89

When tipsy Panaretus snapped his thumb for a late chamberpot (it was already midnight), he was handed a Spoletine flagon, one that he had drained himself and the whole of it had not been enough for him only. With complete accuracy he measured back to the jar its own wine, returning the full contents of his wine-holder.[a] Are you surprised that the flagon held all he had drunk? Stop being surprised, Rufus. He had drunk it neat.

90

Gellia has only one lover. That makes it worse. She's a bigamist.

91

The sacred censorship of our supreme Leader forbids and bans adultery.[b] Congratulations, Zoilus: you don't fuck.[c]

92

A serpent chased by Myron's art is on your wine bowl, Annianus, and you drink Vatican. You drink poison.[d]

---

[a] I.e. bladder. The apparent inconsistency with v. 4 may have escaped M.'s notice.

[b] Cf. 5.75; 6.7.

[c] Cf. 3.82.33.

[d] The wine was bad enough to be snake venom.

93

Tam male Thais olet quam non fullonis avari
    testa vetus, media sed modo fracta via,
non ab amore recens hircus, non ora leonis,
    non detracta cani Transtiberina cutis,
5 pullus abortivo nec cum putrescit in ovo,
    amphora corrupto nec vitiata garo.
virus ut hoc alio fallax permutet odore,
    deposita quotiens balnea veste petit,
psilothro viret aut acida latet oblita creta
10   aut tegitur pingui terque quaterque faba.
cum bene se tutam per fraudes mille putavit,
    omnia cum fecit, Thaida Thais olet.

94

Ponuntur semper chrysendeta Calpetano
    sive foris seu cum cenat in urbe domi.
sic etiam in stabulo semper, sic cenat in agro.
    non habet ergo aliud? non habet immo suum.

94.1 calpetano *cod. unus e familia* γ : palp- γ, *ut vid.* : cal-
petiano β

93

Thais smells worse than the veteran crock of a stingy fuller,[a] recently broken in the middle of the road, or a billy goat fresh from his amours, or a lion's mouth, or a hide from beyond Tiber[b] torn from a dog, or a chicken rotting in an aborted egg, or a jar polluted with putrid garum.[c] In order to exchange this stench for a different odor, whenever she takes off her clothes to get into the bath, the crafty lady is green with depilatory or lurks under a lining of chalk and vinegar, or is coated with three or four layers of thick bean meal. A thousand tricks, and she thinks she's safe. But when all's done, Thais smells of Thais.

94

Gold-inlaid plate is always placed before Calpetanus whether he dines abroad or at home in Rome. He always dines so even in an inn or in the country. Has he no other service then? Not so, he has no service of his own.[d]

[a] Fullers used urine in their trade, and used to collect it at street corners in jars; cf. 12.48.8. "Stingy" because he would keep the crock for a long time.

[b] Where tanners pursued their trade; Juv. 14.202.

[c] Sauce made of the intestines and offal of mackerel; cf. 13.102.

[d] "Calpetanus" is satirized for his ostentatious use of plate which is not his own.

LIBER VII

1

Accipe belligerae crudum thoraca Minervae,
    ipsa Medusaeae quem timet ira comae.
dum vacat haec, Caesar, poterit lorica vocari:
    pectore cum sacro sederit, aegis erit.

2

Invia Sarmaticis domini lorica sagittis
    et Martis Getico tergore fida magis,
quam vel ad Aetolae securam cuspidis ictus
    texuit innumeri lubricus unguis apri:
5 felix sorte tua, sacrum cui tangere pectus
    fas erit et nostri mente calere dei.
i comes et magnos illaesa merere triumphos
    palmataeque ducem, sed cito, redde togae.

---

[a] These lines allude to a cuirass, made of boars' hoofs, either taken from a temple of Minerva, or made for Domitian in imitation of her aegis with the Gorgon's head upon it, and worn by him in his Sarmatian expedition, A.D. 92. It is again alluded to in 14.179.

[b] Meleager's, who slew the Calydonian boar; cf. Sp. 17.1.

BOOK VII

1

Accept the fierce breastplate of war-waging Minerva, dreaded even by Medusa's angry locks. While not in use, this, Caesar, may be called a cuirass. When it rests on your sacred breast, it will be an aegis.[a]

2

Cuirass of our Lord, impervious to Sarmatian shafts and more trusty than the Getic shield of Mars, which the sliding hooves of countless boars wove to be proof even against the strokes of an Aetolian spear,[b] happy are you in your lot; for to you it will be lawful to touch the sacred breast and grow warm with the mind of our divinity.[c] Go with him, and win unscathed great triumphs, and restore — but soon — our Leader to the palm-embroidered gown.[d]

[c] The heart being the seat of the intellect.
[d] A triumphing general formerly wore a purple and gold toga (*picta*) over a tunic embroidered with palm leaves (*tunica palmata*). The palm-embroidered toga is first mentioned here.

3

Cur non mitto meos tibi, Pontiliane, libellos?
ne mihi tu mittas, Pontiliane, tuos.

4

Esset, Castrice, cum mali coloris,
versus scribere coepit Oppianus.

5

Si desiderium, Caesar, populique patrumque
respicis et Latiae gaudia vera togae,
redde deum votis poscentibus. invidet hosti
Roma suo, veniat laurea multa licet:
5 terrarum dominum propius videt ille tuoque
terretur vultu barbarus et fruitur.

6

Ecquid Hyperboreis ad nos conversus ab oris
Ausonias Caesar iam parat ire vias?
certus abest auctor, sed vox hoc nuntiat omnis:
credo tibi, verum dicere, Fama, soles.
5 publica victrices testantur gaudia chartae,
Martia laurigera cuspide pila virent.

ᵃ An abbreviated version of 5.73.
ᵇ Pallor being characteristic of poets (and students generally; cf. Pers. 1.26). Oppianus takes to writing poetry in

3

Why don't I send you my little books, Pontilianus?
For fear you might send me yours, Pontilianus.[a]

4

Because he had a bad color, Castricus, Oppianus
started to write verses.[b]

5

If you have regard, Caesar, for the longing of people
and fathers and the true joy of the Latin gown,
restore their god to the prayers that demand him.[c]
Rome envies her enemy, though many a laurel
come.[d] He sees earth's lord nearer at hand; the bar-
barian quails before your countenance and enjoys it.

6

Does Caesar turn our way from Hyperborean lands,
is he already preparing to tread Ausonian roads?
There is no sure voucher, but every voice reports it.
I believe you, Rumor, you generally speak true. Vic-
torious despatches certify the public joy; the pikes
of Mars are green with laurelled points. Once

order to mask the real cause; cf. 1.77.6.
  [c] Domitian in A.D. 92 was campaigning against the Sar-
matians. He returned in January 93.
  [d] Despatches announcing victory were laurel-wreathed.

rursus, io, magnos clamat tibi Roma triumphos
    invictusque tua, Caesar, in urbe sonas.
sed iam laetitiae quo sit fiducia maior,
10   Sarmaticae laurus nuntius ipse veni.

7

Hiberna quamvis Arctos et rudis Peuce
et ungularum pulsibus calens Hister
fractusque cornu iam ter improbum Rhenus
teneat domantem regna perfidae gentis
5   te, summe mundi rector et parens orbis:
abesse nostris non tamen potes votis.
illic et oculis et animis sumus, Caesar,
adeoque mentes omnium tenes unus
ut ipsa magni turba nesciat Circi
10   utrumne currat Passerinus an Tigris.

8

Nunc hilares, si quando, mihi, nunc ludite, Musae:
    victor ab Odrysio redditur orbe deus.
certa facis populi tu primus vota, December:
    iam licet ingenti dicere voce 'venit.'
5 felix sorte tua! poteras non cedere Iano,
    gaudia si nobis quae dabit ille dares.

7.3 improbum SB^3 : -bus β : -bo γ
8.1 *post* quando *distinxi*

again—huzzah!—Rome shouts your mighty triumphs and in your city, Caesar, your title "Invincible" resounds. But now, that happiness may be more assured, come in person announcing your Sarmatian laurel.

7

Though the wintry Bear and rude Peuce and Hister warming to the beat of hooves and Rhine, whose presumptious horn has now been shattered for the third time,[a] detain you, the world's supreme ruler and earth's parent, as you subdue the realms of a perfidious race, yet you cannot be absent from our prayers. We are there, Caesar, with our eyes and our minds. And so wholly do you alone hold the thoughts of all that the very crowd in the great Circus knows not whether Passerinus runs or Tigris.[b]

8

Now if ever make sport for me merrily, Muses. The god is restored victorious from the Odrysian world. You are first, December, to make certain the people's prayers. Now we may cry with one mighty voice: "He is coming." Happy in your lot! You might not yield to Janus, if you were giving us the joy that

---

[a] River gods were represented with horns. The shattering of the horn meant defeat: cf. 10.7.6.

[b] Racehorses.

festa coronatus ludet convicia miles,
　　inter laurigeros cum comes ibit equos.
fas audire iocos levioraque carmina, Caesar,
10　　et tibi, si lusus ipse triumphus amat.

9

Cum sexaginta numeret Cascellius annos,
　　ingeniosus homo est: quando disertus erit?

10

Pedicatur Eros, fellat Linus: Ole, quid ad te
　　de cute quid faciant ille vel ille sua?
centenis futuit Matho milibus: Ole, quid ad te?
　　non tu propterea, sed Matho pauper erit.
5　in lucem cenat Sertorius: Ole, quid ad te,
　　cum liceat tota stertere nocte tibi?
septingenta Tito debet Lupus: Ole, quid ad te?
　　assem ne dederis crediderisve Lupo.
illud dissimulas ad te quod pertinet, Ole,
10　　quodque magis curae convenit esse tuae:
pro togula debes. hoc ad te pertinet, Ole.
　　quadrantem nemo iam tibi credit: et hoc.

ᵃ If Domitian were actually arriving in December, that
month might never give place to January.
　ᵇ For the license allowed to soldiers in a triumphal pro-
cession cf. 1.4.3.

he will give.[a] The garlanded soldiery will sport in festive insults as they accompany the laurel-bearing horses. Even for you, Caesar, it is lawful to hear jests and lighter verses, if the triumph itself loves jollity.[b]

9

Cascellius counts sixty years and he is a man of talent. When will he be a good speaker?[c]

10

Eros is sodomized, Linus sucks. What's it to you, Olus, what either one of them does with his own skin?[d] Matho fornicates for a hundred thousand. What's it to you, Olus? You won't be a pauper on that account, Matho will. Sertorius dines till daybreak. What's it to you, Olus, when *you* can snore all night? Lupus owes Titus seven hundred thousand. What's it to you, Olus? Don't give or lend Lupus a penny. What *does* have to do with you, Olus, what ought rather to be your concern, you pretend not to know. You owe for your gown: this has to do with you, Olus. Nobody lends you a farthing

[c] He had the ability to make a fine barrister, but had never mastered the technique.

[d] Housman (1182) compared the saying *de suo corio ludere*, "play with (i.e. at the expense of) one's own hide"; cf. 3.16.5.

uxor moecha tibi est: hoc ad te pertinet, Ole.
　　poscit iam dotem filia grandis: et hoc.
15　dicere quindecies poteram quod pertinet ad te:
　　sed quid agas ad me pertinet, Ole, nihil.

11

Cogis me calamo manuque nostra
　　emendare meos, Pudens, libellos.
o quam me nimium probas amasque,
qui vis archetypas habere nugas!

12

Sic me fronte legat dominus, Faustine, serena
　　excipiatque meos qua solet aure iocos,
ut mea nec iuste quos odit pagina laesit
　　et mihi de nullo fama rubore placet.
5　quid prodest, cupiant cum quidam nostra videri
　　si qua Lycambeo sanguine tela madent,
vipereumque vomat nostro sub nomine virus
　　qui Phoebi radios ferre diemque negat?
ludimus innocui: scis hoc bene: iuro potentis
10　　per genium Famae Castaliumque gregem,

　　ᵃ The corrections in the author's hand would put Pudens' copy on a par with an authentic work by a famous artist.

　　ᵇ I.e. favoring or attentive.

any more: this too. Your wife has a lover: this has to do with you, Olus. Your grown-up daughter is already asking for a dowry: this too. I could mention fifteen things that have to do with you, Olus. But your doings, Olus, have nothing to do with me.

11

You make me correct my little books with my own pen and hand, Pudens. Oh, how excessively you approve and love me, wanting to have an original of my trifles![a]

12

So may our Lord read me with unfurrowed brow, Faustinus, and catch my jests with his accustomed ear,[b] as my page has never harmed even those it justly hates, nor do I desire celebrity from anybody's blush. But what's the use, when certain persons are eager for any weapons that drip with Lycambes' blood to be thought mine, and some creature who refuses to bear Phoebus' rays and the light of day vomits his snake venom under my name? I sport harmlessly, you know that well. I swear it by the genius of potent Fame[c] and the Castalian troop and

[c] A curious expression, perhaps to be explained by the custom of slaves and other inferiors swearing by the "genius" (guardian spirit; cf. 7.78.4) of their masters or betters. M. was as it were a client of Fame.

perque tuas aures, magni mihi numinis instar,
    lector inhumana liber ab invidia.

13

Dum Tiburtinis albescere solibus audit
    antiqui dentis fusca Lycoris ebur,
venit in Herculeos colles. quid Tiburis alti
    aura valet! parvo tempore nigra redit.

14

Accidit infandum nostrae scelus, Aule, puellae;
    amisit lusus deliciasque suas:
non quales teneri ploravit amica Catulli,
    Lesbia, nequitiis passeris orba sui,
5 vel Stellae cantata meo quas flevit Ianthis,
    cuius in Elysio nigra columba volat:
lux mea non capitur nugis nec amoribus istis,
    nec dominae pectus talia damna movent:
bis senos puerum numerantem perdidit annos,
10   mentula cui nondum sesquipedalis erat.

14.5 quas β : quam γ 14.7 nec amoribus ς : neque
mor- (*vel* emor-) $\beta\gamma$ 14.9 senos ς : de- $\beta\gamma$

---

[a] The sulphurous exhalations of the springs at Tibur
(cf. 4.4.2) were supposed to have the property of bleaching
things, especially ivory.

[b] M. had probably forgotten that he had published a
prototype of this epigram (4.62) using the same name.
Lycoris. Cf. also 1.72.6.

by your ears, reader free from heartless jealousy, a mighty divinity to me.

13

Hearing that the ivory of an ancient tusk turns white in the suns of Tibur,[a] dusky Lycoris went to Hercules' hills. How potent is the air of lofty Tibur! In a short time she returned black.[b]

14

An unspeakable villainy has afflicted my girl, Aulus: she has lost her plaything and pet — not such as tender Catullus' mistress wept for, Lesbia, bereaved of her sparrow's naughty tricks, or such as Ianthis, sung by my Stella, bewailed,[c] whose black dove flies in Elysium. My beloved is not won by trifles or by such loves[d] as those nor do such losses move my lady's heart. She has lost a boy numbering twice six[e] years, whose cock was not yet eighteen inches long.

[c] I.e. on whose grief for her dead dove Stella wrote his poem (cf. 1.7).

[d] The manuscript reading *neque moribus istis* ("nor by such ways") makes poor sense, and M. never has *neque* before a consonant in dactylic meter (always *nec*).

[e] Some editors keep the absurd *denos*, making the boy twenty years old.

15

Quis puer hic nitidis assistit Ianthidos undis?
  effugit dominam Naida numquid Hylas?
o bene quod silva colitur Tirynthius ista
  et quod amatrices tam prope servat aquas!
5 securus licet hos fontes, Argynne, ministres:
  nil facient Nymphae: ne velit ipse cave.

16

Aera domi non sunt. superest hoc, Regule, solum
  ut tua vendamus munera: numquid emis?

17

Ruris bibliotheca delicati,
vicinam videt unde lector urbem,
inter carmina sanctiora si quis
lascivae fuerit locus Thaliae,
5 hos nido licet inseras vel imo
septem quos tibi misimus libellos
auctoris calamo sui notatos:
haec illis pretium facit litura.
at tu munere †delicata† parvo,

17.1 assistit β : abs- γ 17.9 delicata γ : dedi- β : mun-
erata *temptavi* (SB^3)

---

[a] The statue of Stella's page Argynnus stands among
others (cf. 7.50) beside the stream, beautiful enough to be
Hylas escaped from his Naiad (SB^3). M.'s interpreters,
reading *absistit* ("withdraws") in v. 1, go far afield.

15

What boy stands here by Ianthis' sparkling stream?
Has Hylas escaped his Naiad mistress?[a] Well it is
that the Tirynthian is worshipped in this wood and
watches the amorous waters so close at hand.
Argynnus, you may hand out this fount[b] without
fear. The Nymphs will do nothing; but beware lest
Himself[c] take a fancy.

16

There's no money in the house. My only recourse,
Regulus, is to sell your presents. Are you buying?

17

Library of a dainty villa from which the reader sees
the neighboring city, if there be space for wanton
Thalia among poems of higher tone, you may put in
a niche, even the lowest, these seven little books
that I have sent you, marked by their author's pen;
the corrections give them value. But do you,
presented(?)[d] with a small present, you who shall be

[b] Hand its water to the company, as the original of the
statue would do at banquets.

[c] Hercules.

[d] Translating my conjecture. *Delicata* would be awk-
wardly placed and intolerable after *delicati* in v. 1. On
dedicata, which makes no sense, see my edition. G. P.
Goold suggests *praedicata*, "made known by a small
present" (i.e. M.'s epigram).

10   quae cantaberis orbe nota toto,
      pignus pectoris hoc mei tuere,
      Iuli bibliotheca Martialis.

18

Cum tibi sit facies de qua nec femina possit
      dicere, cum corpus nulla litura notet,
cur te tam rarus cupiat repetatque fututor
      miraris? vitium est non leve, Galla, tibi.
5   accessi quotiens ad opus mixtisque movemur
      inguinibus, cunnus non tacet, ipsa taces.
di facerent ut tu loquereris et ille taceret:
      offendor cunni garrulitate tui.
pedere te mallem: namque hoc nec inutile dicit
10   Symmachus et risum res movet ista simul.
quis ridere potest fatui poppysmata cunni?
      cum sonat hic, cui non mentula mensque cadit?
dic aliquid saltem clamosoque obstrepe cunno,
      et, si adeo muta es, disce vel inde loqui.

19

Fragmentum quod vile putas et inutile lignum,
      haec fuit ignoti prima carina maris.
quam nec Cyaneae quondam potuere ruinae
      frangere nec Scythici tristior ira freti,

18.9 mallem β : uel- Tγ   18.14 et] aut A. Ker

88

recited and famous throughout the world, keep well this pledge of my affection, library of Julius Martialis.

18

Since you have a face about which even a woman could find nothing[a] to say, since no blemish marks your person, do you wonder why a fornicator so seldom wants you and comes again? You have a serious defect, Galla. Whenever I get to work and we move with mingled loins, your cunt is vocal, while you are silent. Would that the gods would make you talk and it be silent! The garrulity of your cunt puts me off. I had rather you farted; Symmachus says that is healthy, and besides it makes one laugh. But who can laugh at the smacking of a silly cunt? Whose cock and spirits don't droop at the sound of it? At least say something and counter your clamorous cunt; and if you are so tongue-tied, learn to talk out of *it*.

19

What you take for a paltry fragment, a useless piece of lumber, was the first keel to sail the unknown sea.[b] What once neither the Cyanean rocks could

[a] I.e. nothing adverse.
[b] The Argo.

5   saecula vicerunt: sed quamvis cesserit annis,
     sanctior est salva parva tabella rate.

20

Nihil est miserius neque gulosius Santra.
rectam vocatus cum cucurrit ad cenam,
quam tot diebus noctibusque captavit,
ter poscit apri glandulas, quater lumbum,

5   et utramque coxam leporis et duos armos,
nec erubescit peierare de turdo
et ostreorum rapere lividos cirros.
buccis placentae sordidam linit mappam;
illic et uvae collocantur ollares

10 et Punicorum pauca grana malorum
et excavatae pellis indecens vulvae
et lippa ficus debilisque boletus.
sed mappa cum iam mille rumpitur furtis,
rosos tepenti spondylos sinu condit

15 et devorato capite turturem truncum.
colligere longa turpe nec putat dextra
analecta quidquid et canes reliquerunt.
nec esculenta sufficit gulae praeda:
mixto lagonam replet ad pedes vino.

20 haec per ducentas cum domum tulit scalas

20.8 buccis placentae *Scriverius* : b- plangentem β : dulci
placenta γ

---

^a The Euxine (Black Sea).
^b I.e. a sow's matrix, a favorite dish: cf. Hor. *Epist*

break nor the grimmer wrath of the Scythian main,[a]
the ages have vanquished. But though it has suc-
cumbed to the years, the small plank is more vener-
able than the ship intact.

20

Santra is the most miserly and the greediest of
beings. When he has an invitation and runs off to a
formal dinner, for which he has been angling for so
many days and nights, he asks for three helpings of
boar's sweetbreads, four of loin, both haunches of
hare and two shoulders; nor does he blush to lie
about a thrush and snatch the livid beards of
oysters. He smears his dirty napkin with mouthfuls
of cake. Therein are assembled preserved grapes
and a few pomegranate grains, and the ugly skin of
a hollowed matrix[b] and an oozy fig and a crippled
mushroom. But when the napkin bursts with a
thousand thefts, he hides gnawed vertebrae in his
warm pocket together with the remains of a pigeon
whose head has been devoured. Nor does he think
shame to collect with a long arm whatever the
sweeper and the dogs have left. Edible plunder is
not enough for his gullet, he fills a flagon at his feet
with mixed wine.[c] When he has carried all this
home up two hundred stairs and anxiously shut

1.15.41. It was served boiled and soused in a vinegar and
brine sauce and other condiments; cf. Athen. 3.58f.
[c] Wines stolen from different glasses rather than wine
and water.

seque obserata clusit anxius cella
gulosus ille, postero die vendit.

21

Haec est illa dies, magni quae conscia partus
　　Lucanum populis et tibi, Polla, dedit.
heu! Nero crudelis nullaque invisior umbra,
　　debuit hoc saltem non licuisse tibi.

22

Vatis Apollinei magno memorabilis ortu
　　lux redit: Aonidum turba, favete sacris.
haec meruit, cum te terris, Lucane, dedisset,
　　mixtus Castaliae Baetis ut esset aquae.

23

Phoebe, veni, sed quantus eras cum bella tonanti
　　ipse dares Latiae plectra secunda lyrae.
quid tanta pro luce precer? tu, Polla, maritum
　　saepe colas et se sentiat ille coli.

21.1 magni quae β : q- m- Rγ　　　23.1 tonanti γ : canenti β

himself in his barred chamber, this greedy fellow—
sells it next day.

21

This is the day that, conscious of a mighty birth,
gave Lucan to mankind and to you, Polla. Ah, cruel
Nero, for no death more hated, this at least should
not not have been permitted you.

22

The day returns made memorable by the mighty
birth of Apollo's poet. Aonian throng, to these rites
be propitious. This day, when it gave you to earth,
Lucan, deserved that Baetis be blended with
Castalia's water.[a]

23

Come, Phoebus, but come in might, as when in per-
son you gave the second quill of the Latin lyre[b] to
him who thunders wars. What prayer should I
make for so great a dawn? Polla, may you often
commemorate your husband, and may he know it.

[a] Lucan was born at Corduba (Cordova) on the Baetis
(Guadalquivir).
[b] Virgil's being the first.

24

Cum Iuvenale meo quae me committere temptas,
    quid non audebis, perfida lingua, loqui?
te fingente nefas Pyladen odisset Orestes,
    Thesea Pirithoi destituissset amor;
5   tu Siculos fratres et maius nomen Atridas
    et Ledae poteras dissociare genus.
hoc tibi pro meritis et talibus imprecor ausis,
    ut facias illud quod, puto, lingua, facis.

25

Dulcia cum tantum scribas epigrammata semper
    et cerussata candidiora cute,
nullaque mica salis nec amari fellis in illis
    gutta sit, o demens, vis tamen illa legi!
5   nec cibus ipse iuvat morsu fraudatus aceti,
    nec grata est facies cui gelasinus abest.
infanti melimela dato fatuasque mariscas:
    nam mihi, quae novit pungere, Chia sapit.

24

False tongue, that try to set me at loggerheads with my Juvenal,[a] what will you not dare to say? With you to invent wickedness, Orestes would have hated Pylades and Pirithous' love forsaken Theseus. You could have parted the Sicilian brethren,[b] and (a greater name) the sons of Atreus[c] and Leda's children.[d] For such deserts, such outrages, thus I curse you: tongue, may you do what methinks you do.

25

You never write epigrams that are not bland and whiter than a white-leaded skin, without a grain of salt in them, not a drop of bitter gall: and yet, you crazy fellow, you want people to read them. There is no relish even in food deprived of vinegar's bite, and a face without a dimple fails to please. Give honey apples and insipid figs to baby: my taste is for the Chian,[e] that knows how to sting.

[a] Very probably, but not quite certainly, the future satirist. The cognomen is not rare.

[b] Amphinomus and Anapius, models of fraternal love and filial piety, who carried their parents from an eruption of Etna; cf. *Aetna* 624ff, *al.*

[c] Agamemnon and Menelaus.

[d] Castor and Pollux.

[e] Fig.

26

Apollinarem conveni meum, scazon,
et si vacabit — ne molestus accedas —,
hoc qualecumque, cuius aliqua pars ipse est,
dabis: hoc facetae carmen imbuant aures.
5   si te receptum fronte videris tota,
noto rogabis ut favore sustentet.
quanto mearum scis amore nugarum
flagret: nec ipse plus amare te possum.
contra malignos esse si cupis tutus,
10 Apollinarem conveni meum, scazon.

27

Tuscae glandis aper populator et ilice multa
    iam piger, Aetolae fama secunda ferae,
quem meus intravit splendenti cuspide Dexter,
    praeda iacet nostris invidiosa focis.
5   pinguescant madido laeti nidore penates
    flagret et exciso festa culina iugo.
sed cocus ingentem piperis consumet acervum
    addet et arcano mixta Falerna garo:
ad dominum redeas, noster te non capit ignis,
10   conturbator aper: vilius esurio.

26.4 hoc (ς) facetae *Gronovius* : haec facetum βγ : h
facetum *Gilbert*   27.5 laeti ς : tetri *vel* teti β : la
γ   madidi lauto *Heinsius*

BOOK VII

26

Limping verse,[a] go meet my Apollinaris, and, if he is not too busy (don't approach him at the wrong time), give him this, such as it is, of which he is himself a part. Let his witty ear be first to hear the verses. If you see yourself received with an unwrinkled brow, ask him to support you with his well-known favor. You know how ardently he loves my trifles. I can't love you more myself. If you want to be safe against ill-wishers, go meet my Apollinaris, limping verse.

27

A boar, ravager of Tuscan acorns and sluggish now with many an ilex, second in fame to the beast of Aetolia,[b] pierced with gleaming spear by my Dexter, a booty to make men envious, lies at my hearth. Let my household gods rejoice and grow fat with the steamy savor and my festal kitchen blaze with the felled hillside. But my cook will consume a huge pile of pepper and add Falernian mixed with his private garum. Go back to your master, my fire is too small for you, bankrupter boar. My hunger comes less expensive.

[a] Cf. 1.96.1.
[b] Cf. 7.2.3n.

28

Sic Tiburtinae crescat tibi silva Dianae
　　et properet caesum saepe redire nemus,
nec Tartesiacis Pallas tua, Fusce, trapetis
　　cedat et immodici dent bona musta lacus;
5　sic fora mirentur, sic te Palatia laudent,
　　excolat et geminas plurima palma fores:
otia dum medius praestat tibi parva December,
　　exige, sed certa, quos legis, aure iocos.
'scire libet verum? res est haec ardua.' sed tu
10　quod tibi vis dici dicere, Fusce, potes.

29

Thestyle, Victoris tormentum dulce Voconi,
　　quo nemo est toto notior orbe puer,
sic etiam positis formosus amere capillis
　　et placeat vati nulla puella tuo:
5　paulisper domini doctos sepone libellos,
　　carmina Victori dum lego parva tuo.
et Maecenati, Maro cum cantaret Alexin,
　　nota tamen Marsi fusca Melaenis erat.

29.1 Victoris ς : -turi βγ

---

　[a] I.e. the law courts. There were at this time three
Romanum, Iulii, and Augusti.
　[b] Palms were affixed to the doors of advocates after suc‑
cess in court cf. Juv. 7.117.
　[c] Deliberately ambiguous: the truth or something
flattering?

28

Fuscus, so may the wood of Tiburtine Diana grow for you and the oft-felled grove hasten to return, and your olives not yield to Tartessian presses, and your overflowing vats give good must, so may the Forums[a] admire you and the Palace praise you and many a palm deck your twin doors:[b] while mid-December affords you a little leisure, judge the jests you read and let your ear be sure. "Do you wish to know the truth? That is a difficult matter." But you can tell me Fuscus, what *you* want to be told.[c]

29

Thestylus, sweet torment of Voconius Victor, than whom no boy in the whole world is better known,[d] so may you be beautiful and loved even when you have put aside your long hair and may no girl please your poet: for a little while put away your master's elegant books while I read my little poems to your Victor. Even to Maecenas, when Maro sang of Alexis, still was Marsus' dusky Melaenis familiar.[e]

[d] Because you are sung of in his poems (*docti libelli*); cf. *ati* in v. 4.

[e] The analogy is not perfect. Marsus corresponds to M. and Alexis to Thestylus, but Maecenas and Virgil do not have separate counterparts, no matter which is thought of as Alexis' master.

30

Das Parthis, das Germanis, das, Caelia, Dacis,
    nec Cilicum spernis Cappadocumque toros;
et tibi de Pharia Memphiticus urbe fututor
    navigat, a rubris et niger Indus aquis;
5 nec recutitorum fugis inguina Iudaeorum,
    nec te Sarmatico transit Alanus equo.
qua ratione facis, cum sis Romana puella,
    quod Romana tibi mentula nulla placet?

31

Raucae chortis aves et ova matrum
et flavas medio vapore Chias
et fetum querulae rudem capellae
nec iam frigoribus pares olivas
5 et canum gelidis holus pruinis
de nostro tibi missa rure credis?
o quam, Regule, diligenter erras!
nil nostri, nisi me, ferunt agelli.

30.3 Phario . . . orbe *Heinsius*

30

You give your favors to Parthians, you give them to
Germans, Caelia, you give them to Dacians, nor do
you despise the beds of Cilicians and Cappadocians;
and to you comes sailing the fornicator of Memphis
from his Pharian city and the black Indian from the
Red Sea.[a] Nor do you shun the loins of circumcised
Jews nor does the Alan pass you by with his Sarma-
tian horse.[b] Why is it, since you are a Roman girl,
that no Roman cock is to your liking?

31

Birds of the cackling poultry yard, eggs of mother
fowl, Chian figs yellow with insufficient heat,[c] and
the youthful offspring of a bleating nanny goat, and
olives no longer able to withstand the cold, and
vegetables blanched by chill frosts — do you think
they are sent to you from my place in the country?
How egregiously[d] you are mistaken, Regulus! My
little fields bear[e] nothing but myself. Whatever

---

[a] "A general name for the sea bounding Arabia" *OLD*.

[b] Perhaps with an obscene double meaning; cf.
11.104.14.

[c] Sometimes understood as "midsummer heat," but M.
seems to be playing down his gifts. For *medius*,
"moderate" (and so insufficient), cf. Sen. *Nat. quaest.* 4b. 12
hoc medio frigore.

[d] Apparently a colloquial use of *diligenter*, not found
elsewhere.

[e] In two senses: "yield" and "support the weight of."

quidquid vilicus Umber aut colonus
10   aut rus marmore tertio notatum
aut Tusci tibi Tusculive mittunt,
id tota mihi nascitur Subura.

32

Attice, facundae renovas qui nomina gentis
    nec sinis ingentem conticuisse domum,
te pia Cecropiae comitatur turba Minervae,
    te secreta quies, te sophos omnis amat.
5   at iuvenes alios fracta colit aure magister
    et rapit immeritas sordidus unctor opes.
non pila, non follis, non te paganica thermis
    praeparat aut nudi stipitis ictus hebes,
vara nec in lento ceromate bracchia tendis,
10   non harpasta vagus pulverulenta rapis,
sed curris niveas tantum prope Virginis undas
    aut ubi Sidonio taurus amore calet.
per varias artes, omnis quibus area servit,
    ludere, cum liceat currere, pigritia est.

31.9 Calenus *Heinsius*   31.12 id γ : in β

---

[a] See *SB* [3]. *Tusci* is regular because the property takes
its name from a region (*Tusci* = Etruria in Cic. *Att*. 8.12
C.1). *Tusculi* is a freak. *Tusculus* = *Tusculanus* occurs
now and then (as in Mart. 4.64.13 and 9.60.2), but Tus-
culum being a municipality a property in its district is
properly called *Tusculanum*, neuter singular adjectival
substantive. Prompted by the jingle, Martial commits a
barbarism, intentionally, no doubt, and facetiously.
[b] I.e. M. has to buy in the market; cf. 10.94.5.

102

your Umbrian bailiff or tenant sends you, or your farm marked by the third milestone, or your Tuscan or Tusculan properties,[a] is produced for me up and down Subura.[b]

32

Atticus, you who renew the name of an eloquent line[c] and permit not a mighty house to fall silent, the pious worshippers of Cecropian Minerva attend you, quiet seclusion and every wise man loves you. Other young fellows are courted by the coach with his broken ears and the dirty masseur pockets undeserved wealth. No hand ball, no follis, no paganica[d] prepares *you* for the warm bath, nor the blunt stroke of the bare[e] stick, neither do you stretch curving[f] arms smeared with sticky wrestler's mud nor dashing here and there do you snatch the dusty harpastum. You just run by the Virgin's snowy waters or where the bull is hot with his Sidonian flame. To play, using the various skills to which every sportsground caters, when it is possible to run, is laziness.

[c] Nothing is known of this family. Cicero's friend Pomponius Atticus had no male children.

[d] Cf. 4.19.7n. On the paganica see 14.45.

[e] Without metal (*nudus* often = "unarmed"). *Stipitis* is usually understood as the wooden post (*palus*) on which swordsmen practiced. But taken so, the genitive after *ictus* is hard to parallel and *nudi* lacks point.

[f] *Vara* = "bent outwards in different directions but with converging extremities" (*OLD*).

33

Sordidior caeno cum sit toga, calceus autem
    candidior prima sit tibi, Cinna, nive,
deiecto quid, inepte, pedes perfundis amictu?
    collige, Cinna, togam; calceus ecce perit.

34

    Quo possit fieri modo, Severe,
    ut vir pessimus omnium Charinus
    unam rem bene fecerit, requiris?
    dicam, sed cito. quid Nerone peius?
5   quid thermis melius Neronianis?
    non deest protinus, ecce, de malignis
    qui sic rancidulo loquatur ore:
    'quid? tu tot domini deique nostri
    praefers muneribus Neronianas?'
10   thermas praefero balneis cinaedi.

34.8 *ita Gruter* : quid te tot *β* : q- tu *vel* ut q- tu *γ*
34.9–10 *de interpunctione vide appendicem* A

33

Your gown is dirtier than mud, whereas your shoe, Cinna, is whiter than fresh snow. Why then, you silly man, do you inundate your feet with your drooping garment? Gather up your gown, Cinna. Look, your shoe is going to waste.[a]

34

Do you want to know, Severus, how it can come about that a thoroughpaced scoundrel like Charinus has done one thing well? I'll tell you, and quickly. What was worse than Nero? What is better than Nero's baths? Look now, forthwith up speaks one of our malice-mongers with a sneer: "Oho, you prefer Nero's baths to all those gifts of our Lord and God, do you?" I prefer warm baths to the establishment of a catamite.[b]

[a] With double sense of *perit*, which also = "is being ruined."

[b] See Appendix A.

35

Inguina succinctus nigra tibi servus aluta
    stat, quotiens calidis tota foveris aquis.
sed meus, ut de me taceam, Laecania, servus
    Iudaeum nulla sub cute pondus habet,
5 sed nudi tecum iuvenesque senesque lavantur.
    an sola est servi mentula vera tui?
ecquid femineos sequeris, matrona, recessus,
    secretusque tua, cunne, lavaris aqua?

36

Cum pluvias madidumque Iovem perferre negaret
    et rudis hibernis villa nataret aquis,
plurima, quae posset subitos effundere nimbos,
    muneribus venit tegula missa tuis.
5 horridus, ecce, sonat Boreae stridore December:
    Stella, tegis villam, non tegis agricolam?

37

Nosti mortiferum quaestoris, Castrice, signum?
    est operae pretium discere theta novum:

35.4 nulla $\beta\gamma$: nuda T   36.6 *interrog. fecit Izaac*

---

[a] I.e. of foreskin; see Housman, 1181f.

[b] For this sense of *rudis* cf. 1.12.5n.

[c] Perhaps the president of the *Triumviri Capitales*, a
court of three which dealt out summary justice to malefac-
tors.

35

Your slave stands with a black strap round his loins whenever you submerge your whole self in the warm water. But my slave, Laecania, to say nothing of me, has a Jewish weight under his lack of skin,[a] and young men and old men bathe with you naked. Is your slave's cock the only genuine article? Madam, why don't you make for the women's rooms and get your cunt washed privately in its own water?

36

When my ramshackle[b] villa refused to withstand the rain that Jupiter poured down and swam in winter waters, there arrived a quantity of tiles to run off sudden showers, sent by your bounty. Hark now to harsh December, loud with shrill Boreas. Stella, do you cover the farmhouse, but fail to cover the farmer?

37

Castricus, do you know the quaestor's[c] fatal signal? This novel death warrant[d] is worth learning. He

[d] The Greek letter theta was used on voting tablets as a symbol for death (θάνατος, thanatos).

exprimeret quotiens rorantem frigore nasum,
    letalem iuguli iusserat esse notam.
5 turpis ab inviso pendebat stiria naso,
    cum flaret madida fauce December atrox:
collegae tenuere manus: quid plura requiris?
    emungi misero, Castrice, non licuit.

38

Tantus es et talis, nostri Polypheme Severi,
    ut te mirari possit et ipse Cyclops.
sed nec Scylla minor. quod si fera monstra duorum
    iunxeris, alterius fiet uterque timor.

39

    Discursus varios vagumque mane
    et fastus et have potentiorum
    cum perferre patique iam negaret,
    coepit fingere Caelius podagram.
5 quam dum vult nimis approbare veram
    et sanas linit obligatque plantas
    inceditque gradu laborioso,
    — quantum cura potest et ars doloris! —
    desît fingere Caelius podagram.

had given orders that whenever he blew his nose, as it dripped with the cold, that should be the deadly sign for slaughter. An ugly icicle hung from the hated nose, when fierce December's damp throat was a-blowing. His colleagues held his hands. Why ask further? The wretched man, Castricus, was not allowed to use his handkerchief.

38

Polyphemus, slave of my friend Severus, your size and aspect are such that the Cyclops himself might be amazed at you. But Scylla is no smaller. If you put the two savage monsters together, each will become the terror of the other.

39

Unwilling any longer to bear and suffer the coursings hither and thither, the early morning rounds, and the haughty salutations of the powerful, Caelius started to feign the gout. In his anxiety to prove it genuine, he anoints and bandages his healthy feet and walks with laboring tread. See what the cultivation and art of pain can do. Caelius has stopped feigning the gout.

40

Hic iacet ille senex Augusta notus in aula,
    pectore non humili passus utrumque deum;
natorum pietas sanctis quem coniugis umbris
    miscuit: Elysium possidet ambo nemus.
5 occidit illa prior viridi fraudata iuventa:
    hic prope ter senas vixit Olympiadas.
sed festinatis raptum tibi credidit annis,
    aspexit lacrimas quisquis, Etrusce, tuas.

41

Cosmicos esse tibi, Semproni Tucca, videris:
    cosmica, Semproni, tam mala quam bona sunt.

42

Muneribus cupiat si quis contendere tecum,
    audeat hic etiam, Castrice, carminibus.
nos tenues in utroque sumus vincique parati:
    inde sopor nobis et placet alta quies.
5 tam mala cur igitur dederim tibi carmina quaeris?
    Alcinoo nullum poma dedisse putas?

40

Here lies that old gentleman, well-known in the Augustan palace, who bore not ignobly our god in either vein.[a] His children's piety mingled him with his wife's hallowed shade. Elysium's grove possesses both. She died first, cheated of her fresh youth; he lived almost thrice six Olympiads.[b] But whoever saw your tears, Etruscus, thought that the years had hurried to snatch him from you.

41

Sempronius Tucca, you think of yourself as a citizen of the cosmos. Cosmics,[c] Sempronius, are as often bad as good.

42

If any man should wish to rival you in gifts, let him also dare, Castricus, to vie with you in poetry. I am weak in both, ready to be outdone; so I love sleep and deep repose. Why then have I given you such bad verses, you ask? Do you suppose nobody gave fruit to Alcinous?[d]

[a] I.e. pleased or angry. As for Claudius Etruscus, see Stat. *Silv.* 3.3. He had been banished and recalled by Domitian: cf. 6.83.

[b] Periods of five years, as generally in M.

[c] A play on *cosmicus*, "citizen of the world," and *cosmica*, "products of Cosmus (the perfumer)" (*SB*[1]).

[d] I.e. carried coals to Newcastle.

43

Primum est ut praestes, si quid te, Cinna, rogabo;
 illud deinde sequens ut cito, Cinna, neges.
diligo praestantem; non odi, Cinna, negantem:
 sed tu nec praestas nec cito, Cinna, negas.

44

Maximus ille tuus, Ovidi, Caesonius hic est,
 cuius adhuc vultum vivida cera tenet.
hunc Nero damnavit, sed tu damnare Neronem
 ausus es et profugi, non tua, fata sequi:
5 aequora per Scyllae magni comes exulis isti,
 qui modo nolueras consulis ire comes.
si victura meis mandantur nomina chartis
 et fas est cineri me superesse meo,
audiet hoc praesens venturaque turba fuisse
10 illi te, Senecae quod fuit ille suo.

44.5 magni *Heinsius* : -nus βγ

43

Best is that you give me anything I ask, Cinna; next best, Cinna, is that you refuse promptly. I like a man who gives; I don't hate a man who refuses, Cinna. But you, Cinna, neither give nor promptly refuse.

44

This, Ovidius,[a] is your[b] friend Caesonius Maximus,[c] whose features the living wax still preserves. Nero condemned him; but you dared to condemn Nero and follow the fate of a fugitive, which was not yours. You passed through Scylla's sea as the great exile's companion, you who but lately had declined to go as companion to a consul. If names consigned to my pages shall live and it is given me to survive my ashes, present and future generations shall hear that you were to him what he was to his Seneca.

[a] Quintus Ovidius, M.'s friend and neighbor at Nomentum; cf. 7.93.3; 10.44.

[b] The short second vowel of *tuus* is lengthened "in arsis"; so too in 10.89.1.

[c] Caesonius or Caesennius Maximus was exiled in 65 (Tac. *Ann.* 15.71). He may have gone to Sardinia with Seneca when the latter was exiled by Claudius.

45

Facundi Senecae potens amicus,
caro proximus aut prior Sereno,
hic est Maximus ille, quem frequenti
felix littera pagina salutat.
5   hunc tu per Siculas secutus undas,
o nullis, Ovidi, tacende linguis,
sprevisti domini furentis iras.
miretur Pyladen suum vetustas,
haesit qui comes exuli parentis.
10   quis discrimina comparet duorum?
haesisti comes exuli Neronis.

46

Commendare tuum dum vis mihi carmine munus
   Maeonioque cupis doctius ore loqui,
excrucias multis pariter me teque diebus,
   et tua de nostro, Prisce, Thalia tacet.
5 divitibus poteris Musas elegosque sonantes
   mittere: pauperibus munera πεζά dato.

47

Doctorum Licini celeberrime Sura virorum,
   cuius prisca gravis lingua reduxit avos,
redderis — heu, qunto fatorum munere! — nobis
   gustata Lethes paene remissus aqua.

46.6 πεζά *Palmer* : pexa β : plena γ : prisce *ex* pi- R

45

The powerful friend of eloquent Seneca, next after his beloved Serenus or before him, this is that Maximus whom the auspicious letter[a] greets on many a page. You, Ovidius, whom all tongues should tell of, followed him through Sicilian waters, despising the mad ruler's wrath. Let antiquity admire its Pylades, who clung companion to one banished by his parent.[b] Who could compare the two risks? You clung companion to one banished by Nero.

46

Wishing to commend your present to me with a poem and to speak more gracefully than Maeonian lips, you torture yourself and me alike, Priscus, for many a day, and your Thalia is silent at my cost. You will be able to send Muses and sonorous elegies to the rich: to the poor give your presents in prose.

47

Licinius Sura, most famed of lettered men, whose old-world tongue brought back our grave grandfathers, you are restored to us (ah, what a gift of the Fates!), sent back when you had all but tasted

---

[a] The s for *salutem* (greeting). These letters of Seneca are unknown.

[b] Orestes, banished by Clytemnestra after the murder of Agamemnon.

5   perdiderant iam vota metum securaque flebat
     †tristitia et lacrimis iamque peractus eras†:
   non tulit invidiam taciti regnator Averni
     et ruptas Fatis reddidit ipse colus.
   scis igitur quantas hominum mors falsa querelas
10   moverit et frueris posteritate tua.
   vive velut rapto fugitivaque gaudia carpe:
     perdiderit nullum vita reversa diem.

48

Cum mensas habeat fere trecentas,
pro mensis habet Annius ministros:
transcurrunt gabatae volantque lances.
has vobis epulas habete, lauti:
5   nos offendimur ambulante cena.

49

Parva suburbani munuscula mittimus horti:
faucibus ova tuis, poma, Severe, gulae.

47.6 *vide SB*[3]   47.8 ruptas *Gronovius* : rap- $\beta\gamma$
49.1 parua γ : pauca β

Lethe's stream. Prayers had already lost their fear
and sorrow wept without anxiety * * *.[a] The odium
was too much for the ruler of silent Avernus, and
with his own hand he gave back to the Fates the
broken thread. Therefore you know how men
lamented your false death, and you enjoy your own
posterity. Live as on plunder[b] and pluck fleeting
joys. Life returned should not lose a day.

48

Though he has some three hundred tables, Annius
has pages instead of tables. The platters speed
across and the dishes fly. You are welcome to such
banquets, my fine gentlemen. A walking dinner
puts me off.

49

I send you the little gifts of a suburban[c] garden:
eggs for your throat,[d] Severus, fruit for your palate.

[a] All hope having been abandoned. Reading and sense
in the pentameter are uncertain.

[b] On borrowed time, in modern idiom.

[c] I.e. not far from Rome, on the Nomentan property.

[d] Pliny (*N.H.* 29.42) recommends yoke of egg for a sore
throat.

50

Fons dominae, regina loci quo gaudet Ianthis,
    gloria conspicuae deliciumque domus,
cum tua tot niveis ornetur ripa ministris
    et Ganymedeo luceat unda choro,
5 quid facit Alcides silva sacratus in ista?
    tam vicina tibi cur tenet antra deus?
numquid Nympharum notos observat amores,
    tam multi pariter ne rapiantur Hylae?

51

Mercari nostras si te piget, Urbice, nugas
    et lasciva tamen carmina nosse libet,
Pompeium quares — et nosti forsitan — Auctum;
    Ultoris prima Martis in aede sedet.
5 iure madens varioque togae limatus in usu
    non lector meus hic, Urbice, sed liber est;
sic tenet absentes nostros cantatque libellos
    ut pereat chartis littera nulla meis:
denique, si vellet, poterat scripsisse videri;
10   sed famae mavult ille favere meae.
hunc licet a decima — neque enim satis ante vacabit —
    sollicites, capiet cenula parva duos;
ille leget, bibe tu; nolis licet, ille sonabit,
    et cum 'iam satis est' dixeris, ille leget.

50.6 tibi β : tui γ

50

Fountain dear to your mistress, in which Ianthis, queen of the spot, delights, glory and favorite of a stately home, since your bank is adorned by so many snow-white pages and the water is bright with a band of Ganymedes, what is Alcides doing, hallowed in yonder wood? Why does the god have a bower so near to you? Does he keep watch upon the Nymphs, whose amours he knows so well, lest so many Hylases be snatched away together?[a]

51

If it irks you to buy my trifles, Urbicus, and nonetheless you have a fancy to know my wanton verses, you will seek out (and perhaps you know him) Pompeius Auctus. He sits at the entrance of Mars the Avenger's temple. Steeped in law and practiced in the various employments of the gown, he is not my reader, Urbicus, he is my book. He remembers and recites my little books in their absence so that not a letter is lost to my pages. In fine, he could pass for their author if he wished, but he prefers to favor my fame. You may solicit him from the tenth hour onward (before that he will be too busy); a small dinner will accommodate the two of you. He will read,[b] you drink. Though you wish he wouldn't, on he will boom. And when you say "That's enough," on he will read.

[a] Cf. 7.15.
[b] Aloud, as usual in antiquity.

52

Gratum est quod Celeri nostros legis, Aucte, libellos,
    si tamen et Celerem quod legis, Aucte, iuvat.
ille meas gentes, Celtas et rexit Hiberos,
    nec fuit in nostro certior orbe fides.
5 maior me tanto reverentia turbat, et aures
    non auditoris, iudicis esse puto.

53

Omnia misisti mihi Saturnalibus, Umber,
    munera, contulerant quae tibi quinque dies:
bis senos triplices et dentiscalpia septem;
    his comes accessit spongea, mappa, calix,
5 semodiusque fabae cum vimine Picenarum
    et Laletanae nigra lagona sapae;
parvaque cum canis venerunt cottana prunis
    et Libycae fici pondere testa gravis.
vix puto triginta nummorum tota fuisse
10   munera, quae grandes octo tulere Syri.
quanto commodius nullo mihi ferre labore
    argenti potuit pondera quinque puer!

54

Semper mane mihi de me mera somnia narras,
    quae moveant animum sollicitentque meum.
iam prior ad faecem, sed et haec vindemia venit,
    exorat noctes dum mihi saga tuas;

52.3 Celtas et *Marx* (cf. 4.55.8, 10.78.9. Xen. *Hell*. 7.1.20,
Pliny *N.H.* 3.8) : et c- βγ   53.6 Laletanae] *cf. ad* 1.26.9

120

52

I am gratified, Auctus, that you read my books to
Celer, that is, if Celer too likes what you read. He
governed my peoples, Celts and Iberians, nor in our
world was good faith ever more sure. So much the
greater reverence confounds me, and I conceive his
ears to be not a listener's but a judge's.

53

You sent me at the Saturnalia, Umber, all the
presents that the five days had brought you: a dozen
three-leaved tablets and seven toothpicks, with
which in addition arrived a sponge, a napkin, a cup,
half a peck of beans with a wicker basket of Picene
olives, and a black flask of Laletanian must. Also
came small Syrian figs along with wrinkled plums[a]
and a jar heavy with the weight of Libyan figs. I
think the gifts, borne by eight strapping Syrians,
were scarce worth thirty sesterces in all. How much
more conveniently could a boy without any trouble
have brought me five pounds of silver plate!

54

Always of a morning you tell me your dreams about
me, nothing but that, to disturb me and cause me
anxiety. Last year's vintage is already down to the
dregs, and this one's too, as the wise woman expi-

[a] I.e. prunes.

5 consumpsi salsasque molas et turis acervos;
  decrevere greges, dum cadit agna frequens;
 non porcus, non chortis aves, non ova supersunt.
  aut vigila aut dormi, Nasidiane, tibi.

55

 Nulli munera, Chreste, si remittis,
 nec nobis dederis remiserisque:
 credam te satis esse liberalem.
 sed si reddis Apicio Lupoque
5 et Gallo Titioque Caesioque,
 linges non mihi — nam proba et pusilla est —
 sed quae de Solymis venit perustis
 damnatam modo mentulam tributis.

56

Astra polumque pia cepisti mente, Rabiri,
 Parrhasiam mira qui struis arte domum.
Phidiaco si digna Iovi dare templa parabit,
 has petet a nostro Pisa Tonante manus.

56.3 parabit ς : -auit βγ   56.4 petet β : petat γ

---

[a] Such persons were notoriously bibulous; cf. 11.49.7f;
Prop. 4.5; Ov. *Am.* 1.8.

[b] All these were used in expiations.

[c] Captured by Titus and burned A.D. 70.

ates your nights for me.[a] I have used up salt
sacrificial cakes and heaps of incense. My flocks
have dwindled, as lamb falls after lamb. No porker
is left, nor poultry, nor eggs.[b] Nasidianus, either
stay awake or sleep for yourself.

55

Chrestus, if you return no man's presents, then
don't give any to me or send any in return for mine; I
shall think you sufficiently generous. But if you
make return to Apicius and Lupus and Gallus and
Titius and Caesius, you will lick a cock — not mine,
which is well-behaved and diminutive, but one that
comes from burned-out Jerusalem,[c] one lately
doomed to pay taxes.[d]

56

Rabirius, your pious mind has comprehended the
stars and sky, builder of the Parrhasian dwelling
with wondrous skill.[e] If Pisa shall prepare to give
Phidias' Jupiter[f] a worthy shrine, she will ask our
Thunderer for these hands.

[d] Cf. Suet. *Dom.* 12.2.

[e] A reference to the domed roof of Domitian's palace,
built by Rabirius, his architect (cf. 10.71), and completed in
A.D. 92.

[f] The statue of Zeus at Olympia by Phidias.

57

Castora de Polluce Gabinia fecit Achillan:
πὺξ ἀγαθός fuerat, nunc erit ἱππόδαμος.

58

Iam sex aut septem nupsisti, Galla, cinaedis,
    dum coma te nimium pexaque barba iuvat.
deinde experta latus madidoque simillima loro
    inguina nec lassa stare coacta manu
5 deseris imbelles thalamos mollemque maritum
    rursus et in similes decidis usque toros.
quaere aliquem Curios semper Fabiosque loquentem,
    hirsutum et dura rusticitate trucem:
invenies; sed habet tristis quoque turba cinaedos.
10   difficile est vero nubere, Galla, viro.

59

Non cenat sine Apro noster, Tite, Caecilianus.
    bellum convivam Caecilianus habet.

---

[a] I.e. she has made a pugilist a knight. The reference is
to Hom. *Il.* 3.237, where πὺξ ἀγαθός (pyx agathos, "good
with his fists") is the epithet of Pollux the boxer and ἱππό-
δαμος (hippodamos, "horse-tamer") that of Castor, the
horseman. There is doubtless an obscene pun, since πυγή
(pygê) or πύξ (pyx) = buttocks. *Hippodamus* is less easily
explained, but see the note in my edition.

57

Gabinia has made Achillas a Castor out of a Pollux; he was *pyx agathos*, now he will be Hippodamus.[a]

58

Galla, you have already married six or seven queens, overmuch attracted by long hair and combed beards. Then, after making trial of their vigor and their members like damp leather, which fail to stand even when urged by a weary hand, you abandon the unwarlike bedchambers and the effeminate husband, only to fall again and again into similar unions. Look for someone who is always talking of Curii and Fabii, some husky boor, hairy and gruff; you will find him. But even the sour-faced brigade[b] has its queens. It's hard, Galla, to marry a real man.

59

Our friend Caecilianus, Titus, never dines without Aper.[c] A charming dinner guest Caecilianus has!

[b] I.e. of so-called philosophers: cf. 9.27 and 47.

[c] Aper, a common name, means "boar." It is usually printed here without a capital. Since ancient script had no capitals, three meanings are possible: "without Aper," "without boar (on the menu)," and "without a boar (as guest)." In v. 2 M. humorously chooses the third.

60

Tarpeiae venerande rector aulae,
quem salvo duce credimus Tonantem,
cum votis sibi quisque te fatiget
et poscat dare quae dei potestis,
5   nil pro me mihi, Iuppiter, petenti
ne suscensueris velut superbo.
te pro Caesare debeo rogare:
pro me debeo Caesarem rogare.

61

Abstulerat totam temerarius institor urbem
    inque suo nullum limine limen erat.
iussisti tenuis, Germanice, crescere vicos,
    et modo quae fuerat semita, facta via est.
5   nulla catenatis pila est praecincta lagonis
    nec praetor medio cogitur ire luto,
stringitur in densa nec caeca novacula turba,
    occupat aut totas nigra popina vias.
tonsor, copo, cocus, lanius sua limina servant.
10   nunc Roma est, nuper magna taberna fuit.

60

Worshipful ruler of the Tarpeian palace,[a] in whom
as Thunderer we believe while our Leader is safe,
while each man wearies you with prayers, asking
for what you gods can give, be not angry with me,
Jupiter, who ask nothing for myself, or think me
proud. I ought to petition you on behalf of Caesar;
on my own behalf I ought to petition Caesar.

61

The audacious retailers had appropriated the entire
city; no threshold kept within its own bounds. You
bade[b] the narrow streets expand, Germanicus, and
what had lately been a track became a road. No
column[c] is girt with chained flagons, and the praetor
is not forced to walk through the mud. The razor is
not drawn blindly in a dense crowd, nor does the
grimy cook shop monopolize the whole street. The
barber, the taverner, the cook, the butcher keep to
their own thresholds. Now it is Rome, it used to be a
big shop.

[a] Jupiter's temple on the Capitol. The word *aulae* suggests the parallel between the god and the Emperor.

[b] Domitian (Germanicus) in A.D. 92 by edict forbade stalls protruding into the street.

[c] Of a wine shop.

62

Reclusis foribus grandes percidis, Hamille,
    et te deprendi, cum facis ista, cupis,
ne quid liberti narrent servique paterni
    et niger obliqua garrulitate cliens.
5   non pedicari se qui testatur, Hamille,
    illud saepe facit quod sine teste facit.

63

Perpetui numquam moritura volumina Sili
    qui legis et Latia carmina digna toga,
Pierios tantum vati placuisse recessus
    credis et Aoniae Bacchica serta comae?
5   sacra cothurnati non attigit ante Maronis
    implevit magni quam Ciceronis opus:
hunc miratur adhuc centum gravis hasta virorum,
    hunc loquitur grato plurimus ore cliens.
postquam bis senis ingentem fascibus annum
10   rexerat asserto qui sacer orbe fuit,
emeritos Musis et Phoebo tradidit annos
    proque suo celebrat nunc Helicona foro.

62.1 *et* 5 Hamille *Friedländer* : am- *vel* anulle βγ

62

You sodomize big youths, Hamillus,[a] behind open doors and want to be caught doing so, for fear that your freedmen and your father's slaves and a malicious client, chattering and hinting, may tell some tale. Anyone who calls to witness that he is not sodomized, Hamillus, does often what he does without witnesses.

63

Reader of the everlasting volumes of immortal Silius, poems worthy of the Latin gown, think you that only Pierian retreats and Bacchic garlands for Aonian locks have pleased the bard? He did not put his hand to buskined Maro's mysteries before he filled the measure of great Cicero's work.[b] The solemn spear[c] of the Hundred Men still wonders at him, and a host of clients speak of him with gratitude. After he had ruled with twelve *fasces* the mighty year made sacred by a world set free,[d] he gave his years of retirement to Phoebus and the Muses, and now frequents Helicon instead of his Forum.

[a] See Appendix B.

[b] Advocacy.

[c] A spear set in the ground was the sign of the Centumviral Court; cf. 6.38.5n.

[d] He was consul in A.D. 68, the year of Nero's death.

64

Qui tonsor fueras tota notissimus urbe
    et post hoc dominae munere factus eques,
Sicanias urbes Aetnaeaque regna petisti,
    Cinname, cum fugeres tristia iura fori.
5 qua nunc arte graves tolerabis inutilis annos?
    quid facit infelix et fugitiva quies?
non rhetor, non grammaticus ludive magister,
    non Cynicus, non tu Stoicus esse potes,
vendere nec vocem Siculis plausumque theatris:
10   quod superest, iterum, Cinname, tonsor eris.

65

Lis te bis decimae numerantem frigora brumae
    conterit una tribus, Gargiliane, foris.
ah miser et demens! viginti litigat annis
    quisquam cui vinci, Gargiliane, licet?

66

Heredem Fabius Labienum ex asse reliquit:
    plus meruisse tamen se Labienus ait.

---

[a] She had given him his qualification, 400,000 sesterces.

[b] Which laws? M. does not say.

64

You were the best-known barber in the whole city
and later became a knight by the gift of your
patroness.[a] Now you have sought Sicanian cities
and the realms of Aetna, Cinnamus, in flight from
the Forum's grim laws.[b] With what skill will you
now in your uselessness bear the heavy years?
What use is your unhappy, banished retirement?
You cannot be a rhetor, or a grammarian, or a
schoolmaster, or a Cynic, or a Stoic. You cannot sell
your voice and applause to Sicilian theaters. Only
one thing is left: Cinnamus, you will be a barber
again.

65

A lawsuit wears you out in the three Forums, Gargi-
lianus, as you count the chills of a twentieth winter.
Unhappy madman! Does anybody litigate for
twenty years, when it is open to him to lose the
case?

66

Fabius left Labienus his sole heir; and yet Labienus
says he deserved more.[c]

[c] The point is unclear. Perhaps it is that L.'s obscene
compliances had gone beyond what money could compen-
sate.

67

Pedicat pueros tribas Philaenis
et tentigine saevior mariti
undenas dolat in die puellas.
harpasto quoque subligata ludit
5   et flavescit haphe, gravesque draucis
halteras facili rotat lacerto,
et putri lutulenta de palaestra
uncti verbere vapulat magistri:
nec cenat prius aut recumbit ante
10   quam septem vomuit meros deunces;
ad quos fas sibi tunc putat redire,
cum coloephia sedecim comedit.
post haec omnia cum libidinatur,
non fellat — putat hoc parum virile —,
15   sed plane medias vorat puellas.
di mentem tibi dent tuam, Philaeni,
cunnum lingere quae putas virile.

68

Commendare meas, Istanti Rufe, Camenas
parce, precor, socero: seria forsan amat.
quod si lascivos admittit et ille libellos,
haec ego vel Curio Fabricioque legam.

67.3 dolat *Gruter* : dolet β : uorat γ 67.11 redire β :
reuerti γ 68.1 Istanti *Munro* : ins- $\beta\gamma$ (*cf. ad* 8.50.21;
73.12.95; 98)

67

Lesbian Philaenis sodomizes boys and, more cruel than a husband's lust, penetrates eleven girls per diem. She also plays with the harpastum high-girt, gets yellow with sand, and with effortless arm rotates weights that would tax an athlete. Muddy from the crumbly wrestling floor, she takes a beating[a] from the blows of an oiled trainer. She does not dine or lie down for dinner before she has vomited six pints of neat wine,[b] to which she thinks she can decently return when she has eaten sixteen collops.[c] When after all this she gets down to sex, she does not suck men (she thinks that not virile enough), but absolutely devours girls' middles. May the god give you your present mind,[d] Philaenis, who think it virile to lick a cunt.

68

Pray don't recommend my Muses to your father-in-law, Istantius Rufus. Perhaps he likes serious poetry. But if even he admits my wanton little books, I would read them to Curius and Fabricius.

[a] Massage.

[b] Seven *deunces* = 77 *cyathi*; cf. 6.78.6n.

[c] Pieces of meat favored by athletes, what sort of meat is uncertain.

[d] I.e. keep you in your present deplorable notions.

69

Haec est illa tibi promissa Theophila, Cani,
  cuius Cecropia pectora dote madent.
hanc sibi iure petat magni senis Atticus hortus,
  nec minus esse suam Stoica turba velit.
5 vivet opus quodcumque per has emiseris aures;
  tam non femineum nec populare sapit.
non tua Pantaenis nimium se praeferat illi,
  quamvis Pierio sit bene nota choro.
carmina fingentem Sappho laudarit amatrix:
10 castior haec et non doctior illa fuit.

70

Ipsarum tribadum tribas, Philaeni,
recte, quam futuis, vocas amicam.

71

Ficosa est uxor, ficosus et ipse maritus,
  filia ficosa est et gener atque nepos,
nec dispensator nec vilicus ulcere turpi
  nec rigidus fossor sed nec arator eget.
5 cum sint ficosi pariter iuvenesque senesque,
  res mira est, ficos non habet unus ager.

69.9 laudarit *ed. Rom.* : -dauit γ : -dabat β : -daret *marg.*
Iunii   71.2 nepos Rβ : socer γ

---

[a] Epicurus.
[b] An otherwise unknown poet of Sappho's circle eulogized by Canius.

BOOK VII

69

Canius, this is your promised bride, Theophila, whose mind is steeped in Cecropian riches. The Attic garden of the great ancient[a] could rightfully claim her, nor less would the Stoic throng wish her theirs. Whatever work you send forth through her ears will live; so unwomanlike is her taste, so far removed from the common. Your Pantaenis[b] would scarcely claim to be her superior, well-known though she be to the Pierian choir. Sappho would love her and praise her verse-making. Theophila is more pure and Sappho was not more accomplished.

70

Lesbia of the very Lesbians, Philaenis, rightly do you call the girl you fuck your girl-friend.[c]

71

The wife has figs,[d] so does the husband, the daughter has figs and the son-in-law and the grandson. Neither the steward nor the bailiff nor the rugged ditcher is without the horrid growth, nor yet the ploughman. Since young and old alike have figs, it is remarkable that only the land is without them.

[c] *Amica* = (a) female friend and (b) mistress.
[d] Cf. 1.65.

72

Gratus sic tibi, Paule, sit December
nec vani triplices brevesque mappae
nec turis veniant leves selibrae,
sed lances ferat et scyphos avorum
5   aut grandis reus aut potens amicus:
seu quod te potius iuvat capitque,
sic vincas Noviumque Publiumque
mandris et vitreo latrone clusos;
sic palmam tibi de trigone nudo
10 unctae det favor arbiter coronae
nec laudet Polybi magis sinistras:
si quisquam mea dixerit malignus
atro carmina quae madent veneno,
ut vocem mihi commodes patronam
15 et quantum poteris, sed usque, clames:
'non scripsit meus ista Martialis.'

73

Esquiliis domus est, domus est tibi colle Dianae,
    et tua Patricius culmina vicus habet;
hinc viduae Cybeles, illinc sacraria Vestae,
    inde novum, veterem prospicis inde Iovem.

72

Paulus, so may December be to your liking, and may no idle three-leaved tablets or exiguous napkins or light half-pounds of incense come your way, but a big defendant or a powerful friend bring dishes and cups of our forebears; or, what pleases you and takes your fancy more, so may you vanquish Novius and Publius, hemming them in with your pawns and glass soldiers;[a] so may the oiled circle's favoring judgment give you a victor's palm from the nude[b] trigon, nor praise Polybius' left-handers more: if any malicious person attributes to me verses dripping with black venom, lend me your advocate voice and shout and shout with all your lungs: "My Martial did not write this stuff."

73

You have a house on the Esquiline, and a house on Diana's hill,[c] and Patrician Row[d] has a roof of yours. From one you view the shrine of bereaved[e] Cybele, from another that of Vesta, from this Jupiter's new

[a] In the game of *latrunculi*, often translated "robbers"; but see 14.20n. The game was played with pieces on a board, and the *latro* was superior to the *mandra*.

[b] Cf. 4.19.7n. "Nude," i.e. semi-naked, refers to the players.

[c] The Aventine.

[d] At the foot of the Esquiline.

[e] By the death of Attis.

5   dic ubi conveniam, dic qua te parte requiram:
      quisquis ubique habitat, Maxime, nusquam habitat

74

Cyllenes caelique decus, facunde minister,
    aurea cui torto virga dracone viret:
sic tibi lascivi non desit copia furti,
    sive cupis Paphien seu Ganymede cales;
5 maternaeque sacris ornentur frondibus Idus
    et senior parca mole prematur avus:
hunc semper Norbana diem cum coniuge Carpo
    laeta colat, primis quo coiere toris.
hic pius antistes Sophiae sua dona ministret,
10   hic te ture vocet fidus et ipse Iovi.

75

Vis futui gratis, cum sis deformis anusque.
    res perridicula est: vis dare nec dare vis.

74.9 sua] *anne* nova?   74.10 vocet *scripsi* : uocat $\beta\gamma$

---

    [a] On the Capitol and on the Quirinal. Seven houses are involved.

    [b] The caduceus or herald's wand, borne by Mercury as the messenger of the gods.

    [c] The Ides of May: cf. 12.67.1. Maia was the mother of Mercury.

temple, from that the old one.[a] Tell me where I am to meet you, in what quarter to look for you. Who lives everywhere, Maximus, lives nowhere.

74

Ornament of Cyllene and of heaven, eloquent lackey, whose golden wand[b] is green with twisted snake, so may abundance of stolen wantonness not fail you, whether you desire the Paphian or are hot for Ganymede, and may your mother's Ides[c] be decked with sacred fronds, and your old grand-father[d] be pressed with not too ponderous a mass: let Norbana with her husband Carpus ever joyfully celebrate this day on which they first joined in wedlock. A pious priest, here let him offer Wisdom[e] the gifts that are hers, here invoke you with incense. He too is loyal to Jupiter.[f]

75

You want to be fucked gratis, though you are an ugly hag. The thing is quite ridiculous: you want to give and not to give.[g]

[d] Atlas, who sustained the weight of the sky.

[e] I.e. philosophy; cf. 1.111.1.

[f] He is faithful to our Jupiter, the Emperor, as you are to the celestial Jupiter.

[g] Play on two meanings of *dare*; cf. 10.75.14.

76

Quod te diripiunt potentiores
per convivia, porticus, theatra,
et tecum, quotiens ita incidisti,
gestari iuvat et iuvat lavari:
5   nolito nimium tibi placere.
delectas, Philomuse, non amaris.

77

Exigis ut nostros donem tibi, Tucca, libellos.
    non faciam: nam vis vendere, non legere.

78

Cum Saxetani ponatur coda lacerti
    et, bene si cenas, conchis inuncta tibi:
sumen, aprum, leporem, boletos, ostrea, mullos
    mittis: habes nec cor, Papyle, nec genium.

76

If important people compete for your company at dinner tables and in the colonnades and theaters and like to ride with you and bathe with you as often as you turn up, don't get too conceited. It's your company they like, Philomusus, not you.[a]

77

You demand that I give you my little books, Tucca. I won't, for you want to sell them, not to read them.

78

The tail of a Saxetanian lizard fish[b] is set in front of you and, if you're dining well, some oiled beans; and you send presents of sow's udder, boar, hare, mushrooms, oysters, mullet. You have neither sense,[c] Papylus, nor the capacity to enjoy.[d]

[a] Lit. "you give them pleasure, you are not loved."

[b] From Sexetanum or Saxetanum in Hispania Baetica, where was a noted saltfishery. The *lacerti*, according to Pliny (*N.H.* 32.146), were very small.

[c] Lit. "heart."

[d] Literally, "nor a Genius," this being a sort of guardian angel, a lifelong spiritual attendant (cf. 7.12.10). But "indulging one's Genius" meant having a good time — of which "Papylus" was incapable.

79

Potavi modo consulare vinum.
quaeris quam vetus atque liberale?
prisco consule conditum: sed ipse
qui ponebat erat, Severe, consul.

80

Quatenus Odrysios iam pax Romana triones
    temperat et tetricae conticuere tubae,
hunc Marcellino poteris, Faustine, libellum
    mittere: iam chartis, iam vacat ille iocis.
5 sed si parva tui munuscula quaeris amici
    commendare, ferat carmina nostra puer,
non qualis Geticae satiatus lacte iuvencae
    Sarmatica rigido ludit in amne rota,
sed Mitylenaei roseus mangonis ephebus
10   vel non caesus adhuc matre iubente Lacon.
at tibi captivo famulus mittetur ab Histro,
    qui Tiburtinas pascere possit oves.

81

'Triginta toto mala sunt epigrammata libro.'
    si totidem bona sunt, Lause, bonus liber est.

79.3 prisco *Housman* : ipso βγ

---

[a] I.e. wine at a consul's table; see Housman, 816.
[b] Alternatively "under an ancient (*prisco*) consul."

79

Recently I drank consular wine.[a] You ask how old and generous it was? It was laid down in Priscus' consulship.[b] But my host who served it, Severus, was the consul.

80

Since the Roman Peace now governs the Odrysian Bears and the harsh trumpets have fallen mute, you will be able, Faustinus, to send this little book to Marcellinus;[c] he has time for reading now, and for jests. But if you wish to commend your friend's trifling present, the boy who carries my poems should not be such a one as plays on frozen river with a Sarmatian hoop, full fed with the milk of a Getic heifer, but a rosy youth from a Mitylenian dealer or a Laconian not yet flogged at his mother's orders.[d] In return you will be sent a slave from captive Hister, who can feed your sheep at Tibur.

81

"There are thirty bad epigrams in the whole book." If there are as many good ones, Lausus, it's a good book.

Three consuls called Priscus are recorded in years not long before 92, when Book VII was published.
  [c] Who had been campaigning in Dacia.
  [d] Spartan boys used to be flogged at the altar of Artemis to teach them endurance.

82

Menophili penem tam grandis fibula vestit
    ut sit comoedis omnibus una satis.
hunc ego credideram — nam saepe lavamur in unum ·
    sollicitum voci parcere, Flacce, suae:
5 dum ludit media populo spectante palaestra,
    delapsa est misero fibula: verpus erat.

83

Eutrapelus tonsor dum circuit ora Luperci
    expingitque genas, altera barba subit.

84

Dum mea Caecilio formatur imago Secundo,
    spirat et arguta picta tabella manu,
i, liber, ad Geticam Peucen Histrumque iacentem:
    haec loca perdomitis gentibus ille tenet.
5 parva dabis caro sed dulcia dona sodali:
    certior in nostro carmine vultus erit;
casibus hic nullis, nullis delebilis annis
    vivet, Apelleum cum morietur opus.

83.2 expungit *Eden* (*cf.* 8.52.8)

---

    [a] Comic actors and singers wore this, as a preventive of
sexual indulgence, to save their voice: cf. 11.75.3; 14.215;
Juv. 6.73, 380.

82

So large a sheath covers Menophilus' penis that it would be enough by itself for all our comic actors.[a] I had supposed (we often bathe together) that he was anxious to spare his voice, Flaccus. But while he was in a game in the middle of the sportsground with everybody watching, the sheath slipped off the poor soul; he was circumcised.

83

While barber Eutrapelus[b] moved round Lupercus' face and painted[c] his cheeks, another beard came up.

84

While my likeness is taking shape for Caecilius Secundus[d] and the canvas, painted by a skilful hand, breathes, go, book, to Getic Peuce and prostrate Hister: these regions with their subjugated nations he rules. You will give my dear friend a small gift but a sweet one; my face will be seen more clearly in my poems. No accidents, no passage of years will efface it; it shall live when Apelles' work shall die.

[b] "Nimble," "dexterous."

[c] Cf. Lucil. 265 *expilor <ex>pingor* and 8.52.8.

[d] Not Pliny the Younger (C. Plinius Caecilius Secundus).

85

quod non insulse scribis tetrasticha quaedam,
    disticha quod belle pauca, Sabelle, facis,
laudo nec admiror. facile est epigrammata belle
    scribere, sed librum scribere difficile est.

86

Ad natalicias dapes vocabar,
essem cum tibi, Sexte, non amicus.
quid factum est, rogo, quid repente factum est,
post tot pignora nostra, post tot annos
5   quod sum praeteritus vetus sodalis?
sed causam scio. nulla venit a me
Hispani tibi libra pustulati
nec levis toga nec rudes lacernae.
non est sportula quae negotiatur;
10 pascis munera, Sexte, non amicos.
iam dices mihi 'vapulet vocator.'

87

Si meus aurita gaudet lagalopece Flaccus,
    si fruitur tristi Canius Aethiope,
Publius exiguae si flagrat amore catellae,
    si Cronius similem cercopithecon amat,

87.1 lagalopece *ed. Rom.* : lagao- *vel sim.* βγ

85

That you write some quatrains not without wit and turn a few couplets prettily, Sabellus, is something I praise but do not wonder at. It's easy to write epigrams prettily, but to write a book is hard.

86

I was invited to your birthday feasts, Sextus, when I was not your friend. What has happened, I ask you, what has suddenly happened after so many mutual pledges, so many years, that I, your old comrade, am passed over? But I know the reason. No pound of Spanish frosted silver[a] nor smooth gown nor unworn cloak came your way from me. Hospitality is not a business deal. You feed presents, Sextus, not friends. Now you'll say to me: "I'll have my secretary[b] flogged."

87

If my Flaccus delights in a long-eared fennec,[c] if Canius enjoys a sombre Ethiop, if Publius is a-fire with love for a tiny lapdog,[d] if Cronius adores a long-tailed monkey that resembles him, if a destruc-

[a] A highly refined sort.
[b] *Vocator*, a slave in charge of sending out invitations. Sextus makes him a scapegoat.
[c] "Hare-fox." "Prob. a fennec" *OLD*.
[d] Cf. 1.109.

147

5   delectat Marium si perniciosus ichneumon,
      pica salutatrix si tibi, Lause, placet,
  si gelidum collo nectit †Gadilla† draconem,
      luscinio tumulum si Telesilla dedit:
  blanda Cupidinei cur non amet ora Labyrtae,
10   qui videt haec dominis monstra placere suis?

88

Fertur habere meos, si vera est fama, libellos
    inter delicias pulchra Vienna suas.
me legit omnis ibi senior iuvenisque puerque
    et coram tetrico casta puella viro.
5   hoc ego maluerim quam si mea carmina cantent
     qui Nilum ex ipso protinus ore bibunt;
quam meus Hispano si me Tagus impleat auro,
    pascat et Hybla meas, pascat Hymettos apes.
non nihil ergo sumus nec blandae munere linguae
10   decipimur: credam iam, puto, Lause, tibi.

87.7 gadilla *β* : glacia *γ* : *varia viri docti*   87.8 dedit *γ* :
facit *β*   87.9 labyrtae *β* : labycae *γ*

tive ichneumon charms Marius, if a magpie that can speak your name pleases you, Lausus, if Glaucilla(?) twines a clammy snake about her neck, if Telesilla gave a tomb to a nightingale, why should not anyone who sees these freaks[a] pleasing their owners not love the face of Cupid's Labyrtas?

88

Fair Vienna[b] is said, if report speak true, to hold my little books in high favor. Everybody there reads me — old man, young man, boy, and virtuous young woman in front of her straight-laced husband. This gives me more pleasure than if drinkers of the Nile from its very fount[c] were to recite my verses, or my own Tagus load me with Spanish gold, or Hybla or Hymettus feed my bees. So I am not nothing, nor deceived by the bounty of a flattering tongue. In future, Lausus,[d] I think I shall believe you.

---

[a] The lapdog and the nightingale might protest, but M. is in no mood to make distinctions.

[b] Vienne on the Rhone.

[c] Cf. Sp. 3.5. *Os* ("mouth") is ordinarily used of a river's outlet; *caput* ("head") also occurs in both senses.

[d] Evidently a eulogist. But in 7.81 "Lausus" is a carper. The name is probably random in both places, though Lausus of the preceding epigram should be real.

89

I, felix rosa, mollibusque sertis
nostri cinge comas Apollinaris;
quas tu nectere candidas, sed olim,
sic te semper amet Venus, memento.

90

Iactat inaequalem Matho me fecisse libellum:
    si verum est, laudat carmina nostra Matho.
aequales scribit libros Calvinus et Umber:
    aequalis liber est, Cretice, qui malus est.

91

De nostro facunde tibi Iuvenalis agello
    Saturnalicias mittimus, ecce, nuces.
cetera lascivis donavit poma puellis
    mentula custodis luxuriosa dei.

92

'Si quid opus fuerit, scis me non esse rogandum'
    uno bis dicis, Baccara, terque die.
appellat rigida tristis me voce Secundus:
    audis et nescis, Baccara, quid sit opus.

89

Go, lucky rose, and with soft garland circle the locks
of my Apollinaris. And do not fail to bind them
when they are white — but long hereafter. So may
Venus love you always.

90

Matho spreads the word that I have made an
uneven book. If so, Matho praises my poems. Cal-
vinus and Umber write even books. An even book,
Creticus, is a bad book.

91

Eloquent Juvenal,[a] I send you, see, Saturnalian
nuts from my little bit of land. The rest of its pro-
duce the lustful cock of its guardian has bestowed on
wanton girls.

92

"If you need anything, you know you don't have to
ask me."[b] So you say, Baccara, two or three times in
one day. Grim Secundus duns me in peremptory
tones; you hear, and you don't know what I need,

[a] Cf. 7.24n. "Eloquent" (*facunde*) may refer to advocacy,
but can cover literary performance generally. Juvenal's
satires were yet to be.

[b] I.e. "you have only to let me know what you need."

5 pensio te coram petitur clareque palamque:
    audis et nescis, Baccara, quid sit opus.
esse queror gelidasque mihi tritasque lacernas:
    audis et nescis, Baccara, quid sit opus.
hoc opus est, subito fias ut sidere mutus,
10   dicere ne possis, Baccara, 'si quid opus.'

93

Narnia, sulphureo quam gurgite candidus amnis
    circuit, ancipiti vix adeunda iugo,
quid tam saepe meum nobis abducere Quintum
    te iuvat et lenta detinuisse mora?
5 quid Nomentani causam mihi perdis agelli,
    propter vicinum qui pretiosus erat?
sed iam parce mihi, nec abutere, Narnia, Quinto:
    perpetuo liceat sic tibi ponte frui.

94

Unguentum fuerat, quod onyx modo parva gerebat:
    olfecit postquam Papylus, ecce, garum est.

92.10 si quid *Gilbert* : quid sit Tβ(?)γ

---

[a] Causing paralysis; cf. 11.85 and *OLD sidus* 6b and
sideratio.

[b] Ovidius.

[c] For this use of *causa* (raison d' être) cf. Sil. 8.81 *solus
regni lucisque fuisti / germanae tu causa meae* ("you alone
were the reason to my sister for living and reigning").

Baccara. My rent is demanded in your presence, Baccara, loudly and publicly; you hear, and you don't know what I need, Baccara. I complain that my cloak is chilly and threadbare; you hear, and you don't know what I need, Baccara. What I need is for a star to strike you suddenly dumb,[a] Baccara, so that you can't say "If you need anything."

93

Narnia, circled by your river white with sulphurous flood, hard of access on your double ridge, why do you like to take my Quintus[b] away from me so often and keep him so lengthily detained? Why do you destroy for me the reason[c] for my little place at Nomentum, which was valuable because of my neighbor? Come now, spare me, Narnia, and don't overdo it with Quintus; so may it be yours to enjoy your bridge[d] for ever.

94

It once was perfume, carried a while ago in its small alabaster jar. After Papylus smelt it, see, it's garum.[e]

[d] A high-level bridge joining the two heights, part of which still stands (Ker).

[e] Cf. 6.93.6n.

95

Bruma est et riget horridus December,
audes tu tamen osculo nivali
omnes obvius hinc et hinc tenere
et totam, Line, basiare Romam.
5   quid posses graviusque saeviusque
percussus facere atque verberatus?
hoc me frigore basiet nec uxor
blandis filia nec rudis labellis.
sed tu dulcior elegantiorque,
10 cuius livida naribus caninis
dependet glacies rigetque barba,
qualem forficibus metit supinis
tonsor Cinyphio Cilix marito.
centum occurrere malo cunnilingis
15 et gallum timeo minus recentem.
quare si tibi sensus est pudorque,
hibernas, Line, basiationes
in mensem rogo differas Aprilem.

96

Conditus hic ego sum Bassi dolor, Urbicus infans,
    cui genus et nomen maxima Roma dedit.
sex mihi de prima deerant trieteride menses,
    ruperunt tetricae cum male pensa deae.
5 quid species, quid lingua mihi, quid profuit aetas?
    da lacrimas tumulo, qui legis ista, meo:
sic ad Lethaeas, nisi Nestore serior, undas
    non eat, optabis quem superesse tibi.

95.5 posses β : -sis Tγ 96.4 male *Heinsius* : mala $\beta\gamma$

95

It's winter and harsh December stiffens. Yet you dare to hold up everyone you meet, come they from here or from there, with your frosty salute, Linus, and kiss all Rome. What could you do more hurtful and cruel if you had been stabbed and flogged? In this cold I would not have my wife kiss me or my innocent daughter with her winsome lips. But you are sweeter, more elegant than they—with a livid icicle hanging from your canine nostrils and a beard as stiff as a Cilician clipper with upturned shears reaps from a Cinyphian husband![a] I'd rather fall in with a hundred cunt-lickers, a priest of Cybele[b] fresh from action alarms me less. So if you have any feeling and shame, please put off your winter kissing, Linus, to the month of April.

96

Here am I buried, Bassus' sorrow, Urbicus, an infant, to whom most mighty Rome gave race and name. Six months were wanting to my first three years, when the stern goddesses unkindly broke my threads. What availed me my beauty, my talk, my tender age? You that read these lines, give tears to my tomb. So may one whom you wish to survive you go not down to Lethe's waters save past the age of Nestor.

[a] Goat-hair blankets came from both Cilicia and Africa.
[b] Cf. 3.81.5n.

97

Nosti si bene Caesium, libelle,
montanae decus Umbriae, Sabinum,
Auli municipem mei Pudentis,
illi tu dabis haec vel occupato.
5   instent mille licet premantque curae,
nostris carminibus tamen vacabit.
nam me diligit ille proximumque
Turni nobilibus legit libellis.
o quantum tibi nominis paratur!
10   o quae gloria! quam frequens amator!
te convivia, te forum sonabit,
aedes, compita, porticus, tabernae.
uni mitteris, omnibus legeris.

98

Omnia, Castor, emis: sic fiet ut omnia vendas.

99

Sic placidum videas semper, Crispine, Tonantem
    nec te Roma minus quam tua Memphis amet:
carmina Parrhasia si nostra legentur in aula
    — namque solent sacra Caesaris aure frui —,
5   dicere de nobis, ut lector candidus, aude:
    'temporibus praestat non nihil iste tuis,
nec Marso nimium minor est doctoque Catullo.'
    hoc satis est: ipsi cetera mando deo.

97

If you know Caesius Sabinus well, little book, Caesius the ornament of hilly Umbria, fellow townsman of my friend Aulus Pudens, you will give him these, even if he be busy. Though a thousand cares press and beset him, yet he will have time for my verses. For he loves me and reads me next to Turnus' famous little volumes. Oh, what renown is in the making for you! Oh, what glory! What a multitude of fans! The dinner tables, the Forum, the houses, the crossroads, the colonnades, the shops will utter you. You are sent to one, you will be read by all.

98

You buy up everything, Castor; so it will come to pass that you sell up everything.

99

So may you ever see the Thunderer in kindly mood, Crispinus, and Rome love you no less than your own Memphis: if my verses shall be read in the Parrhasian palace (for they are wont to enjoy Caesar's sacred ear), venture, as a candid reader, to say of me: "He brings some credit to your times; he is not too much inferior to Marsus and elegant Catullus." That is sufficient. I leave the rest to the god himself.

LIBER VIII

IMPERATORI DOMITIANO CAESARI AUGUSTO
GERMANICO DACICO VALERIUS MARTIALIS S.

Omnes quidem libelli mei, domine, quibus tu
famam, id est vitam, dedisti, tibi supplicant; et, puto,
propter hoc legentur. Hic tamen, qui operis nostri
octavus inscribitur, occasione pietatis frequentius
5   fruitur. minus itaque ingenio laborandum fuit, in
cuius locum materia successerat: quam quidem
subinde aliqua iocorum mixtura variare tempta-
vimus, ne caelesti verecundiae tuae laudes suas,
quae facilius te fatigare possint quam nos satiare,
10   omnis versus ingereret. quamvis autem epigram-
mata a severissimis quoque et summae fortunae
viris ita scripta sint ut mimicam verborum licen-
tiam affectasse videantur, ego tamen illis non per-
misi tam lascive loqui quam solent. cum pars libri
15   et maior et melior ad maiestatem sacri nominis
tui alligata sit, meminerit non nisi religiosa
purificatione lustratos accedere ad templa debere.
quod ut custoditurum me lecturi sciant, in ipso

BOOK VIII

TO THE EMPEROR DOMITIANUS CAESAR
AUGUSTUS GERMANICUS DACICUS,
VALERIUS MARTIALIS SENDS GREETINGS

All my little books, Lord, to which you have given fame, which is to say life, are your petitioners, and will be read, I suppose, for that reason. But this one, entitled the eighth of my works, enjoys more frequent opportunities of showing its devotion. So there was less need to labor with invention, since matter had taken its place. However, from time to time I have tried to vary the same by some admixture of jest, lest every line heap its praises upon your celestial modesty, praises which might more easily weary you than satiate us. Furthermore, although epigrams appearing to aim at the verbal license of mime have been written even by men of the strictest morals and the highest station, I have not allowed these here to talk as wantonly as is their custom. Since the greater and better part of the book is bound up with the majesty of your sacred name, let it remember that only persons purified by religious lustration should approach temples. So that prospective readers may know that I shall observe this principle, I have thought proper to

159

libelli huius limine profiteri brevissimo placuit epi-
20 grammate.

1

Laurigeros domini, liber, intrature penates
    disce verecundo sanctius ore loqui.
nuda recede Venus; non est tuus iste libellus:
    tu mihi, tu, Pallas Caesariana, veni.

2

Fastorum genitor parensque Ianus
victorem modo cum videret Histri,
tot vultus sibi non satis putavit
optavitque oculos habere plures:
5 et lingua pariter locutus omni
terrarum domino deoque rerum
promisit Pyliam quater senectam.
addas, Iane pater, tuam rogamus.

3

'Quinque satis fuerant: iam sex septemve libelli
    est nimium: quid adhuc ludere, Musa, iuvat?

---

^a Because of the Emperor's recent victories on the
Danube.

^b The god Janus presided over the year and the public
records.

^c Four, representing the four seasons (sometimes only
two); cf. 10.28.6.

announce it on the very threshold of this little book in the briefest of epigrams.

1

Book, about to enter the laurelled[a] dwelling of our Lord, learn to speak more chastely with modest utterance. Nude Venus, avaunt! This little book is not yours. Do you come to me, you, Caesar's Pallas.

2

When Janus, progenitor and parent of our annals,[b] lately saw Hister's conqueror, he thought his many faces[c] too few and wished to have more eyes. And speaking with all his tongues in unison, he promised the Lord and God of the world four times the Pylian[d] length of days.[e] We ask you, Father Janus, to add your own.

3

"Five had been enough; six or seven little books is already too much. Why, Muse,[f] do you wish to frolic further? Let there be some shame, and an end.

[d] Nestor's.

[e] So 10.38.14. But here M. may have Janus' four tongues in mind.

[f] Thalia, Muse of comedy and light verse (v. 10).

sit pudor et finis: iam plus nihil addere nobis
    fama potest: teritur noster ubique liber;
5 et cum rupta situ Messalae saxa iacebunt
    altaque cum Licini marmora pulvis erunt,
me tamen ora legent et secum plurimus hospes
    ad patrias sedes carmina nostra feret.'
finieram, cum sic respondit nona sororum,
10   cui coma et unguento sordida vestis erat:
'tune potes dulcis, ingrate, relinquere nugas?
    dic mihi, quid melius desidiosus ages?
an iuvat ad tragicos soccum transferre cothurnos
    aspera vel paribus bella tonare modis,
15 praelegat ut tumidus rauca te voce magister
    oderit et grandis virgo bonusque puer?
scribant ista graves nimium nimiumque severi,
    quos media miseros nocte lucerna videt.
at tu Romano lepidos sale tinge libellos:
20   agnoscat mores vita legatque suos.
angusta cantare licet videaris avena,
    dum tua multorum vincat avena tubas.'

4

Quantus, io, Latias mundi conventus ad aras
    suscipit et solvit pro duce vota suo!

3.3 iam *scripsi* : nam Tβγ   3.19 tange *Heinsius*
4.1 conuentus γ : concentus (*vel* -tos) β

---

  [a] His tomb, no doubt; cf. 10.2.9.
  [b] A rich freedman of Augustus (cf. Juv. 1.109), who
built himself a magnificent tomb.

Fame can confer nothing more on me now. My books are thumbed everywhere; and when Messalla's stones[a] lie broken by decay and the tall marbles of Licinus[b] are dust, I shall still be read and many a stranger shall carry my poems with him to the land of his ancestors." I had done, when the ninth of the Sisters, whose hair and dress were stained with unguent, thus made answer: "Ingrate, can you abandon your sweet trifles? Tell me, what better will you find to do in your idleness? Or do you wish to exchange your slipper for tragic buskins or thunder hard-fought wars in equal measures,[c] to be dictated by a pompous schoolmaster's hoarse voice and hated by big girls and honest lads? Let the ultra-serious and the ultra-severe write such stuff, sad fellows looked upon by the midnight lamp. But do *you* dip your witty little books in Roman salt; let life recognize and read of her ways. Never mind if you seem to sing with a narrow pipe, so long as your pipe outmatches many people's trumpets.

4

Huzza! What a gathering of the world makes and discharges its vows for its Leader at Latin altars![d]

---

[c] I.e. in hexameters.

[d] On 3 January, when throughout the empire vows for the Emperor were taken and discharged (Suet. *Nero* 46.2).

non sunt haec hominum, Germanice, gaudia tantum,
    sed faciunt ipsi nunc, puto, sacra dei.

5

Dum donas, Macer, anulos puellis,
desisti, Macer, anulos habere.

6

Archetypis vetuli nihil est odiosius Eucti
    — ficta Saguntino cymbia malo luto —,
argenti fumosa sui cum stemmata narrat
    garrulus et verbis mucida vina facit:
5 'Laomedonteae fuerant haec pocula mensae:
    ferret ut haec muros struxit Apollo lyra.
hoc cratere ferox commisit proelia Rhoecus
    cum Lapithis: pugna debile cernis opus.
hi duo longaevo censentur Nestore fundi:
10   pollice de Pylio trita columba nitet.
hic scyphus est in quo misceri iussit amicis
    largius Aeacides vividiusque merum.
hac propinavit Bitiae pulcherrima Dido
    in patera, Phrygio cum data cena viro est.'

6.1 eucti *β* : au(c)ti lemm. T*γ* : illo *γ*   3 fumosa *Lipsius* : furiosa T*βγ*   7 Rhoecus] *cf. Lindsay et Housman 1103* : chrocos *vel sim. β* : rhoetus T*γ*

---

[a] I.e. you have lost your qualification as a knight: cf. Juv. 11.43. The *ius anulorum* (right to wear a gold ring) was possessed by senators, knights, and magistrates.

These joys are not of man alone, Germanicus. The gods themselves, methinks, are now at worship.

5

In giving rings to girls, Macer, you have ceased to possess rings, Macer.[a]

6

Nothing is so boring as old Euctus' originals (I had rather have cups shaped from Saguntine clay), when he rehearses the smoky pedigrees[b] of his silver and turns the wine moldy with his chatter: "These goblets once belonged to Laomedon's table: Apollo built the walls with his lyre to get them. With this mixing bowl fierce Rhoecus commenced battle with the Lapiths; you see how the piece was damaged in the struggle. These two bases are valuable because of long-lived Nestor; the dove shines, polished by the Pylian thumb. Here we have a bowl in which Aeacus' grandson[c] bade more and livelier wine to be mixed for his friends. In this dish fairest Dido pledged Bitias, when she gave dinner to the Phrygian hero."[d] After you have much admired the

---

[b] The pedigrees (lists of previous owners) of his treasures hung in Euctus' hall like the family tree with death-mask portraits in the hall of a Roman nobleman (cf. 2.90.6 and *OLD famosus*).

[c] Achilles: cf. Hom. *Il.* 9.203.

[d] Aeneas: cf. Virg. *Aen.* 1.738.

15   miratus fueris cum prisca toreumata multum,
     in Priami calathis Astyanacta bibes.

7

Hoc agere est causas, hoc dicere, Cinna, diserte,
    horis, Cinna, decem dicere verba novem?
sed modo clepsydras ingenti voce petisti
    quattuor. o quantum, Cinna, tacere potes!

8

Principium des, Iane, licet velocibus annis
    et renoves vultu saecula longa tuo,
te primum pia tura rogent, te vota salutent,
    purpura te felix, te colat omnis honos:
5   tu tamen hoc mavis, Latiae quod contigit urbi
    mense tuo reducem, Iane, videre deum.

9

Solvere dodrantem nuper tibi, Quinte, volebat
    lippus Hylas, luscus vult dare dimidium.
accipe quam primum; brevis est occasio lucri:
    si fuerit caecus, nil tibi solvet Hylas.

---

[a] I.e. something immature.

[b] Cf. 6.35.1.

[c] Domitian returned from an eight-months' campaign against the Sarmatians in January 93.

[d] As though the loan was money lost, so that a partial repayment would be clear gain.

antique embossments, in Priam's vessels you will drink—Astyanax.[a]

7

Is this pleading causes, is this fine oratory, Cinna, to utter nine words, Cinna, in ten hours? But you have just demanded four water clocks[b] at the top of your voice. What a capacity you have for saying nothing, Cinna!

8

Although you give their beginnings, Janus, to the fleeting years and renew the long centuries with your countenance, though pious incense petition you first, vows salute you, the fortunate purple and every magistracy pay you court, yet more to you than all this is the fact that in your month, Janus, the Latian city had the happiness of seeing our god return.[c]

9

The other day, Quintus, blear-eyed Hylas wanted to pay you back three quarters of his debt; now with one eye he wants to pay half. Take it at once. The chance for a profit[d] is fleeting. If Hylas goes blind, he will pay you nothing.

10

Emit lacernas milibus decem Bassus
Tyrias coloris optimi. lucrifecit.
'adeo bene emit?' inquis. immo non solvit.

11

Pervenisse tuam iam te scit Rhenus in urbem;
    nam populi voces audit et ille tui:
Sarmaticas etiam gentes Histrumque Getasque
    laetitiae clamor terruit ipse novae.
5 dum te longa sacro venerantur gaudia Circo,
    nemo quater missos currere sensit equos.
nullum Roma ducem, nec te sic, Caesar, amavit:
    te quoque iam non plus, ut velit ipsa, potest.

12

Uxorem quare locupletem ducere nolim
    quaeritis? uxori nubere nolo meae.
inferior matrona suo sit, Prisce, marito:
    non aliter fiunt femina virque pares.

13

Morio dictus erat: viginti milibus emi.
    redde mihi nummos, Gargiliane: sapit.

10.3 soluit β : -uet γ 11.6 sensit $\beta\gamma$: sentis L *ante corr.* : sentit T

---

[a] Because the Emperor was present; cf. Sp. 27.2.
[b] Cf. 14.210 and 6.39.17n.

168

10

Bassus bought a cloak for ten thousand, Tyrian, first-rate color. He made a profit. "Was it such a bargain?" you say. Oh no: he didn't pay for it.

11

Now Rhine knows that you have arrived at your city; for even he hears the voices of your people. The very clamor of novel joy has scared the Sarmatic tribes, and Hister, and the Getae. As protracted applause worshipped you in the sacred[a] Circus, nobody noticed that the horses had four times been started and were running. Rome never so loved a Leader, never so loved you, Caesar. Now she cannot love even you more ardently, though she herself wish to.

12

You all ask why I don't want to marry a rich wife? I don't want to be my wife's wife. The matron, Priscus, should be below her husband. That's the only way man and woman can be equal.

13

He was described as a natural.[b] I bought him for twenty thousand. Give me back my money, Gargilianus. He's no fool.

14

Pallida ne Cilicum timeant pomaria brumam
    mordeat et tenerum fortior aura nemus,
hibernis obiecta Notis specularia puros
    admittunt soles et sine faece diem.
5   at mihi cella datur non tota clusa fenestra,
    in qua nec Boreas ipse manere velit.
sic habitare iubes veterem crudelis amicum?
    arboris ergo tuae tutior hospes ero.

15

Dum nova Pannonici numeratur gloria belli,
    omnis et ad reducem dum litat ara Iovem,
dat populus, dat gratus eques, dat tura senatus,
    et ditant Latias tertia dona tribus.
5   hos quoque secretos memorabit Roma triumphos,
    nec minor ista tuae laurea pacis erit.
quod tibi de sancta credis pietate tuorum,
    principis est virtus maxima nosse suos.

15.5–6 memorabit ... erit β (vide SB¹) : -auit ... erat
γ   6–7 post 6 plenius dist. SB¹, post 7 vulg.

ᵃ Saffron plants are presumably meant; cf. 3.65.2.
ᵇ Cf. 8.68.
ᶜ See 4.29.7n.
ᵈ On his return Domitian had distributed a largesse
(congiarium) to the people, his third.

14

Lest your orchard from Cilicia[a] lose color in dread of winter and a brisker air bite the tender grove, transparent panes facing the wintry south winds admit clear suns and unadulterated daylight.[b] But I am assigned a cubbyhole shut in by a window that doesn't quite close, in which Boreas himself would not care to pass the night. Cruel fellow, is it thus you tell an old friend to lodge? So I shall be safer as the guest of your trees.

15

As the new glory of a Pannonian war is scored up[c] and every altar makes accepted offerings to Jove the Home-bringer, the people and the grateful knights and senate give incense and a third round of gifts enriches the Latin tribes.[d] This private triumph[e] too shall Rome remember, nor shall this laurel of your peace be less esteemed. You trust yourself concerning your people's pure devotion; it is a prince's greatest virtue to know his subjects.[f]

[e] Domitian had waived a triumph, merely dedicating a laurel wreath (*ista laurea*, v. 6) to Jupiter Capitolinus: Suet. *Dom.* 6.1; Stat. *Silv.* 3.3.171.

[f] You know you can rely on the people appreciating your victory even without a triumph. On *quod* ("whereas"), linking the two statements, and the punctuation, see *SB*[1].

16

Pistor qui fueras diu, Cypere,
causas nunc agis et ducena quaeris:
sed consumis et usque mutuaris.
a pistore, Cypere, non recedis:
5   et panem facis et facis farinam.

17

Egi, Sexte, tuam pactus duo milia causam.
   misisti nummos quod mihi mille quid est?
'narrasti nihil' inquis 'et a te perdita causa est.'
   tanto plus debes, Sexte, quod erubui.

18

Si tua, Cerrini, promas epigrammata vulgo,
   vel mecum possis vel prior ipse legi:
sed tibi tantus inest veteris respectus amici
   carior ut mea sit quam tua fama tibi.
5   sic Maro nec Calabri temptavit carmina Flacci,
   Pindaricos nosset cum superare modos,
et Vario cessit Romani laude cothurni,
   cum posset tragico fortius ore loqui.
aurum et opes et rura frequens donabit amicus:
10   qui velit ingenio cedere rarus erit.

---

[a] Per annum.

[b] I.e. you dissipate your earnings, as grain is reduced to the dust of flour.

16

For a long time you were a baker, Cyperus. Now you plead cases and make two hundred thousand.[a] But you spend it and go on borrowing. You are still the baker, Cyperus. You make bread and you make flour.[b]

17

Sextus, I pleaded your case for an agreed two thousand. What do you mean by sending me a thousand sesterces? "You didn't state the facts," you say, "and you lost the case." You owe me all the more, Sextus, for having blushed.[c]

18

Cerrinius, if you were to give your epigrams to the public, you might be read as my equal or my superior. But such is your regard for an old friend that my reputation means more to you than your own. So Maro did not attempt the lyrics of Calabrian Flaccus,[d] though he was capable of surpassing Pindar's measures, and yielded the glory of the Roman buskin to Varius, though he could have spoken more boldly than Varius in the tones of tragedy. Many a friend will give gold and riches and land, but one prepared to yield in talent will be found but seldom.

[c] The facts were discreditable.
[d] Horace; cf. 5.30.2n.

19

Pauper videri Cinna vult; et est pauper.[a]

20

Cum facias versus nulla non luce ducenos,
  Vare, nihil recitas. non sapis atque sapis.

21

Phosphore, redde diem: quid gaudia nostra moraris?
  Caesare venturo, Phosphore, redde diem.
Roma rogat. placidi numquid te pigra Bootae[b]
  plaustra vehunt, lento quod nimis igne venis?
5 Ledaeo poteras abducere Cyllaron astro:
  ipse suo cedet nunc tibi Castor equo.
quid cupidum Titana[c] tenes? iam Xanthus et Aethon[d]
  frena volunt, vigilat Memnonis alma parens.
tarda tamen nitidae non cedunt sidera luci,
10 et cupit Ausonium Luna videre ducem.
iam, Caesar, vel nocte veni: stent astra licebit,
  non deerit populo te veniente dies.

22

Invitas ad aprum, ponis mihi, Gallice, porcum.
  hybrida sum, si das, Gallice, verba mihi.

21.4 igne $\beta\gamma$: axe T   8 uolunt] vorant *Köstlin*

---

[a] He wishes to be thought a rich man pretending
poverty; in fact, he is as poor as he pretends.
  [b] Gemini.   [c] The Sun (Hyperion).
  [d] "Yellow" and "Tawny," horses of the Sun; cf. 3.67.5.

19

Cinna wishes to appear a poor man. And he is a poor man.[a]

20

Although you make two hundred verses every day, Varus, you never recite. You are a fool, and you are no fool.

21

Phosphorus, bring back the day. Why do you retard our joy? Caesar is coming: Phosphorus, bring back the day. Rome asks you. Does the lazy wagon of gentle Bootes carry you, that you come with so slow a fire? You could have taken Cyllaros from Leda's constellation;[b] Castor himself will give up his mount to you now. Why do you hold back the eager Titan?[c] Already Xanthus and Aethon[d] crave the reins, Memnon's fostering mother[e] is awake. Yet the slow stars yield not to shining dawn and the Moon is fain to see the Ausonian Leader. Come now, Caesar, night though it be. Let the stars stand still; at your advent the people will not want for day.

22

You invite me to boar and you serve me pork, Gallicus. I am a hybrid,[f] Gallicus, if you deceive me.[g]

[e] Aurora, goddess of the morning.

[f] Offspring of dissimilar parents, as a sow and a wild boar.   [g] I.e. I can tell the difference.

175

23

Esse tibi videor saevus nimiumque gulosus,
    qui propter cenam, Rustice, caedo cocum.
si levis ista tibi flagrorum causa videtur,
    ex qua vis causa vapulet ergo cocus?

24

Si quid forte petam timido gracilique libello,
    improba non fuerit si mea charta, dato.
et si non dederis, Caesar, permitte rogari:
    offendunt numquam tura precesque Iovem.
5   qui fingit sacros auro vel marmore vultus,
    non facit ille deos: qui rogat, ille facit.

25

Vidisti semel, Oppiane, tantum
aegrum me male: saepe te videbo.

26

Non tot in Eois timuit Gangeticus arvis
    raptor, in Hyrcano qui fugit albus equo,
quot tua Roma novas vidit, Germanice, tigres:
    delicias potuit nec numerare suas.

25.2 *de interpunctione vide SB*[1]

23

You think me cruel and too fond of my stomach, Rusticus, because I beat my cook on account of a dinner. If that seems to you a trivial reason for lashes, for what reason then do you want a cook to be flogged?

24

Should I happen to make some petition in my slender, timid little book, if my page be not overbold, grant it. And if you do not grant it, Caesar, allow yourself to be asked. Incense and prayers never offend Jupiter. He does not make gods who sculpts sacred faces in gold or marble; he makes them who asks of them.

25

When I was very ill, Oppianus, you saw me only once. I shall see you often.[a]

26

The robber[b] of Ganges, who flees pale-faced on his Hyrcanian mount, did not fear so many tigers in eastern lands as your Rome, Germanicus, saw for the first time; she could not even count her darlings.

[a] A sly assumption, wrapped up in what appears to be a promise to return good for evil (SB^1).

[b] Of cubs.

5 vincit Erythraeos tua, Caesar, harena triumphos
    et victoris opes divitiasque dei:
nam cum captivos ageret sub curribus Indos,
    contentus gemina tigride Bacchus erat.

27

Munera qui tibi dat locupleti, Gaure, senique,
    si sapis et sentis, hoc tibi ait, 'morere.'

28

Dic, toga, facundi gratum mihi munus amici,
    esse velis cuius fama decusque gregis?
Apula Ledaei tibi floruit herba Phalanthi,
    qua saturat Calabris culta Galaesus aquis?
5 an Tartesiacus stabuli nutritor Hiberi
    Baetis in Hesperia te quoque lavit ove?
an tua multifidum numeravit lana Timavum,
    quem pius astrifero Cyllarus ore bibit?
te nec Amyclaeo decuit livere veneno
10   nec Miletos erat vellere digna tuo.
lilia tu vincis nec adhuc delapsa ligustra
    et Tiburtino monte quod albet ebur;
Spartanus tibi cedet olor Paphiaeque columbae,
    cedet Erythraeis eruta gemma vadis.

28.12 albet ς (*cf.* 7.13) : alget βγ

---

[a] Bacchus, according to myth, made an expedition into
the East, where he taught the conquered nations the use of
the vine. He was represented as drawn by tigers.

Your arena, Caesar, surpasses Erythraean triumphs and the wealth and riches of the victor god. For when Bacchus led captive Indians behind his chariot, a pair of tigers sufficed him.[a]

27

You are rich, Gaurus, and old. Who gives you presents, says to you, if you have the wit to understand: "Die."

28

Gown, welcome gift of an eloquent friend, tell me, of what flock would you like to be the fame and pride? Did the Apulian grass of Ledean Phalanthus flourish for you, where Galaesus saturates the tilth with Calabrian waters? Or did Baetis, Tartessian nourisher of the Iberian fold, wash you too on the back of a Hesperian ewe? Or did your wool number manycleft Timavus, whom faithful Cyllarus drank with starry[b] mouth? It was not yours to grow grey with Amyclaean dye, nor was Miletus worthy of your fleece. You outdo lilies and privet still unfallen and the ivory that whitens on Tibur's hill.[c] Sparta's swans will yield to you and Paphian doves; the pearl shall yield, dug out from Erythraean shallows. But

[b] By anticipation. Cyllarus had not become part of the constellation Gemini when he drank from the Timavus. Cf. 4.25.6n.

[c] Cf. 4.62n.

15 sed licet haec primis nivibus sint aemula dona,
        non sunt Parthenio candidiora suo.
    non ego praetulerim Babylonos picta superbae
        texta, Samiramia quae variantur acu;
    non Athamanteo potius me mirer in auro,
20   Aeolium dones si mihi, Phrixe, pecus.
    o quantos risus pariter spectata movebit
        cum Palatina nostra lacerna toga!

29

Disticha qui scribit, puto, vult brevitate placere.
    quid prodest brevitas, dic mihi, si liber est?

30

Qui nunc Caesareae lusus spectatur harenae,
    temporibus Bruti gloria summa fuit.
aspicis ut teneat flammas poenaque fruatur
    fortis et attonito regnet in igne manus!
5   ipse sui spectator adest et nobile dextrae
        funus amat: totis pascitur illa sacris.
    quod nisi rapta foret nolenti poena, parabat
        saevior in lassos ire sinistra focos.

30.3 aspicis γ : -cit β : -cite *Gruter*

---

[a] Probably with allusion to the derivation of the name from πάρθενος (parthenos), "virgin," virginity being associated with whiteness; cf. 9.49.6

[b] The ram with the golden fleece: see 6.3.6. Aeolus, the wind god, was Phrixus' grandfather; cf. 8.50.9.

though this gift challenges fresh snow, it is no whiter than Parthenius,[a] its giver I would not rather have the painted fabrics of proud Babylon, embroidered by Semiramis' needle. I would not rather admire myself in gold of Athamas, if Phrixus were to give me the Aeolian ram.[b] Oh, what merriment my cloak will raise, seen along with my Palatine gown![c]

29

He who writes distichs wishes, I suppose, to please by brevity. What use is brevity, tell me, if it's a book?

30

The entertainment now viewed in Caesar's arena was the summit of glory in Brutus' days. You see how the hand grasps the flames and enjoys its punishment and kings it bravely in the astonished fire.[d] He is there as his own spectator and revels in his right hand's noble death. The hand feasts on the entire rite. If the punishment had not been snatched away in its despite, the left, yet fiercer, was making ready to enter the wearied brazier.

[c] A hint for a new cloak.

[d] Cf. 1.21 and 10.25. The story was presented in the amphitheater with a criminal taking the chief role.

scire piget post tale decus quid fecerit ante:
10   quam vidi satis hanc est mihi nosse manum.

31

Nescio quid de te non belle, Dento, fateris,
    coniuge qui ducta iura paterna petis.
sed iam supplicibus dominum lassare libellis
    desine et in patriam serus ab urbe redi:
5 nam dum tu longe deserta uxore diuque
    tres quaeris natos, quattuor invenies.

32

Aëra per tacitum delapsa sedentis in ipsos
    fluxit Aretullae blanda columba sinus.
luserat hoc casus, nisi inobservata maneret
    permissaque sibi nollet abire fuga.
5 si meliora piae fas est sperare sorori
    et dominum mundi flectere vota valent,
haec a Sardois tibi forsitan exulis oris,
    fratre reversuro, nuntia venit avis.

33

De praetoricia folium mihi, Paule, corona
    mittis et hoc phialae nomen habere iubes.

---

[a] The *ius trium liberorum*; cf. 2.91n.

After such achievement I would sooner not know
what this hand had done before; enough for me to
know it as I saw it.

31

You make an admission about yourself and not a
pretty one, Dento, when you seek paternal rights[a]
after marrying a wife. But stop wearying our Lord
with begging memorials and late in time go back
from Rome to your native town. For while you look
for three children so long and so far away from your
deserted wife, you are like to find four.

32

Dropping down through the silent air, a winsome
dove glided into Aretulla's very bosom where she
sat. That might have been a freak of chance, were it
not that the creature stayed all unguarded and,
though permitted to take flight, refused to leave. If
it be no sin for a loving sister to hope for better
things and if prayers can sway the lord of the world,
perhaps this bird came to you as a messenger from
the exile's Sardinian shores, and your brother is
about to return.

33

You send me a leaf, Paulus, from your praetor's gar-
land and you would have it called a bowl. With this

hac fuerat nuper nebula tibi pegma perunctum,
    pallida quam rubri diluit unda croci.
5 an magis astuti derasa est ungue ministri
    brattea, de fulcro quam reor esse tuo?
illa potest culicem longe sentire volantem
    et minimi pinna papilionis agi;
exiguae volitat suspensa vapore lucernae
10   et leviter fuso rumpitur icta mero.
hoc linitur sputo Iani caryota Kalendis,
    quam fert cum parco sordidus asse cliens.
lenta minus gracili crescunt colocasia filo,
    plena magis nimio lilia sole cadunt;
15 nec vaga tam tenui discurrit aranea tela,
    tam leve nec bombyx pendulus urget opus.
crassior in facie vetulae stat creta Fabullae,
    crassior offensae bulla tumescit aquae;
fortior et tortos servat vesica capillos
20   et mutat Latias spuma Batava comas.
hac cute Ledaeo vestitur pullus in ovo,
    talia lunata splenia fronte sedent.
quid tibi cum phiala, ligulam cum mittere possis,
    mittere cum possis vel cocleare mihi, —
25 magna nimis loquimur—cocleam cum mittere possi
    denique cum possis mittere, Paule, nihil?

---

  [a] Cf. 5.25.8n.
  [b] Symbolic gifts like Easter eggs: cf. 13.27: Ov. *Fast.*
1.189.

184

film your platform was lately coated and the pallid stream of red saffron washed it away.[a] Or was it rather a flake scraped off by a cunning servant's nail—I think it is from the leg of your couch. It can feel the flight of a gnat at a distance and be agitated by the wing of the smallest butterfly. It hovers suspended in the heat of a tiny lamp and breaks if lightly splashed when wine is poured. With such spittle is smeared the nut which a shabby client brings along with a frugal copper coin[b] on Janus' Kalends. Less slender is the filament with which grow pliant Egyptian beans, lilies[c] are thicker when they fall in too hot a sun. Neither does the errant spider run to and fro in a web so tenuous or the hanging silkworm ply so light a task. Denser stands the chalk on old Fabulla's face, denser swells a bubble in water when you strike it. Stronger the net that keeps braided hair in place and the Batavian foam that dyes Latin tresses.[d] With such a skin is clothed the chick in Leda's egg, such are the patches sitting on a crescent-bedizened forehead.[e] Why bother with a bowl when you could send a spoon, when you could send me a snail pick even (I talk of things too large), when you could send a snail shell, when in fine, Paulus, you could send nothing?

[c] I.e. their petals.
[d] A kind of soap giving the hair a bright hue; cf. 14.26.
[e] Cf. 2.29.9.

34

Archetypum Myos argentum te dicis habere.
  quod sine te factum est, hoc magis archetypum est?[a]

35

Cum sitis similes paresque vita,
uxor pessima, pessimus maritus,
miror non bene convenire vobis.

36

Regia pyramidum, Caesar, miracula ride;
  iam tacet Eoum barbara Memphis opus:
pars quota Parrhasiae labor est Mareoticus aulae?[b]
  clarius in toto nil videt orbe dies.
5   septenos pariter credas assurgere montes,
  Thessalicum brevior Pelion Ossa tulit;[c]
aethera sic intrat, nitidis ut conditus astris
  inferiore tonet nube serenus apex
et prius arcano satietur lumine Phoebi
10   nascentis Circe quam videt ora patris.
  haec, Auguste, tamen, quae vertice sidera pulsat,
  par domus est caelo, sed minor est domino.

36.9 lumine β : nu- γ

---

  [a] *fictum*, "faked," would make the point clearer.
  [b] On the Palatine; cf. 7.56. Statius too acclaims this
edifice in *Silv.* 4.2.18–31 and elsewhere.
  [c] When the giants attempted to scale heaven in their
war with the gods, they piled Pelion upon Ossa, both
mountains in Thessaly.

34

You say you have a piece of silver, an original by Mys. Is what was made[a] without you any the more an original?

35

Since the two of you are alike and equal in your way of life, a rotten wife and a rotten husband, I am surprised you don't suit one another.

36

Laugh, Caesar, at the royal marvels of the pyramids; barbarous Memphis no longer talks of eastern work. How small a part of the Parrhasian palace[b] is equalled by Mareotic toil! The sun sees nothing more magnificent in all the world. You would think the seven hills rose in unison. Ossa bearing Thessalian Pelion was not so tall.[c] It pierces the ether, so that, concealed in the bright stars, the clear summit thunders with the cloud below; and it is sated with Phoebus' hidden light before Circe[d] sees her nascent father's face. Yet, Augustus, this mansion, whose top strikes the constellations, though it equal heaven, is less than its lord.

[d] Daughter of the Sun, which was said to strike first on her island.

37

Quod Caietano reddis, Polycharme, tabellas,
    milia te centum num tribuisse putas?
'debuit haec' inquis. tibi habe, Polycharme, tabellas
    et Caietano milia crede duo.

38

    Qui praestat pietate pertinaci
    sensuro bona liberalitatis,
    captet forsitan aut vicem reposcat:
    at si quis dare nomini relicto
5   post Manes tumulumque perseverat,
    quaerit quid nisi parcius dolere?
    refert sis bonus an velis videri.
    praestas hoc, Melior, sciente fama,
    qui sollemnibus anxius sepulti
10   nomen non sinis interire Blaesi,
    et de munifica profusus arca
    ad natalicium diem colendum
    scribarum memori piaeque turbae
    quod donas, facis ipse Blaesianum.
15   hoc longum tibi, vita dum manebit,
    hoc et post cineres erit tributum.

37.2 num ς : non β : nunc γ

---

[a] Cf. a similar epigram, 9.102.
[b] *Being* good.
[c] I.e. celebrate; see *OLD facio* 24.

37

Because you return Caietanus his bond, do you think, Polycharmus, that you have given him a hundred thousand? "He owed the money," you say. Keep the bond, Polycharmus, and lend Caietanus two thousand.[a]

38

He who with persevering devotion confers his bounty's benefits on one who will perceive them may be fishing for a legacy or asking a return. But if a man persist in giving to a name, left behind after death and burial, what does he want except to alleviate his sorrow? There is a difference between goodness and pretence. This,[b] Melior, you provide, and fame knows it. With anxious care, by means of ritual observances, you forbid that buried Blaesus' name should perish; from your munificent chest you give lavish funds to the company of scribes, that holds him in loving memory, to celebrate his birthday, and thus you yourself keep[c] the Feast of Blaesus.[d] This tribute you will offer long, while life remains, and even beyond the grave.

[d] *Blaesianum*; cf. Marcellia and Verria, festivals in honor of Marcellus and Verres (Cic. *Verr.* 2.4.151).

39

Qui Palatinae caperet convivia mensae
    ambrosiasque dapes non erat ante locus:
hic haurire decet sacrum, Germanice, nectar
    et Ganymedea pocula mixta manu.
5 esse velis oro serus conviva Tonantis:
    at tu si properas, Iuppiter, ipse veni.

40

Non horti neque palmitis beati
    sed rari nemoris, Priape, custos,
ex quo natus es et potes renasci,
    furaces moneo manus repellas
5 et silvam domini focis reserves:
    si defecerit haec, et ipse lignum es.

41

'Tristis Athenagoras non misit munera nobis
    quae medio brumae mittere mense solet.'
an sit Athenagoras tristis, Faustine, videbo:
    me certe tristem fecit Athenagoras.

39

Formerly there was no place large enough for the banquets and ambrosial repasts of the Palatine board. Here,[a] Germanicus, you may fitly drink sacred nectar and cups mixed by the hand of a Ganymede. I pray it may be long before you choose to dine with the Thunderer. As for you, Jupiter, if you cannot wait, come yourself.

40

Priapus, guardian—not of a garden or fertile vineyard, but of a scattered copse, from which you were born and can be born again—keep off thievish hands, I warn you, and preserve the wood for its owner's hearth. If it gives out, you too are timber.[b]

41

"Athenagoras is sad and has not sent us the presents which he normally sends in the middle of midwinter's month." Whether Athenagoras is sad I'll see later, Faustinus. Athenagoras has certainly saddened me.

[a] In Domitian's palace; cf. 8.36.
[b] And may be burned instead.

42

Si te sportula maior ad beatos
non corruperit, ut solet, licebit
de nostro, Matho, centies laveris.

43

Effert uxores Fabius, Chrestilla maritos,
    funereamque toris quassat uterque facem.
victores committe, Venus: quos iste manebit
    exitus, una duos ut Libitina ferat.

44

Titulle, moneo, vive: semper hoc serum est;
sub paedagogo coeperis licet, serum est.
at tu, miser Titulle, nec senex vivis,
sed omne limen conteris salutator
5   et mane sudas urbis osculis udus,
foroque triplici sparsus ante equos omnes
aedemque Martis et colosson Augusti
curris per omnes tertiasque quintasque.
rape, congere, aufer, posside: relinquendum est.
10 superba densis arca palleat nummis,

---

[a] A hundred farthings (quadrantes) was the client's usual allowance (cf. 3.7.1), and a farthing was the price of a bath.

[b] Lit. "under a paedagogus," a slave in charge of children.

[c] I.e. equestrian statues.

42

If a larger dole at rich men's houses does not bribe you, Matho, as usually happens, you will be able to bathe a hundred times at my expense.[a]

43

Fabius buries his wives, Chrestilla her husbands; each of them brandishes a funeral torch over the marriage bed. Venus, match the winners; the end awaiting them will be one bier to carry the pair.

44

Titullus, I warn you, live. It is always late for that. Though you start in your schooldays,[b] it's late. But you, my poor Titullus, don't live even in your old age. You polish every threshold with your calls and sweat in the early morning, damp with the kisses of the town; and scattering your presence over the three Forums, in front of all the horses[c] and Mars' temple[d] and Augustus' colossus,[e] you keep on the go through every third hour and every fifth.[f] Snatch, amass, seize, possess: it has to be left behind. Though your proud coffer be yellow with packed

[d] Of Mars Ultor, Mars the Avenger (of Julius' Caesar's murder), in the Forum of Augustus.

[e] Which colossal statue is meant is doubtful.

[f] I.e. during the business hours of the day; cf. 4.8.2f.

centum explicentur paginae Kalendarum,
iurabit heres te nihil reliquisse,
supraque pluteum te iacente vel saxum,
fartus papyro dum tibi torus crescit,
15 flentis superbus basiabit eunuchos;
tuoque tristis filius, velis nolis,
cum concubino nocte dormiet prima.

45

Priscus ab Aetnaeis mihi, Flacce, Terentius oris
    redditur: hanc lucem lactea gemma notet;
defluat et lento splendescat turbida lino
    amphora centeno consule facta minor.
5 continget nox quando meis tam candida mensis?
    tam iusto dabitur quando calere mero?
cum te, Flacce, mihi reddet Cythereia Cypros,
    luxuriae fiet tam bona causa meae.

46

Quanta tua est probitas, tanta est praestantia formae
    Ceste puer, puro castior Hippolyto.
te secum Diana velit doceatque natare,
    te Cybele molli mallet habere Phryge;

46.1 tanta R : quanta $\beta\gamma$ praestantia *v.l. in duobus
familiae* β *codd.* : infan- R $\beta\gamma$ 2 puro *Heinsius* : puero
R $\beta\gamma$ 46.4 molli mallet *Housman ex* mollet L :
totum mallet R β, γ (?) : t- uellet E : secum mallet ς,
Brodaeus   Phryge *Brodaeus* : -ga R $\beta\gamma$

coins and a hundred pages of Kalends[a] unfold, your heir will swear you left nothing, and, as you lie on plank or stone and your pyre grows with its stuffing of papyrus, the haughty fellow will be kissing the weeping eunuchs; and your sorrowing son,[b] whether you like it or not, will sleep the first night with your catamite.

45

Priscus Terentius is restored to me, Flaccus, from Aetna's shores. Let a milky pearl mark this day.[c] Let a jar,[d] diminished by a hundred consulships, flow down and its turbidity brighten as it slowly passes through the linen. When shall another night so fair befall my table? When shall I be vouchsafed so good a reason to grow warm with wine? When Cytherean Cyprus returns you to me, Flaccus, there will be as good a cause for my indulgence.

46

Boy Cestus, more chaste than pure Hippolytus, your modesty is equalled by your surpassing beauty. Diana would wish you to swim with her and would be your teacher, Cybele would rather have had you

[a] Records of interest due on the first of the month.

[b] M. seems to forget that the heir (v. 12) and the son would normally be the same person.

[c] Cf. 11.36.1. On the custom, doubtful as to detail, see Conington on Pers. 2.1.

[d] I.e. its contents.

5   tu Ganymedeo poteras succedere lecto,
       sed durus domino basia sola dares.
    felix, quae tenerum vexabit sponsa maritum
       et quae te faciet prima puella virum!

47

Pars maxillarum tonsa est tibi, pars tibi rasa est,
    pars vulsa est. unum quis putet esse caput?

48

Nescit cui dederit Tyriam Crispinus abollam,
    dum mutat cultus induiturque togam.
quisquis habes, umeris sua munera redde, precam
    non hoc Crispinus te, sed abolla rogat.
5   non quicumque capit saturatas murice vestes
    nec nisi deliciis convenit iste color.
si te praeda iuvat foedique insania lucri,
    qua possis melius fallere, sume togam.

47.2 putet β : putat R γ

than her womanish Phrygian.[a] You could have suc-
ceeded to Ganymede's bed, but in your cruelty you
would have given your master naught but kisses.
Happy the bride-to-be that shall torment her tender
husband, the girl that shall first make you a man!

47

Part of your jaws is clipped, part shaved, part
plucked. Who would think it is one head?

48

Crispinus doesn't know to whom he gave his Tyrian
cloak[b] as he was changing his clothes and putting
on his gown. Whoever you are that have it, return
to his shoulders the gift that is theirs,[c] we beg. It is
not Crispinus asking this of you but the cloak. Not
everybody can wear garments saturated with purple
dye. The color suits only elegants. If loot and the
madness of vile gain are what you want, take the
gown; you could better pass with that.[d]

[a] The emasculated Attis; cf. 5.41.2.
[b] Crispinus was a dandy. Juvenal mentions his Tyrian
cloak (1.27).
[c] Given them by Crispinus.
[d] Gowns (togas) were more standardized, though not
altogether so.

49 (50)

Quanta Gigantei memoratur mensa triumphi
    quantaque nox superis omnibus illa fuit,
qua bonus accubuit genitor cum plebe deorum
    et licuit Faunis poscere vina Iovem:
5 tanta tuas, Caesar, celebrant convivia laurus;
    exhilarant ipsos gaudia nostra deos.
vescitur omnis eques tecum populusque patresque
    et capit ambrosias cum duce Roma dapes.
grandia pollicitus quanto maiora dedisti!
10   promissa est nobis sportula, recta data est.

50 (51)

Quis labor in phiala? docti Myos anne Myronos?
    Mentoris haec manus est an, Polyclite, tua?
livescit nulla caligine fusca nec odit
    exploratores nubila massa focos;
5 vera minus flavo radiant electra metallo
    et niveum felix pustula vincit ebur.
materiae non cedit opus: sic alligat orbem,
    plurima cum tota lampade luna nitet.
stat caper Aeolio Thebani vellere Phrixi
10   cultus: ab hoc mallet vecta fuisse soror;
hunc nec Cinyphius tonsor violaverit et tu
    ipse tua pasci vite, Lyaee, velis.

49.5 c(a)esar celebrant β : celebrat c(a)e- γ : celebrant C- ς

---

[a] To go with an inferior meal.
[b] The bowl was not made of gold and silver like genuine

BOOK VIII

49 (50)

Great as was (we are told) the feast at the triumph
over the Giants, great as was that night for all the
High Ones, when the good Father reclined with the
common run of deities and the Fauns had license to
call on Jove for wine: so great, Caesar, is the ban-
quet that celebrates your laurels; our joys cheer the
gods themselves. All the knights eat with you, and
the people and the Fathers; Rome takes ambrosial
fare along with her Leader. Large as were your
promises, how much grander your gifts! We were
promised a dole,[a] we have been given a formal
dinner.

50 (51)

Whose work is in the bowl? Skilled Mys's or
Myron's? Is this Mentor's hand, or yours, Poly-
clitus? No murkiness dulls or darkens it, no cloudy
mass abhors the testing fires. True electrum[b]
shines with a metal less yellow, and the fine frosted
silver surpasses snowy ivory. The workmanship
matches the material. So does the moon complete
her orb when she shines abundant with all her
lamp. There stands a goat clad in the Aeolian fleece
of Theban Phrixus; his sister would have preferred
this mount. No Cinyphian barber would assail him,
and you yourself, Lyaeus, would wish him to feed on

electrum but of silver (v. 6) and some sort of bronze (cf.
SB^1).

terga premit pecudis geminis Amor aureus alis,
    Palladius tenero lotos ab ore sonat:
15 sic Methymnaeo gavisus Arione delphin
    languida non tacitum per freta vexit onus.
imbuat egregium digno mihi nectare munus
    non grege de domini, sed tua, Ceste, manus;
Ceste, decus mensae, misce Setina: videtur
20 ipse puer nobis, ipse sitire caper.
det numerum cyathis Istanti littera Rufi:
    auctor enim tanti muneris ille mihi.
si Telethusa venit promissaque gaudia portat,
    servabor dominae, Rufe, triente tuo;
25 si dubia est, septunce trahar; si fallit amantem,
    ut iugulem curas, nomen utrumque bibam.

51

Formosam sane, sed caecus diligit Asper.
    plus ergo, ut res est, quam videt Asper amat.

50.14 Palladia et *Heinsius*   21 Istanti *Munro* : ins- $\beta\gamma$
(*cf. ad* 7.68)

---

[a] He seems to be a real slave belonging to Istantius,
though in 1.92 the name may be fictitious; cf. 8.46. M. will
have received the gift of the bowl as Istantius' guest.
Alternatively, M. is in his own house, as vv. 23–26 seem to
suggest, and he is the "master" of v. 18, though that verse
better suits a wealthy patron. Either way we have a
problem.

your vine. On the animal's back sits a golden Love with his pair of wings and a pipe of Pallas sounding from his tender mouth. So did the dolphin carry his musical burden through the languid sea, delighting in Methymnean Arion. Let not just any one of the master's troop of slaves, let your hand, Cestus,[a] inaugurate for me this noble gift with nectar worthy of it. Cestus, ornament of the feast, mix Setine; the boy himself, the goat himself seems to me athirst. Let the letters of Istantius Rufus' name supply a number for our measures; for this precious gift comes to me from him. If Telethusa arrives bringing promised joys, I shall keep myself for my lady with your four, Rufus. If she's doubtful, I'll spin out the time with seven.[b] If she cheats her lover, to kill my sorrow I'll drink both names.

51 (49)

Asper's in love with a beauty, to be sure, but he's blind. So Asper, as the fact is, loves more than he sees.[c]

[b] The numbers will represent vocatives, "Rufe" and "Istanti." For the practice cf. 9.93; 11.36.

[c] "Loves more than he sees" might be said of any lover who finds qualities in the loved one that are not there. In Asper's case it is literally true.

52

Tonsorem puerum, sed arte talem
qualis nec Thalamus fuit Neronis,
Drusorum cui contigere barbae,
aequandas semel ad genas rogatus
5   Rufo, Caediciane, commodavi.
dum iussus repetit pilos eosdem,
censura speculi manum regente,
expingitque cutem facitque longam
detonsis epaphaeresin capillis,
10 barbatus mihi tonsor est reversus.

53 (55)

Auditur quantum Massyla per avia murmur,
   innumero quotiens silva leone furit,
pallidus attonitos ad Poena mapalia pastor
   cum revocat tauros et sine mente pecus:
5 tantus in Ausonia fremuit modo terror harena.
   quis non esse gregem crederet? unus erat,
sed cuius tremerent ipsi quoque iura leones,
   cui diadema daret marmore picta Nomas.
o quantum per colla decus, quem sparsit honorem
10   aurea lunatae, cum stetit, umbra iubae!
grandia quam decuit latum venabula pectus
   quantaque de magna gaudia morte tulit!

52.8 expungitque *Eden*

---

[a] Claudius and Nero bore this among their other names, but M. probably uses it loosely to cover the imperial house.

52

A barber—a boy, but a greater artist even than Nero's Thalamus, whose lot it was to tend the beards of the Drususes—[a] I lent to Rufus at his request to smooth his cheeks once, Caedicianus. As the boy, so ordered, went back again and again to the same bristles, his hand guided by the mirror's appraisal, and painted up the skin, and did a lengthy second clipping of the hair he had cut, my barber came back to me with a beard.[b]

53 (55)

Loud as the roaring heard in Massylian wilds when the forest rages with countless lions and the pale herdsman recalls his startled bulls and terrified flock to his Punic steading, so great a terror lately roared in the Ausonian arena. Who would not have thought him a pride? He was but one, but one before whose rule the very lions would tremble, to whom marble-painted Numidia[c] would give a diadem. When his curving mane stood erect, what beauty, what dignity did its golden shadow shed over his neck! How well his broad chest became the long hunting spears, what joy he took from a mighty

[b] Cf. 7.83.
[c] Famous for its colored marble.

unde tuis, Libye, tam felix gloria silvis?
  a Cybeles numquid venerat ille iugo?
15 an magis Herculeo, Germanice, misit ab astro
  hanc tibi vel frater vel pater ipse feram?

54 (53)

Formosissima quae fuere vel sunt,
sed durissima quae fuere vel sunt,
o quam te fieri, Catulla, vellem
formosam minus aut minus pudicam!

55 (56)

Temporibus nostris aetas cum cedat avorum
  creverit et maior cum duce Roma suo,
ingenium sacri miraris deesse Maronis
  nec quemquam tanta bella sonare tuba.
5 sint Maecenates, non deerunt, Flacce, Marones
  Vergiliumque tibi vel tua rura dabunt.
iugera perdiderat miserae vicina Cremonae
  flebat et abductas Tityrus aeger oves:
risit Tuscus eques paupertatemque malignam
10 reppulit et celeri iussit abire fuga.

53.14 iugo γ : iugis β   54.2 durissima *Wiman* : uilis- T
βγ   4 minus (*alt.*) T γ : magis β   55.4 tonare
Heinsius   6 sua *Heinsius*

ᵃ Her car was drawn by lions.
ᵇ Had Titus or Vespasian, now gods, sent down the
Nemean lion slain by Hercules from the constellation Leo?
Cf. 4.57.5.

death! Whence, Libya, got your forests so fortunate a glory? Had he come from Cybele's yoke?[a] Or rather, Germanicus, did your brother or your father himself send you this beast from Hercules' star?[b]

54 (53)

Fairest of women that ever were or are, but cruelest of women that ever were or are, oh, how I would have wished you, Catulla, to become less fair or else less virtuous![c]

55 (56)

Since our grandsires' epoch yields to our own times and Rome has grown greater with her Leader, you wonder that sacred Maro's genius is lacking and that no man sounds of wars with so mighty a trumpet. Let there be Maecenases, Flaccus, and we shall not want for Maros: your own countryside will give you a Virgil. Grieving Tityrus had lost his acres close to hapless Cremona[d] and was bemoaning his ravished sheep: the Tuscan knight smiled and drove back malignant Poverty, telling her be off and

[c] *Vilissima* ("vilest") and *magis pudicam* ("more chaste") is usually read; cf. Ov. *Am.* 3.11a.41 *aut formosa fores minus aut minus improba vellem.* This may be right, though Wiman's reading makes a livelier epigram.

[d] Cf. Virg. *Ecl.* 9.28.

'accipe divitias et vatum maximus esto;
    tu licet et nostrum' dixit 'Alexin ames.'
astabat domini mensis pulcherrimus ille
    marmorea fundens nigra Falerna manu,
15 et libata dabat roseis carchesia labris,
    quae poterant ipsum sollicitare Iovem.
excidit attonito pinguis Galatea poetae
    Thestylis et rubras messibus usta genas;
protinus Italiam concepit et 'arma virumque',
20 qui modo vix Culicem fleverat ore rudi.
quid Varios Marsosque loquar ditataque vatum
    nomina, magnus erit quos numerare labor?
ergo ero Vergilius, si munera Maecenatis
    des mihi? Vergilius non ero, Marsus ero.

56 (54)

Magna licet totiens tribuas, maiora daturus
    dona, ducum victor, victor et ipse tui,
diligeris populo non propter praemia, Caesar,
    te propter populus praemia, Caesar, amat.

57

Tres habuit dentes, pariter quos expuit omnes,
    ad tumulum Picens dum sedet ipse suum;

55.23 ero $\beta\gamma$: ego T   56.4 te propter *Schneidewin* : et
p- β : p- te R γ 57.1 expuit γ : -ulit β

---

[a] Cf. 5.16.12.   [b] In the *Eclogues*.
[c] "Italy" = *Georgics* (cf. 2.136–176), "Arms, etc." =
Aeneid. Housman, however, thought that "Italy" too *might*

quickly. "Take riches and be greatest of poets," he said; "you may even love my Alexis."[a] That beauteous lad was standing by his master's board pouring the dark Falernian with a hand as white as marble and offering goblets tasted by rosy lips, lips that might stir Jove himself. The astonished poet forgot buxom Galatea and Thestylis[b] with her red cheeks tanned by the harvests. Forthwith he conceived Italy[c] and "Arms and the man," though his prentice lips had but lately with difficulty mourned the Gnat.[d] Why should I speak of Varius and Marsus and other names of poets made rich, whom it would be great labor to enumerate? Well then, shall I be a Virgil if you were to give me the gifts of a Maecenas? I shall not be a Virgil, I shall be a Marsus.

56 (54)

Though you give great gifts so often and have greater in store, conqueror of chieftains, conqueror even of yourself,[e] it is not because of your largesses Caesar, that you are beloved of the people; Caesar, the people love your largesses because of you.

57

Picens had three teeth, all of which he spat out together as he sat by his own sepulcher. Collecting

refer to the *Aeneid* (989).

[d] The *Culex* passed for an early work of Virgil (cf. 14.185).   [e] I.e. continually surpassing yourself.

collegitque sinu fragmenta novissima laxi
    oris et aggesta contumulavit humo.
ossa licet quondam defuncti non legat heres:
    hoc sibi iam Picens praestitit officium.

58

Cum tibi tam crassae sint, Artemidore, lacernae,
    possim te Sagarim iure vocare meo.

59

Aspicis hunc uno contentum lumine, cuius
    lippa sub attrita fronte lacuna patet?
ne contemne caput, nihil est furacius illo;
    non fuit Autolyci tam piperata manus.
5   hunc tu convivam cautus servare memento:
    tunc furit atque oculo luscus utroque videt.
pocula solliciti perdunt ligulasque ministri
    et latet in tepido plurima mappa sinu;
lapsa nec a cubito subducere pallia nescit
10   et tectus laenis saepe duabus abit;
nec dormitantem vernam fraudare lucerna
    erubuit fallax, ardeat illa licet.
si nihil invasit, puerum tunc arte dolosa
    circuit et soleas surripit ipse suas.

---

[a] A play on words. *Sagum* was a thick military cloak.
But more is involved; see SB^1.

in his lap the final fragments of his loose mouth, he buried them in a heap of earth. When his time comes, his heir will not need to gather up his bones; Picens has already performed that office for himself.

58

Since your cloak is so thick, Artemidorus, I could properly call you "Sagaris."[a]

59

Do you see him here, making do with a single eye, beneath whose brazen brow a dripping socket gapes? Don't despise the man, he is the most thievish of beings; Autolycus' hand was not so pepper-sharp. When he is your guest, be on your guard and remember to watch him. That's when he goes crazy[b] and, one-eyed though he be, sees with both. The anxious waiters lose cups and spoons, and many a napkin lurks in his warm lap. Nor does he lack skill to abstract the mantle slipped from your elbow and often gets away wearing two cloaks. The cunning rogue has not blushed to cheat a sleeping slave of his lamp, though it be burning. If he has laid hands on nothing, he moves craftily round his boy and purloins his own slippers.

[b] *Furit*, not a very appropriate word for a cunning thief. *Ferit*, "strikes," used in the sense "tricks," is suggested (*SB*[1]); note *fraudare* in v. 11 and *arte dolosa* in v. 13.

60

Summa Palatini poteras aequare Colossi,[a]
    si fieres brevior, Claudia, sesquipede.

61

Livet Charinus, rumpitur, furit, plorat
et quaerit altos unde pendeat ramos:
non iam quod orbe cantor et legor toto,
nec umbilicis quod decorus et cedro
5   spargor per omnes Roma quas tenet gentes,
sed quod sub urbe rus habemus aestivum
vehimurque mulis non, ut ante, conductis.
quid imprecabor, o Severe, liventi?
hoc opto: mulas habeat et suburbanum.[b]

62

Scribit in aversa Picens epigrammata charta,
    et dolet averso quod facit illa deo.[c]

63

Thestylon Aulus amat sed nec minus ardet Alexin,
    forsitan et nostrum nunc Hyacinthon amat.[d]

---

[a] Cf. Sp. 2.1.

[b] With all their worries.

[c] Apollo.

[d] Voconius Victor (cf. 7.29), himself a poet, was his master. Alexis too must be (or at least be thought of as)

60

Claudia, you could measure up to the top of the Palatine colossus[a] if you were shortened by a foot and a half.

61

Charinus is green with envy, he bursts, fumes, weeps, and looks for high branches from which to hang himself—not now because I am recited and read the world over, nor because, handsome with bosses and cedar oil, I am scattered through all the nations under Rome's dominion, but because I have a summer place in the country close to the city and ride on mules no longer hired as formerly. What curse shall I call down on the envious creature, Severus? This I pray: let him own mules and a place near town.[b]

62

Picens writes epigrams on the back of the paper and is upset because the god's[c] back is turned while he composes them.

63

Aulus loves Thestylus,[d] but has no less of a passion for Alexis; and perhaps he now loves my Hya-

a living boy, not Virgil's favorite; also perhaps belonging to Voconius. Aulus is M.'s friend Pudens; cf. 1.31.8n.

i nunc et dubita vates an diligat ipsos,
  delicias vatum cum meus Aulus amet.

64

Ut poscas, Clyte, munus exigasque,
uno nasceris octiens in anno
et solas, puto, tresve quattuorve
non natalicias habes Kalendas.
5 sit vultus tibi levior licebit
tritis litoris aridi lapillis,
sit moro coma nigrior caduco,
vincas mollitia tremente plumas
aut massam modo lactis alligati,
10 et talis tumor excitet papillas
qualis cruda viro puella servat,
tu nobis, Clyte, iam senex videris:
tam multos quis enim fuisse credat
natalis Priamive Nesorisve?
15 sit tandem pudor et modus rapinis.
quod si ludis adhuc semelque nasci
uno iam tibi non sat est in anno,
natum te, Clyte, nec semel putabo.

65

Hic ubi Fortunae Reducis fulgentia late
  templa nitent, felix area nuper erat:

---

[a] Clear proof that birthdays were sometimes celebrated
on the first of the month in which they occurred; see Introduction.

cinthus. Doubt if you can that friend Aulus loves the poets themselves, when he loves the poets' darlings.

64

In order to ask and exact a present, Clytus, you are born eight times in one year and you have only three or four Kalends, I think, that are not birthdays.[a] Your face may be smoother than worn pebbles on a dry beach, your hair may be blacker than a fallen mulberry, your quivering softness may surpass feathers or a mass of freshly curdled milk, and your nipples may stir and swell like those that a virgin keeps for her husband—but, Clytus, we think of you as already an old man. For who would believe that Priam or Nestor had so many birthdays? Let there at length be some discretion, some measure to your plunderings. But if you continue this foolery and to be born once a year is no longer enough for you, I shall not regard you as born even once, Clytus.[b]

65

Here, where shines far and wide the gleaming temple of Fortune[c] the Home-bringer, was but lately a

[b] I.e. I shall look upon you as nonexistent, a nobody; cf. 4.83.4; 10.27.4; 11.65.6.

[c] Built in celebration of Domitian's return from his Sarmatian campaign.

hic stetit Arctoi formosus pulvere belli
  purpureum fundens Caesar ab ore iubar;
5 hic lauru redimita comas et candida cultu
  Roma salutavit voce manuque ducem.
grande loci meritum testantur et altera dona:
  stat sacer et domitis gentibus arcus ovat;
hic gemini currus numerant elephanta frequentem,
10 sufficit immensis aureus ipse iugis.
haec est digna tuis, Germanice, porta triumphis:
  hos aditus urbem Martis habere decet.

66

Augusto pia tura victimasque
pro vestro date Silio, Camenae.
bis senos iubet en redire fasces,
nato consule, nobilique virga
5 vatis Castaliam domum sonare
rerum prima salus et una Caesar.
gaudenti superest adhuc quod optet,
felix purpura tertiusque consul.
Pompeio dederit licet senatus
10 et Caesar genero sacros honores,
quorum pacificus ter ampliavit

---

^a Besides the temple just mentioned.

^b On the face of it, this seems to mean that there was one golden statue of Domitian controlling both chariots, each drawn by a team of elephants.

214

lucky space. Here stood Caesar, beauteous with the dust of northern warfare, pouring brilliant radiance from his countenance. Here Rome, her hair wreathed with laurel and clothed in white, saluted her Leader with voice and hand. Another gift[a] attests the signal merit of the spot: a sacred arch stands exultant over subjugated nations. Here twin chariots number many an elephant, and Himself in gold suffices for the colossal cars.[b] This gate, Germanicus, is worthy of your triumphs; Mars' city deserves such an entrance.

66

Muses, give pious incense and victims to Augustus for your Silius' sake. See, his son is consul. Caesar, the world's chief and only welfare, makes the twice six fasces[c] to return and the poet's Castalian mansion to resound with the noble rod.[d] He rejoices, but there still remains something for him to pray for: happy purple and a third consul.[e] The senate gave to Pompey and Caesar to his son-in-law[f] sacred honors: Janus the peacemaker three times glorified

---

[c] The consul's twelve attendant lictors carried axes and rods symbolic of his authority.

[d] The lictor, escorting the consul to his house, struck on the door with his staff: Liv. 6.34.6.

[e] M. hopes that Silius' second son (who, however, died shortly afterwards) may become consul, three consulships thus falling to one house. The father was consul A.D. 68: 7.36.9.

[f] I.e. Augustus to Agrippa.

Ianus nomina: Silius frequentes
mavult sic numerare consulatus.

67

Horas quinque puer nondum tibi nuntiat, et tu
    iam conviva mihi, Caeciliane, venis,
cum modo distulerint raucae vadimonia quartae
    et Floralicias lasset harena feras.
5 curre, age, et illotos revoca, Calliste, ministros;
    sternantur lecti: Caeciliane, sede.
caldam poscis aquam: nondum mihi frigida venit;
    alget adhuc nudo clusa culina foco.
mane veni potius; nam cur te quinta moretur?
10   ut iantes, sero, Caeciliane, venis.

68

Qui Corcyraei vidit pomaria regis,
    rus, Entelle, tuae praeferet ille domus.
invida purpureos urat ne bruma racemos
    et gelidum Bacchi munera frigus edat,

---

[a] The consular Fasti were kept in the temple of Janus.

[b] Adjourned the court. *Vadimonia* were bonds required
of the parties to a suit to ensure their appearance. "They"
are the presiding officers. *Quartae* is usually taken as
nominative, equivalent to *quarta* (*hora*) or *quattuor horae*,
but that is unexampled. Hence various conjectures, but
with "they" understood as subject, the text can perhaps be
retained. *rauca . . . quarta* (*SB*[3]) would give "at the rau-
cous fourth," i.e. at the end of it.

216

their names.[a] But this is how Silius prefers to number a plurality of consulships.

67

Your boy does not yet announce to you five hours and already, Caecilianus, you arrive as my dinner guest, although they have only just adjourned the bail bonds[b] of the raucous fourth and the arena still tires the beasts at Flora's festival. Quick, Callistus, go and call back the unwashed servants,[c] have the couches spread. Sit down, Caecilianus. You ask for hot water; my cold has not arrived yet.[d] The closed kitchen is still chilly, the fire not laid. Better come in the morning. For why should the fifth hour hold you up?[e] You come too late for breakfast, Caecilianus.

68

He who has seen the orchards of Corcyra's king[f] will prefer the country inside your city mansion, Entellus. Lest envious winter bite the purple clusters, and chill frost devour the gifts of Bacchus, the

[c] They had gone out to bathe.
[d] M. had no water laid on to his house: cf. 9.18.
[e] I.e. why wait for it?
[f] Alcinous; cf. 7.42.6.

5   condita perspicua vivit vindemia gemma
     et tegitur felix nec tamen uva latet:
   femineum lucet sic per bombycina corpus,
     calculus in nitida sic numeratur aqua.
   quid non ingenio voluit natura licere?
10   autumnum sterilis ferre iubetur hiems.

69

Miraris veteres, Vacerra, solos
nec laudas nisi mortuos poetas.
ignoscas petimus, Vacerra: tanti
non est, ut placeam tibi, perire.

70

Quanta quies placidi tanta est facundia Nervae,
   sed cohibet vires ingeniumque pudor.
cum siccare sacram largo Permessida posset
   ore, verecundam maluit esse sitim,
5 Pieriam tenui frontem redimire corona
   contentus, famae nec dare vela suae.
sed tamen hunc nostri scit temporis esse Tibullum
   carmina qui docti nota Neronis habet.

vintage lives enclosed in transparent glass and the blooming grape is covered, yet not hidden. So a woman's body shines through silk, so pebbles are counted in clear water. What license has nature not willed for ingenuity? Barren winter is bidden to bear an autumn.[a]

69

You admire only the ancients, Vacerra, and praise no poets except dead ones. I crave your pardon, Vacerra; your good opinion is not worth dying for.

70

Gentle Nerva is as eloquent as he is tranquil, but modesty restrains his power and genius. Although he could have drained sacred Permessis[b] with ample draughts, he preferred his thirst be moderate, content to wreathe his Pierian brow with a slender chaplet and spread no sail to his fame. Yet, whoever is familiar with poet Nero's verses, knows that Nerva is the Tibullus of our time.

[a] Cf. 8.14.

[b] Properly the Nymph of the river Permessus, which rises on Mt Helicon, here used for the spring itself. Cf. 1.76.11n.

71

Quattuor argenti libras mihi tempore brumae
    misisti ante annos, Postumiane, decem;
speranti plures — nam stare aut crescere debent
    munera — venerunt plusve minusve duae;
5   tertius et quartus multo inferiora tulerunt;
    libra fuit quinto, Septiciana quidem;
besalem ad scutulam sexto pervenimus anno;
    post hunc in cotula rasa selibra data est;
octavus ligulam misit sextante minorem;
10   nonus acu levius vix cocleare tulit.
quod mittat nobis decimus iam non habet annus:
    quattuor ad libras, Postumiane, redi.

72

Nondum murice cultus asperoque
morsu pumicis aridi politus
Arcanum properas sequi, libelle,
quem pulcherrima iam redire Narbo,
5   docti Narbo paterna Votieni,
ad leges iubet annuosque fasces:
votis quod paribus tibi petendum est,
continget locus ille et hic amicus.
quam vellem fieri meus libellus!

71

Ten years ago, Postumianus, you sent me four pounds[a] of silver at the midwinter season. I was hoping for more (for presents should stay the same or grow); but two pounds, more or less, came. A third year and a fourth brought much lower quantities. By the fifth it was one pound, and Septician[b] at that. The sixth year we came down to an eight-ounce dish. The next I was presented with a bare half-pound in the shape of a cup. The eighth sent a spoon weighing less than two ounces. The ninth with difficulty brought a snail pick lighter than a needle. The tenth year has nothing to send me. Back to four pounds, Postumianus!

72

Not yet decked in purple and polished by the bite of dry pumice, you hasten, my little book, to follow Arcanus, whom fairest Narbo, Narbo Paterna[c] of lettered Votienus, bids now return to her laws and annual magistracy. You will find what you should pray for in equal measure: that place and this friend. How I would have liked to become my own little book!

[a] The Roman pound (*libra*) contained twelve ounces (*unciae*).

[b] I.e. inferior; cf. 4.88.3.

[c] The full name appears to have been Colonia Julia Paterna Narbo Marcia, now Narbonne. It was the capital of Gallia Narbonensis.

221

73

Istanti, quo nec sincerior alter habetur
    pectore nec nivea simplicitate prior,
si dare vis nostrae vires animosque Thaliae
    et victura petis carmina, da quod amem.
5 Cynthia te vatem fecit, lascive Properti;
    ingenium Galli pulchra Lycoris erat;
fama est arguti Nemesis formosa Tibulli;
    Lesbia dictavit, docte Catulle, tibi:
non me Paeligni nec spernet Mantua vatem,
10   si qua Corinna mihi, si quis Alexis erit.

74

Oplomachus nunc es, fueras opthalmicus ante.
    fecisti medicus quod facis oplomachus.

75

Dum repetit sera conductos nocte penates
    Lingonus a Tecta Flaminiaque recens,
expulit offenso vitiatum pollice talum
    et iacuit toto corpore fusus humi.
5 quid faceret Gallus, qua se ratione moveret?
    ingenti domino servulus unus erat,
tam macer ut minimam posset vix ferre lucernam:
    succurrit misero casus opemque tulit.

73.1 Istanti *Munro* : -ni β : stant γ : Instanti ς (*cf. ad*
7.68)   75.3 extudit o- luxatum *Heinsius*

73

Istantius, than whose heart none is accounted truer
and of snowier sincerity, if you wish to give strength
and courage to my Thalia and seek verses that will
live, give me something to love. Cynthia made you a
poet, sprightly Propertius; fair Lycoris was Gallus'
genius; beauteous Nemesis is the fame of clear-
voiced Tibullus; Lesbia, elegant Catullus, dictated
your verse. My poetry neither the Paelignians[a] nor
Mantua[b] will spurn, if I find a Corinna or an Alexis.

74

You are a gladiator now, you were formerly an eye-
doctor. You did as a doctor what you do as a
gladiator.[c]

75

A Lingonian fresh from the Covered[d] and Flaminian
Ways was returning late at night to his hired lodg-
ing when he caught his big toe and put his ankle out
of joint; so he lay stretched out full length on the
ground. What was the Gaul to do, how was he to
move? One little slave attended his huge master, so
meagre that he could barely carry the smallest of
lanterns; chance came to the poor fellow's rescue,

[a] Countrymen of Ovid.
[b] Birthplace of Virgil.
[c] Cf. similar epigrams, 1.30 and 47.
[d] Cf. 3.5.5n.

quattuor inscripti portabant vile cadaver,
10 accipit infelix qualia mille rogus;
hos comes invalidus summissa voce precatur,
  ut quocumque velint corpus inane ferant:
permutatur onus stipataque tollitur alte
  grandis in angusta sarcina sandapila.
15 hic mihi de multis unus, Lucane, videtur
  cui merito dici 'mortue Galle' potest.

76

'Dic verum mihi, Marce, dic amabo;
nil est quod magis audiam libenter.'
sic et cum recitas tuos libellos,
et causam quotiens agis clientis,
5 oras, Gallice, me rogasque semper.
durum est me tibi quod petis negare.
vero verius ergo quid sit audi:
verum, Gallice, non libenter audis.

77

Liber, amicorum dulcissima cura tuorum,
  Liber, in aeterna vivere digne rosa,
si sapis, Assyrio semper tibi crinis amomo
  splendeat et cingant florea serta caput;

---

^a Public slaves.

^b In the arena the net-caster (*retiarius*) would thus provoke his opponent, the *murmillo*, who wore a Gaulish helmet. M.'s point is that *this* Gaul was not only called dead

bringing aid. Four branded slaves[a] were bearing a corpse of low degree like a thousand that the pauper's pyre receives. The puny page begs them humbly to take the lifeless body wherever they like. The load is changed and the great bulk crammed in the narrow bier and hoisted high. He, Lucanus, is the only one of many, methinks, who can fairly be addressed as "Dead Gaul."[b]

76

"Tell me the truth, Marcus, now please do. There's nothing I would hear more gladly." So you beg of me, Gallicus, so you always ask, when you are reciting your little books or pleading a client's case. It is hard for me to refuse your request. So hear what is truer than true: the truth, Gallicus, you do not gladly hear.[c]

77

Liber, your friends' sweetest care, Liber, worthy to live wreathed in everlasting roses, if you are wise, let your hair ever glisten with Assyrian unguent and garlands of flowers circle your head. Let the

when really alive (like the *murmillo*) but actually put on a burial cart (*SB*[1]).

[c] Cf. 5.63; 7.28.9.

5 candida nigrescant vetulo crystalla Falerno
      et caleat blando mollis amore torus.
   qui sic vel medio finitus vixit in aevo,
      longior huic facta est quam data vita fuit.

78

   Quos cuperet Phlegraea suos victoria ludos,
      Indica quos cuperet pompa, Lyaee, tuos,
   fecit Hyperborei celebrator Stella triumphi,
      o pudor! o pietas! et putat esse parum.
5 non illi satis est turbato sordidus auro
      Hermus et Hesperio qui sonat orbe Tagus.
   omnis habet sua dona dies; nec linea dives
      cessat et in populum multa rapina cadit:
   nunc veniunt subitis lasciva nomismata nimbis,
10   nunc dat spectatas tessera larga feras,
   nunc implere sinus securos gaudet et absens
      sortitur dominos, ne laceretur, avis.

---

[a] For a similar sentiment, cf. 10.23.7f.

[b] The victory of the gods over the giants in the Phlegraean Plains in Campania: cf. 8.49.1.

[c] Cf. 8.26.7.

[d] Not to be taken literally. Domitian had declined a triumph.

clear crystal grow dark with old Falernian and the
soft couch be warm with a beguiling loved one. He
who has so lived, though he end in mid span, has
made his life longer than it was given to him.[a]

78

Games such as Phlegra's victory[b] would have
wished its own, such as the Indian pageant,
Lyaeus,[c] would have wished yours, did Stella exhi-
bit in celebration of the Hyperborean triumph,[d] and
(what modesty! what devotion!) he thinks them all
too little. Hermus dark with turbid gold does not
suffice him, nor Tagus, resounding in the Hesperian
world. Each day has its gifts. The wealthy cord[e]
takes no holiday and ample plunder falls into the
crowd. Now come sportive tokens[f] in sudden
showers, now the lavish coupon bestows the animals
they have been watching, now birds are happy to fill
safe laps and find masters in absence by lot, lest
they be torn apart.[g] Why should I count the chariots

[e] A cord hung with gifts for the populace. Cf. Suet. *Nero*
11.2.

[f] Entitling the holder to receive presents. Friedländer,
however, thought that *lasciva* refers to tokens giving free
access to brothels or to prostitutes in the theater (cf. Stat.
Silv. 1.6.67).

[g] Birds, instead of being scrambled for and so torn to
pieces, are assigned by lot.

quid numerem currus ter denaque praemia palmae
   quae dare non semper consul uterque solet?
15 omnia sed, Caesar, tanto superantur honore,
   quod spectatorem te tua laurus habet.

79

Omnis aut vetulas habes amicas
aut turpis vetulisque foediores.
has ducis comites trahisque tecum
per convivia, porticus, theatra.
5   sic formosa, Fabulla, sic puella es.

80

Sanctorum nobis miracula reddis avorum
   nec pateris, Caesar, saecula cana mori,
cum veteres Latiae ritus renovantur harenae
   et pugnat virtus simpliciore manu.
5 sic priscis servatur honos te praeside templis
   et Casa tam culto sub Iove numen habet;
sic nova dum condis, revocas, Auguste, priora:
   debentur quae sunt quaeque fuere tibi.

80.4 et pugnat *Gilbert* : et pugnet β : et pugna et γ : ut pug-
net *Gruter*

and the thrice ten victory prizes, such as both consuls are not always apt to give?[a] But all this, Caesar, is surpassed by one signal glory: your triumph has you for its spectator.

79

All your women friends are either old hags or frights uglier than old hags. These are your companions whom you bring with you and trail through dinner parties, colonnades, theaters. In this way, Fabulla, you are a beauty, you are a girl.

80

You give us back, Caesar, the wonders of our venerable forebears, nor suffer ancient epochs to die, when the old usages of the Latian arena are revived and valor fights with simpler hand.[b] Even so under your rule antique temples keep their honors and the Cot[c] beneath a Jupiter so amply worshipped has sanctity.[d] Thus, Augustus, while founding the new, you bring back the old. What is and what was alike are owed to you.

[a] There were thirty races. The consuls exhibited games on their entry into office.

[b] Apparently Domitian had restored unarmed combat in the arena.

[c] Casa Romuli, Romulus' legendary thatched cottage on the Capitol (there was another on the Palatine).

[d] Jove is magnificently honored, yet the humble Cot is hallowed.

81

Non per mystica sacra Dindymenes
nec per Niliacae bovem iuvencae,
nullos denique per deos deasque
iurat Gellia, sed per uniones.
5   hos amplectitur, hos perosculatur,
hos fratres vocat, hos vocat sorores,
hos natis amat acrius duobus.
his si quo careat misella casu,
victuram negat esse se nec horam.
10   eheu, quam bene nunc, Papiriane,
Annaei faceret manus Sereni!

82

Dante tibi turba querulos, Auguste, libellos
nos quoque quod domino carmina parva damus
posse deum rebus pariter Musisque vacare
scimus et haec etiam serta placere tibi.
5 fer vates, Auguste, tuos: nos gloria dulcis,
nos tua cura prior deliciaeque sumus.
non quercus te sola decet nec laurea Phoebi:
fiat et ex hedera civica nostra tibi.

82.8 nostra] *v. annot.*

---

[a] Apis, the sacred Egyptian bull, representing Osiris,
the husband of Isis, who was represented as a heifer: cf.
2.14.8.
[b] Surely Seneca's friend (cf. 7.45.2). For "hand," i.e.
thieving hand, cf. 8.59.4; 11.54.5. The reference will be to

81

Gellia does not swear by the mystic rites of Din-
dymene, nor by the bull of Nile's heifer,[a] nor in fine
by any gods or goddesses, but by her pearls. These
she embraces, these she covers with kisses, these
she calls her brothers, these she calls her sisters,
these she loves more passionately than her two chil-
dren. If the poor thing were by some mischance to
lose them, she says she would not live an hour. Ah,
Papirianus, how well the hand of Annaeus Serenus[b]
might now be employed!

82

While the multitude offer you plaintive petitions,
Augustus, we too offer little poems to our Lord. We
know that your deity has time both for business and
for the Muses and that these garlands too are pleas-
ing to you. Bear with your bards, Augustus. We are
your sweet glory, your erstwhile care and delight.[c]
Not the oak[d] only and Phoebus' laurel[e] beseem you.
Let our[f] civic crown of ivy also be made for you.

some well-known incident otherwise unrecorded.
   [c] Cf. 5.5.7n.
   [d] The *corona civica* of oak leaves given to one who had
preserved the life of a citizen, afterwards given to the
Emperor as the general preserver.
   [e] The crown of victory in war.
   [f] Relating to or coming from us poets. But *nostra* seems
awkward, the idea being sufficiently expressed by *hedera*,
the poets' ivy. Perhaps *nexa*, "woven."

LIBER IX

Have, mi Torani, frater carissime. epigramma,
quod extra ordinem paginarum est, ad Stertinium
clarissimum virum scripsimus, qui imaginem meam
ponere in bibliotheca sua voluit. de quo scribendum
5   tibi putavi, ne ignorares Avitus iste quis vocaretur.
vale et para hospitium.

    Note, licet nolis, sublimi pectore vates,
        cui referet serus praemia digna cinis,
    hoc tibi sub nostra breve carmen imagine vivat,
        quam non obscuris iungis, Avite, viris:
5   'ille ego sum nulli nugarum laude secundus,
        quem non miraris sed, puto, lector, amas.
    maiores maiora sonent: mihi parva locuto
        sufficit in vestras saepe redire manus.'

1

Dum Ianus hiemes, Domitianus autumnos,
Augustus annis commodabit aestates,

BOOK IX

Greetings, my Toranius, my dearest brother. I addressed the epigram which is placed out of paginal order to the illustrious[a] Stertinius,[b] who wished to place a bust of me in his library. I thought I should write to you about it, so that you know who this person I call Avitus is. Good-bye and prepare a welcome.

Bard of soul sublime, known to fame, though you desire it not, to whom long hereafter the grave will render meet reward, let this brief verse live under my bust, which you, Avitus, are placing in company not undistinguished:

"I am he whose trifles are praised second to none, whom, reader, you do not wonder at, but whom, methinks, you love. Let greater men sing greater themes: I speak of little things, and am content to come back often to your hands."

1

So long as Janus shall lend winters, Domitian autumns, and Augustus summers to the years, so

---

[a] I.e. a senator. Stertinius was consul in A.D. 92.
[b] Addressed as Avitus also in 1.16, as in Books X–XII.

dum grande famuli nomen asseret Rheni
Germanicarum magna lux Kalendarum,
5 Tarpeia summi saxa dum patris stabunt,
dum voce supplex dumque ture placabit
matrona divae dulce Iuliae numen:
manebit altum Flaviae decus gentis
cum sole et astris cumque luce Romana.
10 invicta quidquid condidit manus, caeli est.

2

Pauper amicitiae cum sis, Lupe, non es amicae
    et queritur de te mentula sola nihil.
illa siligineis pinguescit adultera cunnis,
    convivam pascit nigra farina tuum.
5 incensura nives dominae Setina liquantur,
    nos bibimus Corsi pulla venena cadi;
empta tibi nox est fundis non tota paternis,
    non sua desertus rura sodalis arat;
splendet Erythraeis perlucida moecha lapillis,
10   ducitur addictus, te futuente, cliens;
octo Syris suffulta datur lectica puellae,
    nudum sandapilae pondus amicus erit.
i nunc et miseros, Cybele, praecide cinaedos:
    haec erat, haec cultris mentula digna tuis.

2.6 corsi β : torti γ : Tusci *Friedländer*

---

    [a] Domitian, copying Augustus, who named August, and
Julius Caesar, who named July, gave the names German-
icus and Domitianus to September and October respec-
tively, because he became Emperor in the one and was
born in the other: Suet. *Dom.* 13.3.

long as the great day of the Kalends of Germanicus shall claim the grand renown of Rhine in thrall,[a] so long as the Tarpeian rock of the Supreme Father shall stand, so long as suppliant matrons shall placate Divine Julia's[b] sweet deity with voice and incense: thus long shall the lofty ornament of the Flavian race[c] endure, together with sun and stars and Roman daylight.[d] Whatever an unconquered hand has founded, belongs to heaven.

2

To friendship, Lupus, you are a poor man, but not to your mistress; and only your cock has no complaint to make of you. The adulteress fattens on wheaten cunts:[e] black meal feeds your guest. For your lady Setine is strained to set snow on fire:[f] *we* drink the dingy poison of a Corsican jar. You buy a part of a night with your paternal estates; your forsaken crony ploughs fields not his own. Your married fancy shines bright with Erythraean pearls: your client is led off into bondage while you fuck. A litter supported by eight Syrians is given to the girl: your friend's naked corpse will load a pauper's bier. Geld if you will, Cybele, hapless queens: this was the cock, yes this, that merited your knife.

[b] Cf. 6.3.6; 6.13.
[c] The temple built by Domitian in honor of the *Gens Flavia*; cf. 9.3.12.
[d] Where the sun shines, Rome rules.
[e] Cf. 14.70.
[f] Cf. 5.64.2; 14.116 and 117.

3

Quantum iam superis, Caesar, caeloque dedisti
    si repetas et si creditor esse velis,
grandis in aetherio licet auctio fiat Olympo
    cogranturque dei vendere quidquid habent,
5 conturbabit Atlans et non erit uncia tota
    decidat tecum qua pater ipse deum.
pro Capitolinis quid enim tibi solvere templis,
    quid pro Tarpeiae frondis honore potest?
quid pro culminibus geminis matrona Tonantis?
10   Pallada praetereo: res agit illa tuas.
quid loquar Alciden Phoebumque piosque Laconas
    addita quid Latio Flavia templa polo?
expectes et sustineas, Auguste, necesse est:
    nam tibi quo solvat non habet arca Iovis.

4

Aureolis futui cum possit Galla duobus
    et plus quam futui, si totidem addideris,
aureolos a te cur accipit, Aeschyle, denos?
    non fellat tanti Galla. quid ergo? tacet.

3.14 quo *Duff*: quod βγ

---

[a] I.e. the heavens, which he supports.

[b] An *uncia* for every as.

[c] Cf. 4.1.6n.

[d] One of them will have been on the Capitol, rebuilt by
Domitian after destruction in 69. The other is unknown.

BOOK IX

3

If you were to claim back what you have already given to the High Ones and the heavens, Caesar, and choose to be their creditor, though a grand auction be held in skyey Olympus and the gods obliged to sell whatever they possess, Atlas[a] would go bankrupt and there would not be a full twelfth[b] for the Father of the Gods himself to make a settlement with you. For what can he pay you for the temples of the Capitol and the honor of the Tarpeian wreath?[c] Or what the Thunderer's lady for her twin towers?[d] Pallas I leave aside: she is your business manager.[e] Why speak of Alcides and Phoebus and the loving Laconians?[f] Or the Flavian temple added to the Latin sky?[g] Augustus, you must needs wait in patience: for Jove's coffer doesn't have the wherewithal to pay you.

4

Since Galla can be fucked for two gold pieces, and more than fucked if you add as many more, why does she get ten gold pieces a time from you, Aeschylus? Galla sucks for less than that. What then? She keeps mum.

[e] Cf. 4.53.2n. Domitian made a special cult of Minerva.

[f] Castor and Pollux. Domitian had built and restored temples to the deities named. He was the greatest imperial builder since Augustus.

[g] I.e. to the Roman Pantheon, the deified Emperors: cf. 9.34.2.

5 (6)

Tibi, summe Rheni domitor et parens orbis,
pudice princeps, gratias agunt urbes:
populos habebunt; parere iam scelus non est.
non puer avari sectus arte mangonis
5   virilitatis damna maeret ereptae,
nec quam superbus computet stipem leno
dat prostituto misera mater infanti.
qui nec cubili fuerat ante te quondam,
pudor esse per te coepit et lupanari.

6 (7)

Dicere de Libycis reducti tibi gentibus, Afer,
    continuis volui quinque diebus 'have':
'non vacat' aut 'dormit' dictum est bis terque reverso.
    iam satis est. non vis, Afer, havere? vale.

7 (8)

Tamquam parva foret sexus iniuria nostri
    foedandos populo prostituisse mares,
iam cunae lenonis erant, ut ab ubere raptus
    sordida vagitu posceret aera puer.
5   immatura dabant infandas corpora poenas.
    non tulit Ausonius talia monstra pater,

---

[a] Cf. 2.60. Domitian seems to have reissued his edict
against castration as part of a new edict against child pros-
titution; see 9.7.

5 (6)

To you, supreme subjugator of the Rhine and father
of the world, virtuous prince, cities offer thanks.
They will have inhabitants; it is no longer a crime to
give birth. No more do boys mutilated by the art of
a greedy slave dealer grieve for the loss of their rav-
ished manhood,[a] nor does a wretched mother give a
mite to her prostituted infant for the haughty pimp
to calculate.[b] Modesty, which before you in days
gone by was not to be found even in the marriage
bed, has through you come to exist even in the
brothel.

6 (7)

For five successive days I have wanted to say good-
day to you, Afer, now that you are back from the
tribes of Libya. "He's engaged" or "He's asleep," I'm
told, as I return twice and thrice. Enough! You
don't want good-day, Afer? Good-bye.

7 (8)

As though it were not outrage enough to our sex to
have exposed males for the public to defile, the cra-
dle had become the pimp's property, so that the boy
snatched from his mother's breast wailed for dirty
coppers. Bodies ungrown suffered unspeakable
inflictions. The Ausonian Father did not brook such

[b] The mother keeps track of him and gives him money,
so that he does not have to beg for it or be punished by his
master for not getting it (SB^1).

idem qui teneris nuper succurrit ephebis,
   ne faceret steriles saeva libido viros.
dilexere prius pueri iuvenesque senesque,
10   at nunc infantes te quoque, Caesar, amant.

8 (9)

Nil tibi legavit Fabius, Bithynice, cui tu
   annua, si memini, milia sena dabas.
plus nulli dedit ille: queri, Bithynice, noli:
   annua legavit milia sena tibi.

9 (10)

Cenes, Canthare, cum foris libenter,
clamas et maledicis et minaris.
deponas animos truces monemus:
liber non potes et gulosus esse.

10 (5)

Nubere vis Prisco: non miror, Paula; sapisti.
   ducere te non vult Priscus: et ille sapit.

11

Nomen cum violis rosisque natum,
quo pars otima nominatur anni,
Hyblam quod sapit Atticosque flores,

---

[a] Ĕărīnos, from ἔαρ (ear), "spring." It will not fit into
any of M.'s meters.

monstrosities, the same who lately succored tender youths to stop cruel lust from sterilizing males. Boys, young men, and old men loved you before, Caesar, but now infants too adore you.

8 (9)

Fabius, to whom, if I remember right, you used to give six thousand a year, has left you nothing, Bithynicus. He has left nobody more. Don't grumble, Bithynicus. He has left you six thousand a year.

9 (10)

Although you like dining out, Cantharus, you shout and curse and threaten. I advise you to put aside your truculence. You can't be free-spoken and greedy both.

10 (5)

You want to marry Priscus. I'm not surprised, Paula. Wise of you. Priscus doesn't want to marry you. Wise of him, too.

11

Name[a] born together with violets and roses, by which is named the best part of the year, which has the flavor of Hybla and Attic flowers[b] and the

[b] The honey of Hybla, in Sicily, and of Hymettus respectively: cf. 5.39.3; 7.88.8.

quod nidos olet alitis superbae;
5   nomen nectare dulcius beato,
quo mallet Cybeles puer vocari
et qui pocula temperat Tonanti,
quod si Parrhasia sones in aula,
respondent Veneres Cupidinesque;
10   nomen nobile, molle, delicatum
versu dicere non rudi volebam:
sed tu, syllaba contumax, rebellas.
dicunt Eiarinon tamen poetae,
sed Graeci, quibus est nihil negatum
15   et quos Ἄρες Ἄρες decet sonare:
nobis non licet esse tam disertis,
qui Musas colimus severiores.

12 (13)

Nomen habes teneri quod tempora nuncupat anni,
cum breve Cecropiae ver populantur apes:
nomen Acidalia meruit quod harundine pingi,
quod Cytherea sua scribere gaudet acu;
5   nomen Erythraeis quod littera facta lapillis,
gemma quod Heliadum pollice trita notet;
quod pinna scribente grues ad sidera tollant;
quod decet in sola Caesaris esse domo.

11.12 rebellas β : repugnas γ

fragrance of the proud bird's[a] nest; name sweeter
than blessed nectar, by which Cybele's boy and he
who mixes the Thunderer's cups[b] would rather be
called, to which, if you sound it in the Parrhasian
palace, Venuses and Cupids answer: that noble,
soft, and dainty name I wished to put into polished
verse. But, contumacious syllable, you rebel. And
yet poets say Eiarinos; but they are Greeks to whom
nothing is denied, whom it beseems to chant "Āres,
Ăres."[c] We, who cultivate more austere Muses, can-
not be so clever.[d]

12 (13)

You have a name that designates the tender season
of the year, when Cecropian bees raid the short-
lived spring, a name that deserved to be painted
with Acidalian reed, that Cytherea rejoices to
inscribe with her own needle, a name to be traced in
letters made of Erythraean pearls or the Heliads'
jewel thumb-rubbed, one that cranes might raise to
the stars with scribal feather,[e] one that belongs only
in Caesar's house.

[a] The phoenix; cf. 6.55.2.

[b] Attis and Ganymede.

[c] In the Homeric line (*Il.* 5.31) beginning Ἄρες, Ἄρες,
βροτολοιγέ (Āres, Ăres, brotoloige).

[d] *Disertis* implies mastery of language and versifi-
cation.

[e] Palamedes was said to have invented certain letters
including Υ (Latin V) from watching cranes in flight. Eari-
nos latinized become Vernus. Cf. 13.75.

13 (12)

Si daret autumnus mihi nomen, Oporinos essem,
    horrida si brumae sidera, Chimerinos;
dictus ab aestivo Therinos tibi mense vocarer:
    tempora cui nomen verna dedere, quis est?

14

Hunc quem mensa tibi, quem cena paravit amicum
    esse putas fidae pectus amicitiae?
aprum amat et mullos et sumen et ostrea, non te.
    tam bene si cenem, noster amicus erit.

15

Inscripsit tumulis septem scelerata virorum
    'se fecisse' Chloe. quid pote simplicius?

16

Consilium formae speculum dulcisque capillos
    Pergameo posuit dona sacrata deo
ille puer tota domino gratissimus aula,
    nomine qui signat tempora verna suo.
5 felix quae tali censetur munere tellus!
    nec Ganymedeas mallet habere comas.

14.1 huic *conieci*

---

    [a] "Chloe" murdered seven husbands and inscribed on
their tombs *Chloe feci*, "I, Chloe, put it (the tomb) up." But
the words could also mean "I, Chloe, did it," i.e. committed
the crime; cf. Juv. 6.638.

BOOK IX

13 (12)

If autumn gave me my name, I should be Oporinos;
if the shivering stars of winter, Chimerinos; named
from summer's season you would call me Therinos;
who is he to whom springtime gave a name?

14

Do you think this fellow whom your table and your
dinner made your friend is a heart of faithful friend-
ship? He loves your boar and mullet and sow's
udder and oysters, not you. If I dined as well as you,
he would be a friend of mine.

15

Chloe the murderess inscribed on the tombs of her
seven husbands that "she did it."[a] What could be
plainer?

16

The boy, his master's favorite in all the palace,
whose name means springtime, has dedicated his
mirror, beauty's counselor, and his sweet locks as
hallowed offerings to the god of Pergamum.[b] Happy
the land appraised by such a gift! It would not
rather possess the hair of Ganymede.

[b] Aesculapius, god of healing, who had a celebrated
temple at Pergamum. Earinus was born there. The dedi-
cation is the subject of Stat. *Silv.* 3.4.

17

Latonae venerande nepos, qui mitibus herbis
    Parcarum exoras pensa brevesque colos,
hos tibi laudatos domino, rata vota, capillos
    ille tuus Latia misit ab urbe puer;
5 addidit et nitidum sacratis crinibus orbem,
    quo felix facies iudice tuta fuit.
tu iuvenale decus serva, ne pulchrior ille
    in longa fuerit quam breviore coma.

18

Est mihi — sitque precor longum te praeside, Caesar
    rus minimum, parvi sunt et in urbe lares.
sed de valle brevi quas det sitientibus hortis
    curva laboratas antlia tollit aquas,
5 sicca domus queritur nullo se rore foveri,
    cum mihi vicino Marcia fonte sonet.
quam dederis nostris, Auguste, penatibus undam,
    Castalis haec nobis aut Iovis imber erit.

19

Laudas balnea versibus trecentis
cenantis bene Pontici, Sabelle,
vis cenare, Sabelle, non lavari.

18.4 tollit β : ducit γ

---

  [a] Water from the great aqueduct was conveyed by lead
pipes into houses. Strabo (5.3.8) says that almost every
house in Rome had it laid on; cf. Hor. *Epist.* 1.10.20. The

17

Revered grandson of Latona, who with gentle herbs prevail upon the threads and short distaffs of the Fates, your boy has sent you from Latium's city these locks his master praised, a vow fulfilled. And to his dedicated tresses he has added the bright disk whose judgment made his blooming countenance secure. Do you preserve his youthful loveliness; let him be no less comely now that his hair is short than when it was long.

18

I own (and may it long be mine under your rule, Caesar) a tiny country place and a small dwelling in the city. But from the narrow valley a curved pump toilsomely brings up water to give to the thirsty villa, whereas my dry town house complains that it is freshened by no liquid, though I hear Marcia's stream hard by.[a] The water that you give, Augustus, to my home shall be to me fount of Castalia or rain of Jupiter.

19

Sabellus, in three hundred[b] verses you extol the baths of Ponticus, who dines well. You want a dinner, Sabellus, not a bath.

aqueduct will have supplied a stream or fountain near M.'s house.

[b] Indefinite, of a large number.

20

Haec, quae tota patet tegiturque et marmore et auro,
    infantis domini conscia terra fuit.
felix o quantis sonuit vagitibus et quas
    vidit reptantis sustinuitque manus!
5 hic steterat veneranda domus quae praestitit orbi
    quod Rhodos astrifero, quod pia Creta polo.
Curetes texere Iovem crepitantibus armis,
    semiviri poterant qualia ferre Phryges:
at te protexit superum pater et tibi, Caesar,
10   pro iaculo et parma fulmen et aegis erat.

21

Artemidorus habet puerum sed vendidit agrum;
    agrum pro puero Calliodorus habet.
dic uter ex istis melius rem gesserit, Aucte:
    Artemidorus amat, Calliodorus arat.

22

Credis ob haec me, Pastor, opes fortasse rogare
    propter quae populus crassaque turba rogat,

22.2 populus β : uulgus γ

---

[a] The Sun (born in Rhodes by some accounts; cf. Housman, 989) and Jupiter.

20

This piece of ground, that lies all open and is being covered with marble and gold, knew our Lord in infancy. O happy ground, with what mighty wailings it echoed, what crawling hands it saw and sustained! Here had stood the venerable house that gave the world what Rhodes and pious Crete gave the starry sky.[a] The Curetes sheltered Jove with their clashing arms, such arms as half-men Phrygians could bear.[b] But you the Father of the High Ones did protect, and for you, Caesar, thunderbolt and aegis took the place of spear and buckler.

21

Artemidorus has a boy, but has sold his land; Calliodorus has land instead of a boy. Which of the two has made the better bargain, Auctus? Artemidorus plays, Calliodorus plows.[c]

22

Perhaps you think I ask for wealth, Pastor, for the same purposes as the thick-witted, vulgar herd

[b] The Curetes (demigods) clashed their arms to drown the infant's cries, lest his father Cronos should hear and eat him. They are sometimes assimilated with the Corybantes, priests of Cybele.

[c] Or, with Gaselee's *arat* for *amat* (lit. "loves"): "A. plows (*sens. obsc.*) and C. plows," a much sharper point.

ut Setina meos consumat gleba ligones
    et sonet innumera compede Tuscus ager;
5 ut Mauri Libycis centum stent dentibus orbes
    et crepet in nostris aurea lamna toris,
nec labris nisi magna meis crystalla terantur
    et faciant nigras nostra Falerna nives;
ut canusinatus nostro Syrus assere sudet
10 et mea sit culto sella cliente frequens;
aestuet ut nostro madidus conviva ministro,
    quem permutatum nec Ganymede velis;
ut lutulenta linat Tyrias mihi mula lacernas
    et Massyla meum virga gubernet equum.
15 est nihil ex istis: superos et sidera testor.
    ergo quid? ut donem, Pastor, et aedificem.

23

O cui virgineo flavescere contigit auro,
    dic ubi Palladium sit tibi, Care, decus.
'aspicis en domini fulgentes marmore vultus?
    venit ad has ultro nostro corona comas.'
5 Albanae livere potest pia quercus olivae,
    cinxerit invictum quod prior illa caput.

22.15 superos et sidera *Heraeus* : su- ad si- γ : sideraque et
supera β

---

^a Canusium was celebrated for its tawny-colored wool
(Pliny *N.H.* 8.190f); cf. 14.127; 129.
    ^b The suggestion that "Pastor," like "Gellius" in 9.46,
made building an excuse for not giving seems to be right.
M. says that *he* would like to be rich enough to do both.

asks: that Setine clods may wear out my hoes and Tuscan land clang with countless chains; that a hundred round Moorish tables may stand on Libyan tusks and gold foil rattle on my couches; that only large crystal cups be rubbed by my lips and my Falernian blacken snow; that a Syrian in Canusian wool[a] sweat at my pole and my chair be attended by many a well-dressed client; that a tipsy dinner guest steam for my page, whom you would not wish to change for Ganymede; that a muddy mule smear my Tyrian cloak and a Massylian rod guide my horse. No, none of these, I call the High Ones and the stars to witness. Then what? To give, Pastor, and to build.[b]

23

Carus, whose fortune it was to turn blond with the Virgin's gold, tell me where you keep the Palladian prize. "Look. You see the Lord's countenance shining in marble? My wreath came to this hair of its own accord."[c] The loyal oak may envy Alba's olive in that the latter was first to circle the unconquered head.[d]

[c] Carus had won the golden olive wreath, the prize for poetry, at the annual contest in honor of Minerva at Domitian's Alban villa: cf. 4.1.5. This he had transferred to the Emperor's bust.

[d] Cf. 4.1.4n. M. suggests that Carus will go on to win the oak-leaf crown in the Capitoline competition and will place that too on a portrait bust of Domitian.

24

Quis Palatinos imitatus imagine vultus
    Phidiacum Latio marmore vicit ebur?
haec mundi facies, haec sunt Iovis ora sereni:
    sic tonat ille deus cum sine nube tonat.
5 non solam tribuit Pallas tibi, Care, coronam;
    effigiem domini, quam colis, illa dedit.

25

Dantem vina tuum quotiens aspeximus Hyllum,
    lumine nos, Afer, turbidiore notas.
quod, rogo, quod scelus est mollem spectare ministrur
    aspicimus solem, sidera, templa, deos.
5 avertam vultus, tamquam mihi pocula Gorgon
    porrigat, atque oculos oraque nostra tegam?
trux erat Alcides, et Hylan spectare licebat;
    ludere Mercurio cum Ganymede licet.
si non vis teneros spectet conviva ministros,
10 Phineas invites, Afer, et Oedipodas.

26

Audet facundo qui carmina mittere Nervae,
    pallida donabit glaucina, Cosme, tibi,

25.6 tegam β : petat T γ, L ex tegat

---

[a] M. goes one better than Ov. *Ex. P.* 2.8.19f: "When I
look at this portrait I seem to see Rome; for he (Augustus)
bears the face of his fatherland."

[b] The reading *petat* ("were assaulting"), preferred by
editors, is wrong. The Gorgon did not attack faces, she
turned people who looked upon her face to stone.

BOOK IX

24

Who surpassed Phidias' ivory in Latin marble with this bust portraying the Palatine countenance? This is the face of the firmament,[a] this is the aspect of unclouded Jove. So the god thunders when he thunders from a clear sky. It was not merely a wreath, Carus, that Pallas accorded you; she gave you the Lord's effigy, which you worship.

25

Whenever we look at your Hyllus as he pours the wine, you mark us, Afer, with a troubled eye. What crime is there, I ask you, in gazing at a soft page? We gaze at the sun, the stars, temples, gods. Am I to avert my face as though the Gorgon were offering me a cup, and cover my eyes and countenance?[b] Alcides was fierce, yet Hylas could be looked at. Mercury is allowed to play with Ganymede. If you don't want your guests to look at tender pages, Afer, you should invite Phineuses and Oedipuses.[c]

26

He that dares send poems to eloquent Nerva[d] will give you pale glaucine,[e] Cosmus; he will give violets

[c] Phineus and Oedipus were blind.

[d] The future Emperor: cf. 8.70.

[e] *Glaucina* seems to have been an unguent made from the plant *glaucium*—greater celandine rather than horned poppy (Ker).

253

Paestano violas et cana ligustra colono,
    Hyblaeis apibus Corsica mella dabit:
5 sed tamen et parvae nonnulla est gratia Musae;
    appetitur posito vilis oliva lupo.
nec tibi sit mirum, modici quod conscia vatis
    iudicium metuit nostra Thalia tuum:
ipse tuas etiam veritus Nero dicitur aures,
10   lascivum iuvenis cum tibi lusit opus.

27

Cum depilatos, Chreste, coleos portes
et vulturino mentulam parem collo
et prostitutis levius caput culis,
nec vivat ullus in tuo pilus crure,
5 purgentque saevae cana labra vulsellae;
Curios, Camillos, Quintios, Numas, Ancos,
et quidquid usquam legimus pilosorum
loqueris sonasque grandibus minax verbis,
et cum theatris saeculoque rixaris.
10 occurrit aliquis inter ista si draucus,
iam paedagogo liberatus et cuius
refibulavit turgidum faber penem,
nutu vocatum ducis, et pudet fari
Catoniana, Chreste, quod facis lingua.

27.7 usquam β : umq- γ

and white privet to a Paestan gardener and Corsican honey to Hybla's bees.[a] And yet even a petty Muse is not altogether without charm; when bass is served, cheap olives are in request. Nor be surprised that my Thalia, aware of her bard's humble quality, is afraid of your judgment. Nero himself is said to have feared your ears, when in youth he lightly turned out for you some playful piece.[b]

27

You carry depilated testicles, Chrestus, and a cock like a vulture's neck and a head smoother than prostituted arses, there is not a hair alive on your shins and the cruel tweezers purge your white jowls. But your talk is of Curius, Camillus, Quinctius, Numa, Ancus, and every hairy worthy we ever found in books; you are loud and threatening with big words, and you quarrel with the theaters and the times. If, as this goes on, some young athlete comes your way, now freed from tutelage,[c] whose swollen penis has been unpinned by the smith, you summon him with a nod and lead him off; and I shouldn't like to say, Chrestus, what you do with your Catonian tongue.

[a] I.e. will send things—and inferior things—where they are not wanted. Corsican honey was bitter from the abundance of yews on the island; cf. Virg. *Ecl.* 9.30.

[b] Cf. 8.70.7f.

[c] Lit. "from his paedagogus"; cf. 3.58.30n.

28

Dulce decus scaenae, ludorum fama, Latinus
    ille ego sum, plausus deliciaeque tuae,
qui spectatorem potui fecisse Catonem,
    solvere qui Curios Fabriciosque graves.
5 sed nihil a nostro sumpsit mea vita theatro
    et sola tantum scaenicus arte feror;
nec poteram gratus domino sine moribus esse:
    interius mentes inspicit ille deus.
vos me laurigeri larasitum dicite Phoebi,
10   Roma sui famulum dum sciat esse Iovis.

29

Saecula Nestoreae permensa, Philaeni, senectae
    rapta es ad infernas tam cito Ditis aquas?
Euboicae nondum numerabas longa Sibyllae
    tempora: maior erat mensibus illa tribus.
5 heu quae lingua silet! non illam mille catastae
    vincebant, nec quae turba Sarapin amat,
nec matutini cirrata caterva magistri,
    nec quae Strymonio de grege ripa sonat.
quae nunc Thessalico lunam deducere rhombo,
10   quae sciet hos illos vendere lena toros?

28.8 inspicit β : susp- *vel sim.* γ : persp- *Heinsius*

---

  [a] Connotative of loose living.
  [b] Inscriptions show that comic actors (mimes) were so called. There seems to have been a society of "Apollo's Parasites."
  [c] The Sibyl of Cumae in Campania, a colony from

28

Famed Latinus am I, darling pride of the stage,
glory of the festivals, your applause and delight,
who could have made a theater-goer out of Cato and
got a laugh from solemn Curius and Fabricius. But
my life has borrowed nothing from my performance,
it is simply and solely for my art that I am called
actor.[a] I could not have pleased our Lord without
good morals; that god looks deep into men's hearts.
You may call me laureled Phoebus' parasite,[b] so
long as Rome knows me as the servant of her
Jupiter.

29

Philaenis, after measuring out the centuries of aged
Nestor, have you so early been snatched away to the
nether waters of Dis? Not yet were you numbering
the Euboean Sybil's[c] length of days; she was older
by three months. Ah, what a tongue is silent! A
thousand slave auctions did not outdo it, nor yet the
crowd of Serapis-worshippers, nor the curly-headed
troop of the matutinal schoolmaster, nor the bank
that resounds with Strymon's flock. Who now will
have the skill to draw down the moon with Thes-
salian wheel?[d] Or what procuress to sell this

Chalcis in Euboea. Sibyls were women inspired with pro-
phetic power. The Cumaean Sibyl was said to have been
700 years old when Aeneas landed.

[d] Witches were supposed to have this power: cf.
12.57.17.

sit tibi terra levis mollique tegaris harena,
    ne tua non possint eruere ossa canes.

30

Cappadocum seavis Antistius occidit oris
    Rusticus. o tristi crimine terra nocens!
rettulit ossa sinu cari Nigrina mariti
    et questa est longas non satis esse vias;
5 cumque daret sanctam tumulis, quibus invidet, urnam
    visa sibi est rapto bis viduata viro.

31

Cum comes Arctois haereret Caesaris armis
    Velius, hanc Marti pro duce vovit avem;
luna quater binos non tota peregerat orbes,
    debita poscebat iam sibi vota deus:
5 ipse suas anser properavit laetus ad aras
    et cecidit sanctis hostia parva focis.
octo vides patulo pendere nomismata rostro
    alitis? haec extis condita nuper erant:
quae litat argento pro te, non sanguine, Caesar,
10   victima iam ferro non opus esse docet.

---

[a] Similarly *Anth. Pal.* 11.226, by Ammianus, a contemporary.

[b] A goose was representative of the safety of Rome, these birds having given the alarm that saved the Capitol from capture by the Gauls.

marriage bed or that? Let earth be light upon you and soft sand be your covering, lest the dogs be unable to dig up your bones.[a]

30

Antistius Rusticus has died in the cruel land of Cappadocia. O guilty region, grievous crime! Nigrina brought back her dear husband's bones in her bosom and complained that the journey was not long enough. When she gave the hallowed urn to the tomb she envies, she felt robbed of her man and widowed a second time.

31

When Velius was at Caesar's side in Arctic warfare, he vowed this bird[b] to Mars for his general's behoof. The moon had not quite completed eight orbits before the god was demanding the vow already due.[c] The goose hurried joyfully to its appointed altar,[d] and fell, a small offering, victim to the sacred hearth. Do you see eight coins hanging from the bird's open beak? These were but now hidden in its entrails. A sacrifice that gives a good omen on your behalf with silver, not blood, Caesar, tells us that there is no further need for steel.

[c] The Sarmatian war did not last eight months.
[d] It was a good omen when the victim went willingly to the sacrifice.

32

Hanc volo quae facilis, quae palliolata vagatur,
    hanc volo quae puero iam dedit ante meo,
hanc volo quam redimit totam denarius alter,
    hanc volo quae pariter sufficit una tribus.
5   poscentem nummos et grandia verba sonantem
    possideat crassae mentula Burdigalae.

33

Audieris in quo, Flacce, balneo plausum,
Maronis illic esse mentulam scito.

34

Iuppiter Idaei risit mendacia busti,
    dum videt Augusti Flavia templa poli,
atque inter mensas largo iam nectare fusus,
    pocula cum Marti traderet ipse suo,
5   respiciens Phoebum pariter Phoebique sororem,
    cum quibus Alcides et pius Arcas erat:
'Gnosia vos' inquit 'nobis monumenta dedistis:
    cernite quam plus sit Caesaris esse patrem.'

35

Artibus his semper cenam, Philomuse, mereris,
plurima dum fingis, sed quasi vera refers.

32

I want an easy girl, who walks around in a mantle.
I want one who has already obliged my slave, I want
one who sells all she is for a couple of denarii, I want
one who can cope with three at once. She that
demands coin and talks big, let thick-headed
Burdigala's cock have her.

33

When you hear applause in a bath, Flaccus, you
may be sure that Maro's cock is there.

34

Jupiter laughed at the falsehood of his Idaean tomb
when he saw the Flavian temple of the Augustan
heaven;[a] and at table, already drenched with copi-
ous nectar, as he handed the cup to son Mars, look-
ing the while at Phoebus and Phoebus' sister
(Alcides and the loyal Arcadian[b] were there too),
"You gave me," he said, "a Gnosian monument. See
how much greater a thing it is to be Caesar's
father."

35

These are the arts, Philomusus, by which you
always earn your dinner: you invent a deal of news,

[a] Cf. 9.3.12.
[b] Hercules and Mercury.

scis quid in Arsacia Pacorus deliberet aula,
    Rhenanam numeras Sarmaticamque manum,
5 verba ducis Daci chartis mandata resignas,
    victricem laurum quam venit ante vides,
scis quotiens Phario madeat Iove fusca Syene,
    scis quota de Libyco litore puppis eat,
cuius Iuleae capiti nascantur olivae,
10   destinet aetherius cui sua serta pater.
tolle tuas artes; hodie cenabis apud me
    hac lege, ut narres nil, Philomuse, novi.

36

Viderat Ausonium posito modo crine ministrum
    Phryx puer, alterius gaudia nota Iovis:
'quod tuus ecce suo Caesar permisit ephebo,
    tu permitte tuo, maxime rector' ait;
5 'iam mihi prima latet longis lanugo capillis,
    iam tua me ridet Iuno vocatque virum.'
cui pater aetherius 'puer o dulcissime', dixit,
    'non ego quod poscis, res negat ipsa tibi:
Caesar habet noster similis tibi mille ministros
10   tantaque sidereos vix capit aula mares;
at tibi si dederit vultus coma tonsa viriles,
    quis mihi qui nectar misceat alter erit?'

---

[a] I.e. you know the prospects for the harvest in Africa, main source of Rome's grain supply.

[b] I.e. who is going to win at the Alban and Capitoline competitions.

but retail it as though it were true. You know what Pacorus is deliberating in his Arsacian palace, you number the Rhenish and Sarmatian hosts, you unseal words that the Dacian chieftain has put to paper, you see the victorious laurel before it comes. You know how many times dusky Syene is drenched by Pharian rain,[a] you know how many ships leave the Libyan shore, for whose head the Julian olives are born, to whom the celestial Father destines his wreaths.[b] Away with your arts! You shall dine with me this evening on one condition, Philomusus, that you tell me no news.

36

The Phrygian boy, famed joy of the other Jupiter, had seen the Ausonian page[c] with his hair newly shorn: "What your Caesar (look!) has allowed *his* young man, please allow yours, greatest of rulers," said he. "Already the first down lies hidden by my long locks; already your Juno laughs at me and calls me a man." To him said the Heavenly Father: "Sweetest boy, not I but the case itself denies you what you ask. My Caesar has a thousand pages like yourself; the vast palace has scarcely room for so many star-like youths. But if shorn hair gives you a manly look, whom else shall I have to mix the nectar?

[c] Ganymede had seen Earinus.

37

Cum sis ipsa domi mediaque ornere Subura,
    fiant absentes et tibi, Galla, comae,
nec dentes aliter quam Serica nocte reponas,
    et iaceas centum condita pyxidibus,
5 nec tecum facies tua dormiat, innuis illo
    quod tibi prolatum est mane supercilio,
et te nulla movet cani reverentia cunni,
    quem potes inter avos iam numerare tuos.
promittis sescenta tamen; sed mentula surda est,
10   et sit lusca licet, te tamen illa videt.

38

Summa licet, velox Agathine, pericula ludas,
    non tamen efficies ut tibi parma cadat.
nolentem sequitur tenuisque reversa per auras
    vel pede vel tergo, crine vel ungue sedet;
5 lubrica Corycio quamvis sint pulpita nimbo
    et rapiant celeres vela negata Noti,
securos pueri neglecta perambulat artus,
    et nocet artifici ventus et unda nihil.
ut peccare velis, cum feceris omnia, falli
10   non potes: arte opus est ut tibi parma cadat.

---

[a] Cf. 11.29.5–8. *Sescenta* may be taken as "600,000 sesterces" or (since that is a very large sum) "any number of things"; not "an infinity of delights."

[b] Cf. 6.23.

[c] A juggler with a small shield. He cannot let it fall even if he tries.

37

You are at home yourself, Galla, but you are made up in the middle of Subura. Your hair is manufactured in your absence. You lay your teeth aside at night as you do your silks, and lie stored in a hundred caskets. Your face does not sleep with you. Yet you ogle with an eyebrow that is brought out for you every morning and have no respect for your hoary cunt, which you can now number among your ancestors. However, you promise the earth;[a] but my cock is deaf, and though it be one-eyed, it sees you.[b]

38

Nimble Agathinus,[c] you play very dangerous games, but you will not manage to let your little shield fall. It follows you against your will, and returns through the air to sit on your foot or your back, your hair or your fingernail. Though the stage be slippery from a Corycian shower[d] and swift south winds tear away the awning denied us, the neglected shield roams over the boy's heedless limbs; wind and water do not impair the artistry.[e] Though you want to make a mistake, whatever you do, you cannot slip; skill is needed to make your shield fall.

[d] Of saffron.
[e] Lit. "artist."

39

Prima Palatino lux est haec orta Tonanti,
    optasset Cybele qua peperisse Iovem;
hac et sancta mei genita est Caesonia Rufi:
    plus debet matri nulla puella suae.
5 laetatur gemina votorum sorte maritus,
    contigit hunc illi quod bis amare diem.

40

Tarpeias Diodorus ad coronas
Romam cum peteret Pharo relicta,
vovit pro reditu viri Philaenis
illam lingeret ut puella simplex
5 quam castae quoque diligunt Sabinae.
dispersa rate tristibus procellis
mersus fluctibus obrutusque ponto
ad votum Diodorus enatavit.
o tardus nimis et piger maritus!
10 hoc in litore si puella votum
fecisset mea, protinus redissem.

39

This dawn was the first to rise for the Palatine
Thunderer,[a] dawn on which Cybele would have
wished to give birth to Jupiter. And on this day was
born Caesonia, revered wife of my Rufus;[b] no girl
owes her mother more.[c] The happy husband's
prayer is doubly granted;[d] good fortune has let him
love this day twice over.

40

When Diodorus left Pharos and made for Rome to
seek the Tarpeian wreath,[e] Philaenis made a vow
for her man's return, namely to lick, innocent girl,
what even chaste Sabine women love. His ship was
wrecked in a dreadful storm, but though Diodorus
sank in the waves and the sea overwhelmed him,
yet he swam out to land, to the vow. What a very
tardy, lazy husband! If my girl had made that vow
on the shore, I should have returned right away.[f]

[a] Domitian, born on 24 October.

[b] Which Rufus is uncertain; probably not Canius, who
presumably married his Theophila (7.69).

[c] Her mother gave her the same birthday as Domitian's.

[d] Vows made on the previous birthday for the safety
and welfare of Caesonia and the Emperor.

[e] To compete in the Capitoline contest (cf. 4.1.6n).

[f] Without embarking from Egypt at all.

41

Pontice, quod numquam futuis, sed paelice laeva
    uteris et Veneri servit amica manus,
hoc nihil esse putas? scelus est, mihi crede, sed ingens,
    quantum vix animo concipis ipse tuo.
5 nempe semel futuit, generaret Horatius ut tres;
    Mars semel, ut geminos Ilia casta daret.
omnia perdiderat, si masturbatus uterque
    mandasset manibus gaudia foeda suis.
ipsam crede tibi naturam dicere rerum:
10   'istud quod digitis, Pontice, perdis, homo est.'

42

Campis dives, Apollo, sic Myrinis,
sic semper senibus fruare cycnis,
doctae sic tibi serviant sorores
nec Delphis tua mentiatur ulli,
5 sic Palatia te colant amentque:
bis senos cito te rogante fasces
det Stellae bonus annuatque Caesar.
felix tunc ego debitorque voti
casurum tibi rusticas ad aras
10 ducam cornibus aureis iuvencum.
lecta est hostia, Phoebe; quid moraris?

42.1 Myrinis ς : mur- β : murinus γ   11 lecta *scripsi* :
nata βγ

ᵃ The Horatii who fought against the Curiatii; see
Index.

BOOK IX

41

Ponticus, do you think it nothing that you never fuck but use your left hand as a mistress and make it a kindly servant to your lust? It's a crime, believe me, and a heinous one, how great a crime your mind can scarcely grasp. Horatius, we may suppose, fucked once to beget triplets,[a] Mars once for chaste Ilia to give him twins.[b] All had been lost if both of them had masturbated, consigning their loathsome pleasure to their hands. Imagine the very nature of things as saying to you: "What you waste with your fingers, Ponticus, is a human being."

42

Apollo, so may you forever enjoy the wealth of the Myrine[c] plains and aged swans,[d] so may the poetic sisters[e] serve you and your Delphic prophetess tell no man lies, so may the Palace worship you and love you: let gracious Caesar at your behest quickly give Stella the twice six fasces[f] with assenting nod. Then, owing my vow, I shall happily lead a steer with gilded horns to fall at your rustic altar. The victim is chosen, Phoebus. Why delay?

[b] Romulus and Remus.
[c] Of Myrina, a town in Mysia, in Asia Minor. In the neighborhood was Grynium with a temple of Apollo.
[d] Cf. 5.37.1; 13.77.
[e] The Muses.
[f] The consulship; cf. 8.66.3.

43

Hic qui dura sedens porrecto saxa leone
  mitigat, exiguo magnus in aere deus,
quaeque tulit spectat resupino sidera vultu,
  cuius laeva calet robore, dextra mero:
5 non est fama recens nec nostri gloria caeli;
  nobile Lysippi munus opusque vides.
hoc habuit numen Pellaei mensa tyranni,
  qui cito perdomito victor in orbe iacet;
hunc puer ad Libycas iuraverat Hannibal aras;
10 iusserat hic Sullam ponere regna trucem.
offensus variae tumidis terroribus aulae
  privatos gaudet nunc habitare lares,
utque fuit quondam placidi conviva Molorchi,
  sic voluit docti Vindicis esse deus.

44

Alcides modo Vindicem rogabam
esset cuius opus laborque felix.
risit, nam solet hoc, levique nutu
'Graece numquid' ait 'poeta nescis?
5 inscripta est basis indicatque nomen.'
Lysippum lego, Phidiae putavi.

44.1 Alcides . . . Vindicem *ed. Rom.* : -en . . . -cem γ : -en . . .
-cis β   6 Lysippu *Calderinus* : Λυσίππου *Aldus*

ᵃ This and the following epigram are on a statuette of
Hercules, allegedly by Lysippus, Alexander the Great's
favorite sculptor, who gave it to him as a table ornament
(*epitrapezios*, Stat. *Silv.* 4.6). The god was represented

43

He[a] that sits on hard rocks made softer by an outspread lion skin, a great god in a small piece of bronze, and with upturned face watches the stars he bore,[b] whose left hand is busy with a club, his right with wine: he is no recent fame nor the glory of a Roman chisel; you see the noble gift and work of Lysippus. The table of the tyrant of Pella, him who lies low in the world he so swiftly subdued, once possessed this deity, by him boy Hannibal took an oath at a Libyan altar,[c] he ordered fierce Sulla to resign his monarchy. Irked by the tumid terrors of different courts, he now rejoices to inhabit a private dwelling, and, as once he was the dinner guest of peaceful Molorchus, so now the god has chosen to be lettered Vindex's.

44

I recently asked Vindex whose work and happy labor Alcides was. He laughed, for that is his way, and with a slight nod, "Poet," he said, "don't you know Greek? The base is inscribed and shows the name." I read Lysippus. I thought it was Phidias's.[d]

---

sitting on a rock, with his club in one hand and a wine cup in the other. See Statius' poem.

[b] Hercules for a time took the place of Atlas in upholding the sky; cf. 7.74.6.

[c] Hannibal when a boy swore undying hatred to Rome.

[d] Sculptor of the great Zeus of Olympia. The little statue had an air of majesty (cf. Stat. *Silv.* 4.6.36).

45

Miles Hyperboreos modo, Marcelline, triones
 et Getici tuleras sidera pigra poli:
ecce Prometheae rupes et fabula montis
 quam prope sunt oculis nunc adeunda tuis!
5 videris immensis cum conclamata querelis
 saxa senis, dices 'durior ipse fuit.'
et licet haec addas: 'potuit qui talia ferre,
 humanum merito finxerat ille genus.'

46

Gellius aedificat semper: modo limina ponit,
 nunc foribus claves aptat emitque seras,
nunc has, nunc illas reficit mutatque fenestras:
 dum tantum aedificet, quidlibet ille facit,
5 oranti nummos ut dicere possit amico
 unum illud verbum Gellius 'aedifico.'

47

Democritos, Zenonas inexplicitosque Platonas
 quidquid et hirsutis squalet imaginibus,
sic quasi Pythagorae loqueris successor et heres;
 praependet sane nec tibi barba minor.
5 sed, quod et hircosis carum est et turpe pilosis,
 in molli rigidam clune libenter habes.

45.3 promethe(a)e β : -thei γ 47.4 sane T β : tamen γ :
Samia *Heinsius* 5 carum est et SB^1 : serum est et β :
om. γ

BOOK IX

45

Lately, Marcellinus, you had endured as a soldier the Hyperborean Oxen and the lazy stars of the Getic firmament. Look, Prometheus' crags and the fable of the mountain—how near your eyes must now approach them! When you see the rocks that echoed with the ancient's huge groans, you will say: "He was harder than they." And you may add: "He that could endure such pains had deserved to mold the human race."[a]

46

Gellius is forever building. Now he lays down thresholds, now fits keys to doors and buys bolts, remodels and changes now these windows, now those. Gellius does anything you name, just so long as he's building, so that he can say to a friend who asks for money that one word: "Building."

47

You talk of Democritus, Zeno, inexplicable Plato, any original of a hirsute, unkempt bust, as though you were Pythagoras' successor and heir; and sure it is that the beard which hangs in front of you is as long as theirs. But (an expensive taste for the smelly and a discreditable one for the hairy) you like to have a stiff cock in your soft rump. You know the

[a] Cf. 10.39.4. Also Virg. *Georg.* 1.63 *homines . . . durum genus.*

273

tu, qui sectarum causas et pondera nostri,
    dic mihi, percidi, Pannyche, dogma quod est?

48

Heredem cum me partis tibi, Garrice, quartae
    per tua iurares sacra caputque tuum,
credidimus — quis enim damnet sua vota libenter? —
    et spem muneribus fovimus usque datis;
5 inter quae rari Laurentem ponderis aprum
    misimus: Aetola de Calydone putes.
at tu continuo populumque patresque vocasti;
    ructat adhuc aprum pallida Roma meum:
ipse ego — quis credat? — conviva nec ultimus haesi,
10   sed nec costa data est caudave missa mihi.
de quadrante tuo quid sperem, Garrice? nulla
    de nostro nobis uncia venit apro.

49

Haec est illa meis multum cantata libellis,
    quam meus edidicit lector amatque togam.
Partheniana fuit quondam, memorabile vatis
    munus: in hac ibam conspiciendus eques,
5   dum nova, dum nitida fulgebat splendida lana,
    dumque erat auctoris nomine digna sui:
nunc anus et tremulo vix accipienda tribuli,
    quam possis niveam dicere iure tuo.

48.8 pallida *Dousa* : ca- T $\beta\gamma$

---

[a] I.e. it was as huge as the boar slain by Meleager: cf.
7.27.2.   [b] *Uncia*, a twelfth part.

origins and authorities of the schools: tell me, Pan-
nychus, to be sodomized—what sort of dogma is
that?

48

When you swore to me by all you hold sacred, by
your head, Garricus, that I was heir to a quarter of
your estate, I believed you—for who would willingly
renounce his prayers?—and I kept my expectations
warm with continual presents. Among them I sent
a Laurentian boar of unusual weight—you would
think he came from Aetolian Calydon.[a] You at once
invited people and senate. Rome is still bilious,
belching my boar. I myself (who would believe it?)
was not even at the tail end of your guest list, not so
much as a rib or a tail was sent to me. What am I to
hope for from your quarter, Garricus? Not an
ounce[b] of my own boar came my way.

49

This is the gown much sung of in my little books, the
gown my readers have learned by heart and love.[c]
Once it was Parthenius' gown, a poet's memorable
gift. I used to go about in it, a conspicuous knight,
while it was new and shone resplendent with its
bright wool, while it was worthy of its giver's name.[d]
Now it is an old crone scarce worth acceptance by a
doddering pauper; you could rightly call it "snowy."[e]

---

[c] An exaggeration? Cf. 8.28.

[d] "Virginal"; cf. 8.28.16n.   [e] Cf. 4.34.2n.

quid non long dies, quid non consumitis anni?
10   haec toga iam non est Partheniana, mea est.

50

Ingenium mihi, Gaure, probas sic esse pusillum,
    carmina quod faciam quae brevitate placent.
confiteor. sed tu bis senis grandia libris
    qui scribis Priami proelia, magnus homo es?
5   nos facimus Bruti puerum, nos Langona vivum:
    tu magnus luteum, Gaure, Giganta facis.

51

Quod semper superos invito fratre rogasti,
    hoc, Lucane, tibi contigit, ante mori.
invidet ille tibi; Stygias nam Tullus ad umbras
    optabat, quamvis sit minor, ire prior.
5   tu colis Elysios nemorisque habitator amoeni
    esse tuo primum nunc sine fratre cupis;
et si iam nitidis alternus venit ab astris,
    pro Polluce mones Castora ne redeat.

52

Si credis mihi, Quinte, quod mereris,
natalis, Ovidi, tuas Aprilis
ut nostras amo Martias Kalendas.

50.5 langona β : ling- γ : lagone T

---

[a] The number of Books in Statius' *Thebaid*.
[b] Cf. 2.77.4.

Length of days, years, what do you not devour? This gown is no longer Parthenius's, it's mine.

50

You argue that my talent is inconsiderable, Gaurus, because I make poems that please by brevity. I confess it. But you that write of Priam's mighty battles in twice six books,[a] are you a great man? I make a live Brutus' Boy,[b] a live Langon:[c] you, Gaurus, great man that you are, make a giant of clay.

51

The fortune for which you always asked the High Ones, Lucanus, against your brother's will is yours: to die before him. He envies you; for Tullus, though he is the younger, prayed to go first to the Stygian shades. You dwell in Elysium and, denizen of the pleasant grove, now for the first time wish to be without your brother. And if Pollux has already come alternate from the shining stars, you tell Castor not to go back in his place.

52

If you believe me, Quintus Ovidius, I love your birthday Kalends of April[d] as much as my own of

---

[c] Another statuette of a boy, by Lyciscus (Pliny *N.H.* 34.79). The (Greek) word is said in glossaries to mean "lazy" or "tricky." See *RE*, Langon.

[d] Cf. 8.64.4n.

felix utraque lux diesque nobis
5   signandi melioribus lapillis!
hic vitam tribuit, sed hic amicum.
plus dant, Quinte, mihi tuae Kalendae.

53

Natali tibi, Quinte, tuo dare parva volebam
    munera; tu prohibes: imperiosus homo es.
parendum est monitis; fiat quod uterque volemus
    et quod utrumque iuvat: tu mihi, Quinte, dato.

54

Si mihi Picena turdus palleret oliva,
    tenderet aut nostras silva Sabina plagas,
aut crescente levis traheretur harundine praeda
    pinguis et implicitas virga teneret avis:
5   cara daret sollemne tibi cognatio munus,
    nec frater nobis nec prior esset avus.
nunc sturnos inopes fringuillarumque querelas
    audit et arguto passere vernat ager;
inde salutatus picae respondet arator,
10   hinc prope summa rapax miluus astra volat.

54.10 miluus astra *Palmer* : m- ad a- T γ : m- in a- β

---

[a] Cf. 8.45.2n.

[b] Cf. *pallida* = "bilious" in 9.48.8.

[c] A cane smeared with birdlime, which could be elongated like a fishing rod: cf. 14.216.

[d] On 22 February was held the festival of the Caristia or Cara Cognatio, when relations met and exchanged

March—you deserve it. Happy both days, days to be
marked by me with superior pebbles.[a] The one gave
me life, but the other a friend. Quintus, your
Kalends give me more.

53

I wished to give you a trifling birthday present,
Quintus. You forbid it. You are an imperious fel-
low; I must obey your admonition. Let it be as both
of us will wish, as gives both of us pleasure: you give
me something, Quintus.

54

If my thrushes were stuffed yellow[b] with Picene
olives or a Sabine woodland stretched my snares or
my buoyant booty were drawn down by a lengthen-
ing reed and a greasy rod[c] held entangled birds,
Dear Kindred[d] would give you the customary
present, neither brother nor grandfather would
come ahead of you with me. As it is, my land hears
pauper starlings and the plaints of chaffinches,
makes springtime with the chattering sparrow. On
that side the plowman answers the magpie's greet-
ing, on this the greedy kite flies close to the upper-

presents and arranged differences. It was a kind of family
love feast: cf. Ov. *Fast.* 2.617: Val. Max. 2.1.8. The follow-
ing epigram shows that friends as well as relatives were
involved. I suspect that a couplet may be missing contain-
ing the name of the addressee, who appears from v. 12 not
to have been related to M.

mittimus ergo tibi parvae munuscula chortis,
    qualia si recipis, saepe propinquus eris.

55

Luce propinquorum, qua plurima mittitur ales,
    dum Stellae turdos, dum tibi, Flacce, paro,
succurrit nobis ingens onerosaque turba,
    in qua se primum quisque meumque putat.
5 demeruisse duos votum est; offendere plures
    vix tutum; multis mittere dona grave est.
qua possum sola veniam ratione merebor:
    nec Stellae turdos nec tibi, Flacce, dabo.

56

Spendophoros Libycas domini petit armiger urbis:
    quae puero dones tela, Cupido, para,
illa quibus iuvenes figis mollesque puellas:
    sit tamen in tenera levis et hasta manu.
5 loricam clypeumque tibi galeamque remitto;
    tutus ut invadat proelia, nudus eat:
non iaculo, non ense fuit laesusve sagitta,
    casside dum liber Parthenopaeus erat.
quisquis ab hoc fuerit fixus, morietur amore.
10   o felix, si quem tam bona fata manent!
dum puer es, redeas, dum vultu lubricus, et te
    non Libye faciat, sed tua Roma virum.

---

[a] Lit. "first and mine."
[b] *Nudus* can also mean "unarmed."

most stars. So I send you a humble present from my little poultry yard; if you accept such gifts, you shall often be my relative.

55

On Kinsfolk Day, when many a bird is sent as a present, as I make thrushes ready for Stella and for you, Flaccus, a great, burdensome crowd comes to my mind, in which each thinks himself my prime favorite.[a] To oblige two is my desire; but to offend more is hardly safe, while to send presents to many is onerous. I shall earn pardon the only way I can, and give thrushes neither to Stella nor to you, Flaccus.

56

Spendophorus heads for Libya's cities as his master's armour-bearer. Cupid, prepare weapons to give the boy, those with which you pierce young men and soft girls. But let there be also a smooth spear in his tender hand. I don't ask you for breastplate, shield, and helmet; so that he go into battle safely, let him go naked.[b] Parthenopaeus took no harm from javelin or sword or arrow so long as he was free of a casque. Whoever is pierced by this boy, will die of love. Happy he, whomsoever so good a death awaits! Come back while you are a boy, while your face is slippery-smooth; let not Libya but your native Rome make a man of you.

57

Nil est tritius Hedyli lacernis:
non ansae veterum Corinthiorum,
nec crus compede lubricum decenni,
nec ruptae recutita colla mulae,
5   nec quae Flaminiam secant salebrae,
nec qui litoribus nitent lapilli,
nec Tusca ligo vinea politus,
nec pallens toga mortui tribulis,
nec pigri rota quassa mulionis,
10   nec rasum cavea latus visontis,
nec dens iam senior ferocis apri.
res una est tamen — ipse non negabit —,
culus tritior Hedyli lacernis.

58

Nympha sacri regina lacus, cui grata Sabinus
    et mansura pio munere templa dedit,
sic montana tuos semper colat Umbria fontes
    nec tua Baianas Sassina malit aquas:
5 excipe sollicitos placide, mea dona, libellos;
    tu fueris Musis Pegasis unda meis.
'Nympharum templis quisquis sua carmina donat,
    quid fieri libris debeat ipse monet.'

58.8 monet β : docet γ

---

a I.e. "slow-moving," necessarily so with such a wagon.
b Caesius Sabinus.
c As to their reception by the Nymph, or by Sabinus.

57

Nothing is worn smoother than Hedylus' cloak: not
the handles of old Corinthian bronzes, not a shin
polished by a ten-year shackle, not the skinned neck
of a ruptured mule, not the ruts that cleave the
Flaminian Way, not the pebbles shining on the
beaches, not a hoe polished by a Tuscan vineyard,
not the yellowing gown of a dead pauper, not the
shaken wheel of a lazy[a] muleteer, not a bison's flank
shaven by the cage, not the aging tusk of a ferocious
boar. One thing though (he won't deny it himself),
Hedylus' arse, is worn smoother than his cloak.

58

Nymph, queen of the sacred lake, to whom Sabinus[b]
pious bounty gave a shrine, pleasing to you and long
to endure, so may hilly Umbria ever honor your
spring nor your Sassina prefer the waters of Baiae:
receive kindly my gifts, my anxious[c] little books.
You shall be Pegasus' fountain[d] to my Muses.
"Whosoever gives his poems to Nymphs' temples
tells us himself what should be done with his
books."[e]

[d] Hippocrene, the fountain of the Muses, created by the
stroke of the hoof of Pegasus.
[e] The pages should be sponged clean or the books
thrown into the water; cf. 1.5; 3.100.4; 4.10.6. So the
Nymph replies.

59

In Saeptis Mamurra diu multumque vagatus,
    hic ubi Roma suas aurea vexat opes,
inspexit molles pueros oculisque comedit,
    non hos quos primae prostituere casae,
5   sed quos arcanae servant tabulata catastae
    et quos non populus nec mea turba videt.
inde satur mensas et opertos exuit orbes
    expositumque alte pingue poposcit ebur,
et testudineum mensus quater hexaclinon
10 ingemuit citro non satis esse suo.
consuluit nares an olerent aera Corinthon,
    culpavit statuas et, Polyclite, tuas,
et turbata brevi questus crystallina vitro
    murrina signavit seposuitque decem.
15 expendit veteres calathos et si qua fuerunt
    pocula Mentorea nobilitata manu
et viridis picto gemmas numeravit in auro,
    quidquid et a nivea grandius aure sonat;
sardonychas veros mensa quaesivit in omni
20 et pretium magnis fecit iaspidibus.
undecima lassus cum iam discederet hora,
    asse duos calices emit et ipse tulit.

59.19 veros *Aldus* : uero β : uiro γ

59

Wandering long and often in the Enclosure, where golden Rome rummages among her wealth, Mamurra inspected tender boys, devouring them with his eyes; not the ones exposed in the booths in front, but those kept in reserve on the boards of a privy platform, unseen of the public and common folk like me. Sated therewith, he stripped the coverings from round tabletops and called for the oiled ivory exhibited aloft;[a] and after four times measuring a tortoise-shell couch for six, lamented that it was not large enough for his citrus. He enquired of his nostrils whether the bronzes smelt of Corinth,[b] and was critical of Polyclitus' statues. Complaining that the crystals were vitiated by fragments of glass, he marked and set aside ten pieces of murrine.[c] He weighed antique goblets and any cups ennobled by Mentor's hand, counted green jewels in ornamented gold, and anything large that tinkles from a snow-white ear.[d] He looked for genuine sardonyxes at every counter and priced big jaspers. As he finally left tired out at the eleventh hour, he bought two wine cups for a copper and carried them off himself.[e]

[a] Asked for the ivory supports to be brought down for closer inspection.

[b] Connoisseurs will have professed to detect an odor in genuine Corinthian bronze: cf. Petr. 50.7.

[c] Cf. 3.26.2n.

[d] Such as a pearl.

[e] He had not even a slave of his own.

60

Seu tu Paestanis genita es seu Tiburis arvis,
    seu rubuit tellus Tuscula flore tuo,
seu Praenestino te vilica legit in horto,
    seu modo Campani gloria ruris eras:
5   pulchrior ut nostro videare corona Sabino,
    de Nomentano te putet esse meo.

61

In Tartesiacis domus est notissima terris,
    qua dives placidum Corduba Baetin amat,
vellera nativo pallent ubi flava metallo
    et linit Hesperium brattea viva pecus.
5   aedibus in mediis totos amplexa penates
    stat platanus densis Caesariana comis,
hospitis invicti posuit quam dextera felix,
    coepit et ex illa crescere virga manu.
auctorem dominumque nemus sentire videtur:
10   sic viret et ramis sidera celsa petit.
saepe sub hac madidi luserunt arbore Fauni
    terruit et tacitam fistula sera domum;
dumque fugit solos nocturnum Pana per agros,
    saepe sub hac latuit rustica fronde Dryas.
15   atque oluere lares comissatore Lyaeo
    crevit et effuso laetior umbra mero;
hesternisque rubens †delecta† est herba coronis
    atque suas potuit dicere nemo rosas.

61.17 delecta γ : del- *vel* deiecta β : distincta *Gilbert* :
depicta *SB*[1]

60

Whether you were born in Paestum's fields or in Tibur's, or Tusculum's soil blushed with your bloom, or a bailiff's wife picked you in a Praenestine garden, or you were lately the glory of Campania's countryside: to make you more beautiful a garland in my friend Sabinus' eyes, let him think you come from my place at Nomentum.

61

There is a famous house in the land of Tartessus, where wealthy Corduba loves tranquil Baetis and yellow fleeces are pale with native ore and living foil coats the Hesperian flock.[a] In the midst of the mansion, embracing the entire dwelling, stands a plane, Caesar's plane, with dense foliage, planted by the unconquered guest's auspicious hand;[b] from that hand the shoot began to grow. The tree seems to feel its author and lord: so green is it, so it seeks the high stars with its branches. Often did tipsy Fauns play under this tree and a late pipe alarm the silent house; and by night fleeing Pan through the lonely fields, a rustic Dryad often hid below these leaves. And the dwelling was fragrant with reveling Lyaeus; the shade grew more luxuriant with wine's

[a] Cf. 5.37.7n.
[b] Julius Caesar will have planted it when he visited Gades (Cadiz) during his Spanish campaign in 44 B.C. (*Bell. Hisp.* 39.3).

o dilecta deis, o magni Caesaris arbor,
20   ne metuas ferrum sacrilegosque focos.
perpetuos sperare licet tibi frondis honores:
     non Pompeianae te posuere manus.

62

Tinctis murice vestibus quod omni
et nocte utitur et die Philaenis,
non est ambitiosa nec superba:
delectatur odore, non colore.

63

Ad cenam invitant omnes te, Phoebe, cinaedi.
     mentula quem pascit, non, puto, purus homo est.

64

Herculis in magni vultus descendere Caesar
     dignatus Latiae dat nova templa viae,
qua Triviae nemorosa petit dum regna, viator
     octavum domina marmor ab urbe legit.
5 ante colebatur votis et sanguine largo,
     maiorem Alciden nunc minor ipse colit.

---

[a] She wishes to drown her own peculiar odor. Tyrian-dyed garments had a rank smell: cf. 4.4.6.

[b] In two, or perhaps three, senses: see my edition.

effusion, and the blushing grass was painted with
yesternight's garlands: nobody could tell which
roses were his own. O beloved of the gods, o great
Caesar's tree, fear not steel or sacrilegious hearths.
You may expect the glories of your foliage to last for
ever: the hands that planted you were not Pompey's.

62

Philaenis wears purple-dyed garments every night
and day, but she is not ostentatious or haughty; she
likes the odor, not the color.[a]

63

All the queens, Phoebus, ask you to dinner.
Methinks a fellow fed by a cock[b] is not undefiled.

64

Deigning to descend into the countenance of great
Hercules, Caesar gives a new temple to the Latin
Way,[c] where, as he seeks the bosky realms of
Trivia,[d] the traveller reads the eighth milestone
from the imperial city. Alcides used to be wor-
shipped with vows and unstinted bloodshed; now he,
the lesser, himself worships the greater.[e] Him one

[c] Domitian dedicated a temple to Hercules with a
statue bearing his own features.

[d] The temple and grove of Diana of the Crossways
(*Trivia*) at Aricia.

[e] The Emperor.

hunc magnas rogat alter opes, rogat alter honores;
    illi securus vota minora facit.

65

Alcide, Latio nunc agnoscende Tonanti,
    postquam pulchra dei Caesaris ora geris,
si tibi tunc isti vultus habitusque fuissent,
    cesserunt manibus cum fera monstra tuis,
5 Argolico famulum non te servire tyranno
    vidissent gentes saevaque regna pati,
sed tu iussisses Eurysthea; nec tibi fallax
    portasset Nessi perfida dona Lichas,
Oetaei sine lege rogi securus adisses
10   astra patris summi, quae tibi poena dedit,
Lydia nec dominae traxisses pensa superbae
    nec Styga vidisses Tartareumque canem.
nunc tibi Iuno favet, nunc te tua diligit Hebe;
    nunc te si videat Nympha, remittet Hylan.

66

Uxor cum tibi sit formosa, pudica, puella,
    quo tibi natorum iura, Fabulle, trium?
quod petis a nostro supplex dominoque deoque
    tu dabis ipse tibi, si potes arrigere.

65.3 fuissent β : -et γ

---

    [a] By Jupiter Capitolinus, as his son.
    [b] Omphale, queen of Lydia, who wore Hercules' lion
skin while he spun her wool.
    [c] It was one of the labors of Hercules to fetch Cerberus
from the shades.

asks for wealth, another for honors; to the other unconcerned they make lesser vows.

65

Alcides, worthy to be recognized by the Latin Thunderer[a] now that you bear the fair features of our god Caesar, if that countenance and mien had been yours in the days when savage monsters yielded to your hands, the nations would not have seen you serve the Argive tyrant in thraldom and suffer his cruel dominion; you would have given orders to Eurystheus. Neither would treacherous Lichas have brought you Nestor's perfidious gift, and without the requirement of Oeta's pyre you would have attained untroubled the stars of the supreme Father, which suffering gave you. Nor would you have drawn out the Lydian wool of a haughty mistress,[b] nor seen Styx and Tartarus' hound.[c] Now Juno wishes you well, now your Hebe loves you,[d] now the Nymph, if she sees you, will send Hylas back.

66

Since you have a wife, beautiful, virtuous, and young, Fabullus, what do you want with the Rights of Three Children?[e] What you seek as a petitioner from our Lord and God, you will give yourself, if you can erect.

[d] As never before.
[e] Cf. 2.91.6n.

67

Lascivam tota possedi nocte puellam,
    cuius nequitias vincere nemo potest.
fessus mille modis illud puerile poposci:
    ante preces totum primaque verba dedit.
5 improbius quiddam ridensque rubensque rogavi:
    pollicita est nulla luxuriosa mora.
sed mihi pura fuit; tibi non erit, Aeschyle, si vis
    accipere hoc munus condicione mala.

68

Quid tibi nobiscum est, ludi scelerate magister,
    invisum pueris virginibusque caput?
nondum cristati rupere silentia galli:
    murmure iam saevo verberibusque tonas.
5 tam grave percussis incudibus aera resultant,
    causidicum medio cum faber aptat equo:
mitior in magno clamor furit Amphitheatro,
    vincenti parmae cum sua turba favet.
vicini somnum — non tota nocte — rogamus:
10   nam vigilare leve est, pervigilare grave est.
discipulos dimitte tuos. vis, garrule, quantum
    accipis ut clames, accipere ut taceas?

67.2 nemo T γ : nulla β 4 totum *A. Ker* : totas T$\beta\gamma$:
anne totas pluraque *?*

---

^a Cf. 2.60.2.   ^b Explained by Housman, 725 (cf. *SB*¹).
  ^c Successful lawyers were in the habit of erecting eques-
trian statues of themselves in their vestibules: cf. Juv
7.125.

67

All night long I enjoyed a wanton girl, whose naughtinesses no man can exhaust. Tired by a thousand different modes, I asked for the boy routine;[a] before I begged or started to beg, she gave it in full. Laughing and blushing, I asked for something more indecent; the lustful hussy promised without hesitation. But so far as I am concerned, she was undefiled; she won't be so far as you are concerned, Aeschylus, if you choose to accept this present on bad terms.[b]

68

What have you to do with me, cursed schoolmaster, creature hateful to boys and girls? The crested cocks have not yet broken silence and already you make a din with your savage roaring and your thwacks. The bronze resounds as loudly from smitten anvils, when the smith is fitting a barrister[c] to the horse's middle. The shouting rages less wildly in the great Amphitheater when the winning buckler[d] is applauded by its backers. We your neighbors ask for sleep—not all night through; to lie awake is nothing much, but to lie awake all night is a cross. Dismiss your pupils. Will you take as much for holding your tongue as you get for shouting?

[d] Carried by gladiators called Thracians. Domitian was accused of a prejudice against them (Suet. *Dom.* 10.1) and they seldom won; cf. 14.213. When they did win, the applause would be all the louder.

69

Cum futuis, Polycharme, soles in fine cacare.
    cum pedicaris, quid, Polycharme, facis?

70

Dixerat 'o mores! o tempora!' Tullius olim,
    sacrilegum strueret cum Catilina nefas,
cum gener atque socer diris concurreret armis
    maestaque civili caede maderet humus.
5 cur nunc 'o mores!' cur nunc 'o tempora!' dicis?
    quod tibi non placeat, Maeciliane, quid est?
nulla ducum feritas, nulla est insania ferri;
    pace frui certa laetitiaque licet.
non nostri faciunt tibi quod tua tempora sordent,
10   sed faciunt mores, Maeciliane, tui.

71

Massyli leo fama iugi pecorisque maritus
    lanigeri mirum qua coiere fide.
ipse licet videas, cavea stabulantur in una
    et pariter socias carpit uterque dapes:
5 nec fetu nemorum gaudent nec mitibus herbis,
    concordem satiat sed rudis agna famem.
quid meruit terror Nemees, quid portitor Helles,
    ut niteant celsi lucida signa poli?

70.6 *et* 10 m(a)eciliane β : c(a)e- T γ

---

[a] See my edition.   [b] Cic. *Cat.* 1.2.
[c] Pompey married Caesar's daughter Julia.

69

When you fornicate, Polycharmus, it is your habit to
finish with a shit. What do you do, Polycharmus,
when you are sodomized?[a]

70

"What morals! What times!" said Tully long ago,
when Catiline was plotting impious villainy,[b] when
daughter's spouse and father[c] were clashing in mur-
derous combat and the sad soil was doused with civil
slaughter. But why do you now say "What morals!"
why now "What times!" What is there to displease
you, Maecilianus? No brutality of war lords, no
madness of the sword is here. We can enjoy assured
peace and happiness. It's not *our* morals that make
you despise your times, Maecilianus, it's your own.

71

A lion, fame of Massylian mountains, and a husband
of the woolly flock have joined in a marvellous bond
of trust. You may see for yourself, they are stalled
in one pen and both together eat their shared victu-
als. Nor do they relish the produce of the woods or
gentle herbs: a young lamb sates their consentient
hunger. How did the terror of Nemea, how did the
carrier of Helle[d] deserve to shine as lustrous con-

[d] The lion slain by Hercules and the ram that carried
Helle respectively, afterwards two of the signs of the
Zodiac.

        sidera si possent pecudesque feraeque mereri,
10   hic aries astris, hic leo dignus erat.

72

    Liber, Amyclaea frontem vittate corona,
        qui quatis Ausonia verbera Graia manu,
    clusa mihi texto cum prandia vimine mittas,
        cur comitata dapes nulla lagona venit?
5   atqui digna tuo si nomine munera ferres,
        scis, puto, debuerint quae mihi dona dari.

73

    Dentibus antiquas solitus producere pelles
        et mordere luto putre vetusque solum,
    Praenestina tenes decepti regna patroni,
        in quibus indignor si tibi cella fuit;
5   rumpis et ardenti madidus crystalla Falerno
        et pruris domini cum Ganymede tui.
    at me litterulas stulti docuere parentes:
        quid cum grammaticis rhetoribusque mihi?
    frange leves calamos et scinde, Thalia, libellos,
10   si dare sutori calceus ista potest.

73.3 decepti regna β : defuncti rura T γ

---

    [a] A charioteer or jockey, who had won a race at a Greek
festival. Whether *Amyclaea* stands, as Housman says
(725f), for *Castorea* (because of Castor's connection with
horses) or refers to both Dioscuri as patrons of sport

stellations of the lofty sky? If animals, tame and wild, could merit the stars, this ram, this lion were worthy thereof.

72

Liber,[a] whose brow is circled with an Amyclean wreath, whose Ausonian hand cracks a Grecian whip, when you send me lunch in a wicker hamper, why does no flask come to keep the victuals company? And yet, if you bore presents worthy of your name,[b] you know, methinks, what gifts should have been given me.

73

You used to stretch ancient hides with your teeth and bite an old shoe sole rotten with mud: now you possess the Praenestine realm of your patron, gone before his time.[c] It makes me indignant if you ever had a cubbyhole therein. And in your liquor you burst crystal with hot Falernian and lust with your master's Ganymede. But my foolish parents taught me my ABC. What use to me are grammarians and rhetors? Break your puny pens and tear up your little books, Thalia, if a shoe can give all that to a cobbler.

(Pindar *Ol.* 3.36; *Nem.* 10.49) or has a local reference is perhaps not certainly to be determined (*SB*[1]).

[b] Liber, alias Bacchus.

[c] For this rendering of *decepti* see *SB*[3].

74

Effigiem tantum pueri pictura Camoni
    servat et infantis parva figura manet.
florentes nulla signavit imagine vultus,
    dum timet ora pius muta videre pater.

75

Non silice duro structilive caemento
nec latere cocto, quo Samiramis longam
Babylona cinxit, Tucca balneum fecit:
sed strage nemorum pineaque compage,
5 ut navigare Tucca balneo possit.
idem beatas lautus extruit thermas
de marmore omni, quod Carystos invenit,
quod Phrygia Synnas, Afra quod Nomas misit
et quod virenti fonte lavit Eurotas.
10 sed ligna desunt: subice balneum thermis.

76

Haec sunt illa mei quae cernitis ora Camoni,
    haec pueri facies primaque forma fuit.

75.7 Carystides venae *Heinsius*

74

The painting preserves Camonius' likeness only as a child;[a] the baby's little form survives. His loving father did not record his face in manhood with a portrait, fearing to see lips that did not speak.[b]

75

Tucca did not make his bath of hard flint or concrete or burnt brick, with which Semiramis girdled the length of Babylon, but with the wreckage of woods and a framework of pine, so that Tucca could go to sea in his bath. The same luxurious Tucca constructed fine warm baths of every marble that Carystus discovered, that Phrygian Synnas or African Numidia exported, that Eurotas laved with his verdant stream.[c] But wood is lacking: put the first bath under the second.

76

The face you see belongs to my Camonius; these were his features as a child, his earliest form. His

[a] Cf. 6.85; 9.76.

[b] The oddity of this explanation has passed unremarked. I can only take it to mean that when Camonius as a young man left for a lengthy absence in a far-off land, his father chose not to have a portrait painted, as most fathers would have done, because he was afraid the sight of the silent face would distress rather than console him (SB[3]). *Muta* cannot refer to the young man's death.

[c] Cf. 6.42.11. Laconian marble was green.

creverat hic vultus bis denis fortior annis
   gaudebatque suas pingere barba genas,
5 et libata semel summos modo purpura cultros
   sparserat. invidit de tribus una soror
et festinatis incidit stamina pensis
   absentemque patri rettulit urna rogum.
sed ne sola tamen puerum pictura loquatur,
10   haec erit in chartis maior imago meis.

77

Quod optimum sit disputat convivium
   facunda Prisci pagina,
et multa dulci, multa sublimi refert,
   sed cuncta docto pectore.
5 quod optimum sit quaeritis convivium?
   in quo choraules non erit.

78

Funera post septem nupsit tibi Galla virorum,
   Picentine: sequi vult, puto, Galla viros.

76.4 pingere γ : ci- β

countenance had grown more manly in twice ten years[a] and a beard rejoiced to adorn its parent cheeks; the reddish down, shorn but once, had only lately besprinkled the razor's tip. One sister of the three[b] begrudged, and as the wool hastened on, she cut the thread. An urn returned the absent dead to his father.[c] But not alone shall the painting tell of him in childhood; here in my pages there shall be a larger likeness.

77

Priscus' fluent page discusses what is the best sort of dinner party. Much of what he writes is charming, much of it elevated, all of it accomplished. Do you want to know what is the best sort of dinner party? One that doesn't have a flute player.

78

Galla married you after burying seven husbands, Picentinus. Galla, methinks, wants to follow her men.[d]

[a] Generally taken as meaning that Camonius was twenty when he died (cf. 6.85.8n). The wording, however, rather favors understanding "twenty years after the portrait was painted."

[b] Fates.

[c] Camonius junior died in Cappadocia; cf. 6.85.3.

[d] Galla and Picentinus were poisoners; cf. 8.43.

79

Oderat ante ducum famulos turbamque priorem
    et Palatinum Roma supercilium:
at nunc tantus amor cunctis, Auguste, tuorum est
    ut sit cuique suae cura secunda domus.
5 tam placidae mentes, tanta est reverentia nostri,
    tam pacata quies, tantus in ore pudor.
nemo suos — haec est aulae natura potentis —,
    sed domini mores Caesarianus habet.

80

Duxerat esuriens locupletem pauper anumque:
    uxorem pascit Gellius et futuit.

81

Lector et auditor nostros probat, Aule, libellos,
    sed quidam exactos esse poeta negat.
non nimium curo: nam cenae fercula nostrae
    malim convivis quam placuisse cocis.

82

Dixerat astrologus periturum te cito, Munna,
    nec, puto, mentitus dixerat ille tibi.
nam tu dum metuis ne quid post fata relinquas,
    hausisti patrias luxuriosus opes,

79

'ime was when Rome hated the servants of her
ᶫeaders, the retinue of those days, the supercilious
ᵢirs of the Palatine. But now, Augustus, your fol-
ᵢwing is so loved of all men that each of us puts his
ᵥwn household in second place; so gentle are their
ᶫearts, so great their respect for us, so unruffled
ᵗheir calm, such modesty in their faces. None of
ᵓaesar's servants has his own manners, but only
ᶠor such is the nature of an imperial court) his
ᵓrd's.

80

ᶫ hungry pauper, Gellius married a rich old woman.
ᶫe feeds[a] his wife and fucks her.

81

ᶫeader and listener approve my little books, Aulus,
ᵤut a certain poet says they lack finish. I don't care
ᵓo much; for I had rather the courses at my dinner
ᶫeased the diners than the cooks.

82

ᵢn astrologer said you would go to pot shortly,
ᶫunna, and I don't think he lied when he said it.
ᵒor fearing that you would leave something behind
ᶠter your death, you drained your patrimony with

[a] I.e. *irrumat.*

5 bisque tuum deciens non toto tabuit anno:
   dic mihi, non hoc est, Munna, perire cito?

83

Inter tanta tuae miracula, Caesar, harenae,
   quae vincit veterum munera clara ducum,
multum oculi, sed plus aures debere fatentur
   se tibi, quod spectant qui recitare solent.

84

Cum tua sacrilegos contra, Norbane, furores
   staret pro domino Caesare sancta fides,
haec ego Pieria ludebam tutus in umbra,
   ille tuae cultor notus amicitiae.
5 me tibi Vindelicis Raetus narrabat in oris
   nescia nec nostri nominis Arctos erat:
o quotiens veterem non infitiatus amicum
   dixisti 'meus est iste poeta, meus!'
omne tibi nostrum quod bis trieteride iuncta
10   ante dabat lector, nunc dabit auctor opus.

84.5 Raetus *Rutgers* : raptas γ : mestus β

---

[a] *Perire cito* = (a) "die soon," (b) "be ruined quickly."

[b] And cannot bore us: cf. Juv. 1.7–14.

[c] Not the conqueror of Saturninus, whose names, as we now know, did not include Norbanus, but perhaps a Norbanus who was Praetorian Prefect in 96; cf. B. W. Jones, *Parola del Passato* 29 (1974), 189–191.

your extravagance, and your two millions melted away in less than a year. Tell me, Munna, isn't that going to pot shortly?[a]

83

Among the mighty marvels of your arena, Caesar, which outdoes the famous shows of the old Leaders, our eyes acknowledge that they owe you much, but our ears more, in that habitual reciters become spectators.[b]

84

When your untarnished loyalty, Norbanus,[c] was standing firm for Lord Caesar against impious madness, I, well known as a cultivator of your friendship, was turning out these trifles, safe in Pierian shade. The Rhaetian would tell you of me in the land of Vindelicia, nor was the Bear ignorant of my name. How often you said, not denying your old friend: "He's mine, that poet, mine"! All my work that in twice three years' space[d] a reader[e] used to give you, the author will give you now.

[d] Lit. "in a three-year period (*trieteris*) twice put together."

[e] Either a friend, who bought and read the books and then sent them on to Norbanus (cf. 9.99.7; 7.80); or (less likely, I think) "your reader" (*lector*, ἀναγνώστης), a slave in Rome with whom he had left instructions to send him M.'s works as they appeared.

85

Languidior noster si quando est Paulus, Atili,
    non se, convivas abstinet ille suos.
tu languore quidem subito fictoque laboras,
    sed mea porrexit sportula, Paule, pedes.[a]

86

Festinata sui gemeret quod fata Severi
    Silius, Ausonio non semel ore potens,[b]
cum grege Pierio maestus Phoeboque querebar.
    'ipse meum flevi' dixit Apollo 'Linon':
5 respexitque suam quae stabat proxima fratri
    Calliopen et ait: 'tu quoque vulnus habes.
aspice Tarpeium Palatinumque Tonantem:
    ausa nefas Lachesis laesit utrumque Iovem.
numina cum videas duris obnoxia Fatis,
10   invidia possis exonerare deos.'

87

Septem post calices Opimiani
    denso cum iaceam triente blaesus,
affers nescio quas mihi tabellas
    et dicis 'modo liberum esse iussi
5 Nastam — servulus est mihi paternus —:
    signa.' cras melius, Luperce, fiet:

---

a Lit. "stretched its feet out," used of a corpse laid out
with feet pointing to the doorway.
b As orator and poet: cf. 7.63.

85

Whenever our friend Paulus is out of sorts, Atilius, he doesn't deprive himself, he deprives his dinner guests. To be sure you have come down with a sudden fictitious ailment, Paulus, but my dole has given up the ghost.[a]

86

Because Silius, doubly lord of Ausonian language,[b] was bewailing the untimely death of his Severus, I made sad complaint to the Pierian flock and to Phoebus. Apollo said: "I myself wept for my Linus"; and he looked at his sister Calliope standing next to him and said: "You too have your hurt. Look at the Thunderers, Tarpeian and Palatine: daring sacrilege, Lachesis injured both Jupiters. When you see divinities subject to the harsh Fates, you may relieve the gods of odium."[c]

87

When after seven cups of Opimian I lie thick of speech from the continual bumpers, you bring me some document or other and say: "I have just given Nasta (he was a slave of my father's) his freedom. Please seal."[d] Tomorrow will be better for that,

---

[c] *Invidia*, the odium attaching to them for the loss of Severus (cf. 1.12.10; 7.47.7; 12.14.8). Not "jealousy."

[d] As a witness.

nunc signat meus anulus lagonam.

88

Cum me captares, mittebas munera nobis:
  postquam cepisti, das mihi, Rufe, nihil.
ut captum teneas, capto quoque munera mitte,
  de cavea fugiat ne male pastus aper.

89

Lege nimis dura convivam scribere versus
  cogis, Stella: 'licet scribere nempe malos.'

90

Sic in gramine florido reclinis,
qua gemmantibus hinc et inde rivis
curva calculus excitatur unda,
exclusis procul omnibus molestis,
5   pertundas glaciem triente nigro,
frontem sutilibus ruber coronis;
sic uni tibi sit puer cinaedus
et castissima pruriat puella:
infamem nimio calore Cypron
10   observes moneo precorque, Flacce,
messes area cum teret crepantis
et fervens iuba saeviet leonis.
at tu, diva Paphi, remitte nostris
illaesum iuvenem, remitte, votis.

---

^a To prevent theft: Pliny *N.H.* 33.26; Juv. 14.132; Cic. *Fam.* 16.26.2.

Lupercus. For now, my ring seals the flagon."[a]

88

When you were hunting[b] me, you used to send me presents. Now you have caught me, you give me nothing, Rufus. Caught though I be, to keep your catch, go on sending presents; otherwise the ill-fed boar may fly the pen.

89

That rule of yours, Stella, that your dinner guest must write verses, is too hard. "You can write bad ones, of course."

90

So, lying in flowery grass, where on either hand pebbles are stirred by winding waters in a sparkling brook, all worries banished afar, may you bore through ice with a black bumper,[c] your brow ruddy with stitched garlands; so may you have a boy queen to yourself and the purest of girls lust only for you: I warn and beg you, Flaccus, beware of Cyprus, ill-reputed for her excessive heat, when the floor threshes the rattling harvests and the Lion's[d] glowing mane waxes fierce. But you, goddess of Paphos, send the young man back unharmed, back to our

[b] *Captare* ("try to catch") is regularly used of legacy-hunting.

[c] Of Falernian; cf. 8.55.14.

[d] The constellation Leo.

15   sic Martis tibi serviant Kalendae
et cum ture meroque victimaque
libetur tibi candidas ad aras
secta plurima quadra de placenta.

91

Ad cenam si me diversa vocaret in astra
   hinc invitator Caesaris, inde Iovis,
astra licet propius, Palatia longius essent,
   responsa ad superos haec referenda darem:
5 'quaerite qui malit fieri conviva Tonantis:
   me meus in terris Iuppiter ecce tenet.'

92

Quae mala sint domini, quae servi commoda, nescis,
   Condyle, qui servum te gemis esse diu.
dat tibi securos vilis tegeticula somnos,
   pervigil in pluma Gaius ecce iacet.
5 Gaius a prima tremebundus luce salutat
   tot dominos, at tu, Condyle, nec dominum.
'quod debes, Gai, redde' inquit Phoebus et illinc
   Cinnamus: hoc dicit, Condyle, nemo tibi.
tortorem metuis? podagra cheragraque secatur
10   Gaius et mallet verbera mille pati.

91.1 astra] *vide annot.*

---

^a At the festival of the Matronalia men sent presents to their mistresses: cf. 5.84.11.

^b *Astra* is clumsy after *diversa . . . astra* in v. 1. Perhaps read *ista*, "those (i.e. Jupiter's) stars."

^c The Olympian, though Domitian is sometimes so

vows. So may Mars' Kalends serve you[a] and many a square of cut cake be offered at your fair altars, with incense, wine, and sacrifice.

91

If I were invited to dinner in different heavens by Caesar's summoner on the one hand and Jupiter's on the other, though the stars[b] were closer and the Palace farther off, I should give this answer to be returned to the High Ones: "Seek on for one who would rather be the Thunderer's[c] guest: my Jupiter, see, keeps me on earth."[d]

92

Condylus, you lament that you have been so long a slave; you don't know a master's afflictions and a slave's advantages. A cheap little mat gives you carefree slumbers: there's Gaius lying awake all night on feathers. From daybreak on Gaius in fear and trembling salutes so many masters: but you, Condylus, do not salute even your own. "Gaius, pay me back what you owe," says Phoebus, and from yonder so says Cinnamus: nobody says that to you, Condylus. You fear the torturer?[e] Gaius is cut by gout in foot and hand and would rather take a thousand lashes. You don't vomit of a morning or

called, as in 7.99.1.

[d] It has been suggested that the epigram acknowledges an actual invitation from the Emperor.

[e] Slaves were often tortured to extract evidence.

quod nec mane vomis nec cunnum, Condyle, lingis,
    non mavis quam ter Gaius esse tuus?

93

Addere quid cessas, puer, immortale Falernum?
    quadrantem duplica de seniore cado.
nunc mihi dic, quis erit cui te, Cataciase, deorum
    sex iubeo cyathos fundere? 'Caesar erit.'
5 sutilis aptetur deciens rosa crinibus, ut sit
    qui posuit sacrae nobile gentis opus.
nunc bis quina mihi da basia, fiat ut illud
    nomen ab Odrysio quod deus orbe tulit.

94

Santonica medicata dedit mihi pocula virga —
    os hominis! —, mulsum me rogat Hippocrates.
tam stupidus numquam nec tu, puto, Glauce, fuisti,
    χάλκεα donanti χρύσεα qui dederas.
5 dulce aliquis munus pro munere poscit amaro?
    accipiat, sed si potat in elleboro.

93.3 Cataciase *Heraeus* : calac- γ : galac- β   94.1 santonica β : sardo- T γ

---

   [a] I.e. it would keep indefinitely; cf. 11.36.5.
   [b] A variation of the practice illustrated in 1.71 and elsewhere.
   [c] Domitian(us), who founded the temple of the Gens Flavia.
   [d] If the name is Germanicus, *Odrysio* (properly "Thracian") must = "northern," as in 10.7.2. Some suppose it

lick a cunt, Condylus; isn't that better than being your Gaius three times over?

93

What are you waiting for, boy? Pour in the immortal[a] Falernian. Double three measures from the older jar. Tell me now, Catacissus, which of the gods will it be for whom I bid you pour six? "It will be Caesar." Let stitched roses be ten times fitted to my hair,[b] making his number who founded the noble monument of the sacred family.[c] Now give me twice five kisses, adding up to the name which our god brought from the Odrysian world.[d]

94

Hippocrates[e] gave me cups drugged with Santonian twig[f] and (the impudence of the fellow!) asks me for mead. Glaucus, methinks even you were never so stupid, who presented gold armor to him that gave you bronze.[g] Does anybody ask for a sweet gift in return for a bitter one? Let him take it, but only if he drinks it in hellebore.[h]

was "Sarmaticus," referring to Domitian's Thracian campaign, but he is not known to have taken this title. Cf. 9.101.20.

  [e] Name of the founder of medicine. See Appendix B.

  [f] Absinth.

  [g] Diomedes, in the *Iliad* (6.234). Homer says that Zeus deprived Glaucus of his wits.

  [h] A supposed cure for madness.

95

Alfius ante fuit, coepit nunc Olfius esse,
    uxorem postquam duxit Athenagoras.

95 b

Nomen Athenagorae quaeris, Callistrate, verum.
    si scio, dispeream, qui sit Athenagoras.
sed puta me verum, Callistrate, dicere nomen:
    non ego sed vester peccat Athenagoras.

96

Clinicus Herodes trullam subduxerat aegro:
    deprensus dixit 'stulte, quid ergo bibis?'

97

Rumpitur invidia quidam, carissime Iuli,
    quod me Roma legit, rumpitur invidia.

95.1 Alfius ... Olfius *Heraeus* : alphius (alpicius γ) ...
olfius *vel sim.* (olficius γ) αβγ   95b.1 quaeris α : credis
βγ

---

a His supposed name was Alfius Athenagoras, presumably a freedman, Alfius being a recognized gentile name. The point of the epigram is in doubt, but the best guess, as I now think, is Calderini's: Olfius = *cunnilingus* (*olfacere* = "smell").

95

Athenagoras was Alfius formerly, but has now
begun to be Olfius since he married a wife.[a]

95 b

You ask[b] Athenagoras' real name, Callistratus.
Damned if I know who Athenagoras is. But suppose
I am giving a real name, Callistratus. The fault is
not with me but with your[c] Athenagoras.

96

Doctor Herodes had purloined a ladle from a
patient. When caught he said: "You fool, why are
you drinking then?"[d]

97

A certain person, dearest Julius, is bursting with
envy because Rome reads me—bursting with envy.

[b] *Quaeris* is the right choice. The question is answered
in verse 2. "Actually," says M., "I was not writing about a
real person. There is no Athenagoras. But suppose there
was, and that I attacked him, not (as you think) under a
pseudonym, but under his real name: it would be his own
fault for doing what I said he did." *Credis* makes little
sense. Why should C. believe that A. is a real name if he
did not know who A. was?

[c] The plural *vester* implies that others beside Callis-
tratus had made the enquiry.

[d] As though he had removed the ladle out of concern for
the patient's health.

rumpitur invidia quod turba semper in omni
    monstramur digito, rumpitur invidia.
5 rumpitur invidia tribuit quod Caesar uterque
    ius mihi natorum, rumpitur invidia.
rumpitur invidia quod rus mihi dulce sub urbe est
    parvaque in urbe domus, rumpitur invidia.
rumpitur invidia quod sum iucundus amicis,
10   quod conviva frequens, rumpitur invidia.
rumpitur invidia quod amamur quodque probamur:
    rumpatur quisquis rumpitur invidia.

98

Vindemiarum non ubique proventus
cessavit, Ovidi; pluvia profuit grandis.
centum Coranus amphoras aquae fecit.

99

Marcus amat nostras Antonius, Attice, Musas,
    charta salutatrix si modo vera refert:
Marcus Palladiae non infitianda Tolosae
    gloria, quem genuit Pacis alumna Quies.
5 tu qui longa potes dispendia ferre viarum,
    i, liber, absentis pignus amicitiae.

316

He is bursting with envy because fingers always point me out in every crowd—bursting with envy. He is bursting with envy because both Caesars gave me the Right of Children[a]—bursting with envy. He is bursting with envy because I have a pleasant country place near Rome and a small house in the city—bursting with envy. He is bursting with envy because my friends enjoy my company and I am often asked out to dinner—bursting with envy. He is bursting with envy because I am liked and approved of. Whosoever is bursting with envy, let him burst.[b]

98

The vintage has not been a failure everywhere, Ovidius. Heavy rains did good. Coranus has made a hundred jars of—water.[c]

99

Marcus Antonius loves my Muses, Atticus, if only his letter of greeting says true; Marcus, glory undeniable of Palladian Tolosa, child of tranquility the nursling of Peace. Book, who can bear long stretches of travel, go, pledge of absent friendship.

[a] Cf. 2.91.6n.

[b] I.e. "be damned." *Rumpatur* = διαρραγείη. M. juxtaposes two idiomatic uses of *rumpi.*

[c] I.e. wine that is hardly more than water; cf. 1.56.

vilis eras, fateor, si te nunc mitteret emptor;
    grande tui pretium muneris auctor erit:
multum, crede mihi, refert a fonte bibatur
10   quae fluit an pigro quae stupet unda lacu.

100

Denarîs tribus invitas et mane togatum
    observare iubes atria, Basse, tua,
deinde haerere tuo lateri, praecedere sellam,
    ad viduas tecum plus minus ire decem.
5 trita quidem nobis togula est vilisque vetusque:
    denarîs tamen hanc non emo, Basse, tribus.

101

Appia, quam simili venerandus in Hercule Caesar
    consecrat, Ausoniae maxima fama viae,
si cupis Alcidae cognoscere facta prioris,
    disce: Libyn domuit, aurea poma tulit,
5 peltatam Scythico discinxit Amazona nodo,
    addidit Arcadio terga leonis apro,
aeripedem silvis cervum, Stymphalidas astris
    abstulit, a Stygia cum cane venit aqua,

100.4 uiduas β : uetulas γ 5 uetusque β : putrisque γ
101.4 aurea γ : raraque β

ou would have been worth little, I grant, if a buyer
ere now sending you; the author of the gift[a] will
1ake you precious. There's a great difference,
elieve me, between drinking water from a flowing
tream and water stagnating in an idle pond.

100

ou invite me for three denarii[b] and tell me, Bassus,
) attend your hall in the morning, gowned; then to
eep at your side, walk in front of your chair, and go
ith you to ten widows, more or less. My poor gown
s worn and cheap and old, but, Bassus, I don't buy it
ir three denarii.[c]

101

ppia, whom Caesar, to be worshipped in the like-
ess of Hercules,[d] hallows, greatest glory of an
usonian way, if you desire to know the deeds of the
arlier Alcides, learn them: he tamed Libya, carried
ff the golden apples, ungirt the target-bearing
mazon of her Scythian belt, added the lion's skin to
1e Arcadian boar, took the brazen-footed stag from
1e forests and the Stymphalian birds from the
eavens, came with the hound from the waters of

[a] Not "the author's giving"; see Housman, 990f.

[b] Twelve sesterces, almost twice the usual dole. But
assus' demands were exorbitant.

[c] The toga symbolizes client service, which M. implies is
a his case worth more than Bassus is offering.

[d] Cf. 9.64.

fecundam vetuit reparari mortibus Hydram,
10   Hesperias Tusco lavit in amne boves.
haec minor Alcides: maior quae gesserit audi,
     sextus ab Albana quem colit arce lapis.
asseruit possessa malis Palatia regnis,
     prima suo gessit pro Iove bella puer;
15   solus Iuleas cum iam retineret habenas,
     tradidit inque suo tertius orbe fuit;
cornua Sarmatici ter perfida contudit Histri,
     sudantem Getica ter nive lavit equum;
saepe recusatos parcus duxisse triumphos
20   victor Hyperboreo nomen ab orbe tulit;
templa deis, mores populis dedit, otia ferro,
     astra suis, caelo sidera, serta Iovi.
Herculeum tantis numen non sufficit actis:
     Tarpeio deus hic commodet ora patri.

102

Quadringentorum reddis mihi, Phoebe, tabellas:
     centum da potius mutua, Phoebe, mihi.
quaere alium cui te tam vano munere iactes:
     quod tibi non possum solvere, Phoebe, meum est.

---

[a] The Tiber.

[b] Domitian.

[c] Does *suo* refer to Domitian's poem? Cf. 5.5.7n.

[d] In his three campaigns against the tribes on the Danube. As to the shattering of the horn, cf. 10.7.6.

[e] Cf. 8.15.5.

Styx, forbade the fecund Hydra to renew herself by
her deaths, bathed Hesperian oxen in the Tuscan
river.[a] So much did Alcides the Lesser achieve.
Here now what the Greater[b] has accomplished he
whom the sixth stone from Alba's height worships.
He freed the Palatine held under evil dominion, and
in boyhood waged his first war for his[c] Jupiter;
though he alone already held the Julian reins,
he gave them up and became third in the world
that was his own; three times he smashed the
treacherous horns of Sarmatian Hister,[d] three times
he bathed his sweating steed in Getic snow; spar-
ingly celebrating triumphs often rejected,[e] he bore
victorious a name from the Hyperborean world; he
gave temples to the gods, morals to the people, peace
to the sword, heaven to his kindred, stars to the sky,
garlands to Jupiter.[f] Hercules' divinity does not
match such exploits: let this god lend his features to
the Tarpeian Father.[g]

102

You return me my bond for four hundred thousand,
Phoebus. Lend me a hundred instead, Phoebus.
Find somebody else to hear you boast so empty a
gift. What I can't pay you, Phoebus, is mine.

[f] Allusion to the Capitoline festival.
[g] Jupiter of the Capitol.

103

Quae nova tam similis genuit tibi Leda ministros?
    quae capta est alio nuda Lacaena cycno?
dat faciem Pollux Hiero, dat Castor Asylo,
    atque in utroque nitet Tyndaris ore soror.
5   ista Therapnaeis si forma fuisset Amyclis,
    cum vicere duas dona minora deas,
mansisses, Helene, Phrygiamque redisset in Iden
    Dardanius gemino cum Ganymede Paris.

103

What new Leda bore for you servitors so like? What
naked Laconian girl was caught by another swan?
Pollux gives his features to Hierus, Castor his to
Asylus;[a] and in both faces shines their sister, Tyn-
dareus' daughter. If there had been such beauty in
Therapnaean Amyclae[b] when lesser gifts defeated
two goddesses,[c] you would have stayed behind,
Helen, and Dardanian Paris would have gone back
to Phrygian Ida with twin Ganymedes.

[a] The unnamed owner of the two boys was one Ti. Clau-
dius Livianus; see Heraeus' index under Asylus.
[b] Therapnae and Amyclae, towns near Sparta, were
both associated with Helen and her brothers, but the com-
bination is probably only a verse-filling periphrasis for
Sparta or Laconia.
[c] When Venus' promise to Paris of Helen overweighed
the promises of Juno and Minerva in the contest of beauty.

LIBER X

1

Si nimius videor seraque coronide longus
    esse liber, legito pauca: libellus ero.
terque quaterque mihi finitur carmine parva
    pagina: fac tibi me quam cupis ipse brevem.

2

Festinata prius, decimi mihi cura libelli
    elapsum manibus nunc revocavit opus.
nota leges quaedam sed lima rasa recenti;
    pars nova maior erit: lector, utrique fave,
5   lector, opes nostrae: quem cum mihi Roma dedisse
    'nil tibi quod demus maius habemus' ait.
'pigra per hunc fugies ingratae flumina Lethes
    et meliore tui parte superstes eris.
marmora Messallae findit caprificus et audax
10   dimidios Crispi mulio ridet equos:

1.3 parva *Immisch* : -uo βγ   2.1 prius *Reitzenstein* :
prior βγ

---

[a] Lit. "too hurried before, the completion of my tenth
little book has now recalled"—a strained expression of a

324

BOOK X

1

If I seem too large and long a book with colophon
that comes too late, read a few items only: I shall
then be a little book. My small pages quite often
end with the end of a poem. Make me as brief for
yourself as you like.

2

In composing my tenth little book, too hastily issued
earlier,[a] I have now recalled the work that then
slipped from my hands. Some of the pieces you will
read are already known, but polished with a recent
file, the greater part will be new. Reader, wish well
to both—reader, who are my riches. When Rome
gave you to me, she said: "I have nothing greater to
give you. Through him you will escape ungrateful
Lethe's idle waters and survive in the better part of
yourself. The fig tree splits Messalla's marble, the
bold muleteer laughs at Crispus' halved horses.[b]

---

simple idea. The tenth Book as we have it is a revised and
enlarged edition; see Introduction.
  [b] Cf. 8.3.5. Crispus is probably C. Passienus Crispus of
the time of Claudius, stepfather of Nero.

at chartis nec furta nocent et saecula prosunt,
solaque non norunt haec monumenta mori.'

3

Vernaculorum dicta, sordidum dentem,
et foeda linguae probra circulatricis,
quae sulphurato nolit empta ramento
Vatiniorum proxeneta fractorum,
5 poeta quidam clancularius spargit
et vult videri nostra. credis hoc, Prisce?
voce ut loquatur psittacus coturnicis
et concupiscat esse Canus ascaules?
procul a libellis nigra sit meis fama,
10 quos rumor alba gemmeus vehit pinna:
cur ego laborem notus esse tam prave,
constare gratis cum silentium possit?

4

Qui legis Oedipoden caligantemque Thyesten,
Colchidas et Scyllas, quid nisi monstra legis?
quid tibi raptus Hylas, quid Parthenopaeus et Attis,
quid tibi dormitor proderit Endymion,

4.2 nisi] *malim* mihi (*SB*^{3})

---

[a] Glass beakers with long spouts, named after Vatinius a Beneventan cobbler of Nero's time who gained notoriety as a buffoon and a delator; cf. 14.96 and Juv. 5.46. For the bartering of broken glass cf. 1.41.5.

But thefts do not harm paper and the centuries do it good. These are the only memorials that cannot die."

3

Quips of home-bred slaves, vulgar abuse, and the ugly railings of a hawker's tongue, such as a dealer in broken Vatinians[a] would not want to buy for a sulphur match—these a certain skulker of a poet scatters abroad and wishes people to think them mine. Do you believe it, Crispus? Shall a parrot speak with the voice of a quail, and shall Canus crave to play the bagpipes? May black fame be far from my little books, that jewelled report wafts on white wings. Why should I strive for such evil notoriety, when silence can be had free?

4

You that read of Oedipus and Thyestes in the dark[b] and Colchian dames[c] and Scyllas, of what do you read but monstrosities?[d] What good will ravished Hylas be to you, or Parthenopaeus and Attis, or Endymion the sleeper, or the boy who was stripped

[b] Alluding to the eclipse of the sun which followed the atrocity.

[c] Meaning Medea.

[d] Or, with *mihi*, "why, pray, do you read of monstrosities?"

5 exutusve puer pinnis labentibus, aut qui
  odit amatrices Hermaphroditus aquas?
quid te vana iuvant miserae ludibria chartae?
  hoc lege, quod possit dicere vita 'meum est.'
non hic Centauros, non Gorgonas Harpyiasque
10 invenies: hominem pagina nostra sapit.
sed non vis, Mamurra, tuos cognoscere mores
  nec te scire: legas Aetia Callimachi.

5

Quisquis stolaeve purpuraeve contemptor
quos colere debet laesit impio versu,
erret per urbem pontis exul et clivi,
interque raucos ultimus rogatores
5 oret caninas panis improbi buccas.
illi December longus et madens bruma
clususque fornix triste frigus extendat:
vocet beatos clamitetque felices
Orciviana qui feruntur in sponda.
10 at cum supremae fila venerint horae
diesque tardus, sentiat canum litem
abigatque moto noxias aves panno.
nec finiantur morte simplici poenae,

5.9 orciniana *duo ex familia* β   13 simplici *vel* suppl-
SB¹ : supplicis βγ : simplices *Scriverius*

ᵃ Icarus.
ᵇ On the construction see *SB*³.
ᶜ A poem on the legendary origins of names, customs, etc., full of recondite lore. Considerable fragments survive.

of his dropping wings,[a] or Hermaphroditus, who hates the amorous waters? What pleasure do you find in the empty sham of a wretched sheet? Read *this*, of which life can say: "It's mine."[b] You won't find Centaurs here or Gorgons or Harpies: my page smacks of humanity. But you don't want to recognize your own behavior, Mamurra, or to know yourself: you should read the *Origins* of Callimachus.[c]

5

Whoever he be, despiser of stole or purple,[d] that has assailed with impious verses those whom he ought to respect, let him wander through the city, exiled from bridge and slope,[e] and, last among hoarse beggars, crave morsels of shameless bread,[f] fit only for dogs. May a long December and a wet winter and a closed archway drag out for him miserable cold. May he call them happy, acclaim them fortunate who are borne in an Orcivian litter.[g] But when the threads of his final hour have come and his tardy day of death, let him hear the wrangling of dogs and flap his rags to drive off noxious birds. And let not his punishments end with a simple death, but let him weary all the fables of the poets, now lashed by

[d] I.e. of married ladies or magistrates or senators.
[e] Resorts of beggars: cf. 2.19.3; 12.32.10, 25.
[f] With no proper claim to be human food.
[g] A pauper's bier. The meaning of the epithet is uncertain (cf. *SB*[1]).

      sed modo severi sectus Aeaci loris,
15   nunc inquieti monte Sisyphi pressus,
      nunc inter undas garruli senis siccus
      delasset omnis fabulas poetarum:
      et cum fateri Furia iusserit verum,
      prodente clamet conscientia 'scripsi.'

6

Felices, quibus urna dedit spectare coruscum
    solibus Arctois sideribusque ducem.
quando erit ille dies, quo campus et arbor et omnis
    lucebit Latia culta fenestra nuru?
5 quando morae dulces longusque a Caesare pulvis
    totaque Flaminia Roma videnda via?
quando eques et picti tunica Nilotide Mauri
    ibitis et populi vox erit una 'venit'?

7

      Nympharum pater amniumque, Rhene,
      quicumque Odrysias bibunt pruinas,
      sic semper liquidis fruaris undis
      nec te barbara contumeliosi
5   calcatum rota conterat bubulci;

---

   [a] Tantalus.

   [b] Evidently a senatorial delegation to Trajan, chosen by lot.

   [c] The sun and stars are imagined as in attendance upon the Emperor (Trajan, expected from the Rhine in A.D. 98).

the thongs of stern Aeacus, now crushed by the mountain of restless Sisyphus, now dry amidst the waters of the old chatterbox.[a] And when the Fury commands him to confess the truth, let conscience betray him and let him cry out: "I wrote it."

6

Happy they[b] to whom the urn has granted it to see our Leader gleaming with northern suns and stars.[c] When shall be the day on which ground and tree shall shine and every window, adorned by Latium's daughters?[d] When shall be the sweet delays, the long trail of dust behind Caesar, and all Rome to be seen on the Flaminian Way? When shall the cavalry ride and the painted Moors in their tunics of Nile, and one voice of the people be heard: "He comes."

7

Rhine, father of Nymphs and rivers, all that drink Odrysian[e] frosts, so may you ever enjoy clear waters and the barbarian wheel of the insolent cattle-driver never trample and fret you; so may you flow with

[d] Seemingly with reference to gaily dressed people on the ground, lights or decorations in the trees, and women at the windows.

[e] Properly = "Thracian," here "northern"; cf. 9.93.8.

sic et cornibus aureis receptis
et Romanus eas utraque ripa:
Traianum populis suis et urbi,
Thybris te dominus rogat, remittas.

8

Nubere Paula cupit nobis, ego ducere Paulam
nolo: anus est. vellem, si magis esset anus.

9

Undenis pedibusque syllabisque
et multo sale nec tamen protervo
notus gentibus ille Martialis
et notus populis — quid invidetis? —
5   non sum Andraemone notior caballo.

10

Cum tu, laurigeris annum qui fascibus intras,
    mane salutator limina mille teras,
hic ego quid faciam? quid nobis, Paule, relinquis,
    qui de plebe Numae densaque turba sumus?
5 qui me respiciat dominum regemque vocabo?
    hoc tu — sed quanto blandius! — ipse facis.

10.5 respiciat ς : -ciet β : -cies γ

---

a Previously shattered by defeat; cf. 7.7.3; 9.101.17.
b Elegiacs and hendecasyllables.

your golden horns[a] recovered, Roman on either
bank: send Trajan back to his peoples and his city—
Tiber, your lord, bids you.

8

Paula wants to marry me, I don't want to marry
Paula; she's an old woman. I should have wanted, if
she were older still.

9

I, Martial, known to the nations, known to the
peoples for my verses of eleven feet and eleven
syllables,[b] and my wit, abundant but not over-bold
(why do you all envy me?), am no better known than
Andraemon the horse.

10

When you who enter the year with laureled *fasces*[c]
tread a thousand thresholds paying your respects of
a morning, what am I to do here? What do you leave
for us, Paulus, us of Numa's commons, the close-
packed crowd? Shall I address a prospective protec-
tor as "lord" and "patron"? You do that yourself, and
how much more blandly! Shall I follow litter or

[c] As consul, on the first of the year. Men of position
often did not scruple to add to their income by taking the
sportula. Juvenal (1.99, 117) also alludes to this abuse.

333

lecticam sellamve sequar? nec ferre recusas,
 per medium pugnas et prior ire lutum.
saepius assurgam recitanti carmina? tu stas
10 et pariter geminas tendis in ora manus.
quid faciet pauper cui non licet esse clienti?
 dimisit nostras purpura vestra togas.

11

Nil aliud loqueris quam Thesea Pirithoumque
 teque putas Pyladi, Calliodore, parem.
dispeream, si tu Pyladi praestare matellam
 dignus es aut porcos pascere Pirithoi.
5 'donavi tamen' inquis 'amico milia quinque
 et lotam, ut multum, terve quaterve togam.'
quid quod nil umquam Pylades donavit Orestae?
 qui donat quamvis plurima, plura negat.

12

Aemiliae gentes et Apollineas Vercellas
 et Phaethontei qui petis arva Padi,
ne vivam, nisi te, Domiti, dimitto libenter,
 grata licet sine te sit mihi nulla dies:
5 sed desiderium tanti est, ut messe vel una
 urbano releves colla perusta iugo.
i precor et totos avida cute combibe soles —
 o quam formosus, dum peregrinus eris!

11.6 ve … ve *Haupt* : que … que T $\beta\gamma$ 7 Pylades
donavit Orestae *Heinsius* (*cf. ad* 7.24.3) : pyladi d- orestes
T β : ila donauitur esse γ

chair? You don't refuse even to shoulder one and fight your way in front through the middle of the mud. Shall I keep on rising in my seat at his poetry recitation? You are on your feet stretching out both hands at once towards his face. What shall a poor man do, who isn't allowed to be a client? You and your like with your purple have discharged our gowns.

11

Calliodorus, you talk of nothing but Theseus and Pirithous, and think yourself the equal of Pylades. Damned if you are fit to hold a chamber pot to Pylades or feed Pirithous' pigs. "All the same," you say, "I gave a friend five thousand and a gown washed three or four times at most." Well, but Pylades never gave Orestes anything. A giver, however generous, denies more than he gives.

12

Domitius, now heading for the folk of the Aemilian Way and Apollo's Vercellae and the fields of Po, Phaethon's river, upon my oath I let you go gladly, though no day is pleasant to me without you. But it is worth while missing you, so that for one summer at least you may rest your neck galled by the city's yoke. Go, I beg, and let your greedy hide drink sunshine in full measure. How handsome you will be, so long as you stay abroad! And you will come

et venies albis non cognoscendus amicis
10   livebitque tuis pallida turba genis.
sed via quem dederit rapiet cito Roma colorem,
      Niliaco redeas tu licet ore niger.

13 (20)

Ducit ad auriferas quod me Salo Celtiber oras,
      pendula quod patriae visere tecta libet,
tu mihi simplicibus, Mani, dilectus ab annis
      et praetextata cultus amicitia,
5   tu facis; in terris quo non est alter Hiberis
      dulcior et vero dignus amore magis.
tecum ego vel sicci Gaetula mapalia Poeni
      et poteram Scythicas hospes amare casas.
si tibi mens eadem, si nostri mutua cura est,
10   in quocumque loco Roma duobus erit.

14 (13)

Cum cathedrata litos portet tibi raeda ministros
      et Libys in longo pulvere sudet eques,
strataque non unas tingant triclinia Baias
      et Thetis unguento palleat uncta tuo,
5   candida Setini rumpant crystalla trientes,
      dormiat in pluma nec meliore Venus:

12.9 cognoscendus β : adno- γ 14.1 cathedrata litos
Heraeus : -ratalios β : -ras alius γ : cotathedratos T :
cathedralicios ς 3 tingant SB^1 : -at γ : pingat β :
cingant ς : pi- *"Italus" unus*   4 uncta] aucta *Heinsius*

336

back unrecognizable to your whey-faced friends; the pallid throng will envy your cheeks. But Rome will soon rob you of the color the road has given, though you return black-faced as a son of Nile.

13 (20)

If Celtiberian Salo draws me to gold-bearing lands, if I would gladly see the roofs of my native town perched on the hill, you, Manius, dear to me from my years of innocence, whose friendship I cultivated in my boyhood gown, you are the cause; in Iberia's land there is no sweeter man, none worthier of true affection. With you I could be a stranger in the Gaetulian huts of the sun-parched Carthaginian or the cottages of Scythia and love them. If you are of the same mind, if you care for me in return, any place will be Rome for us two.

14 (13)

Although a carriage fitted with armchairs bears your painted minions and a Libyan horseman sweats in a long trail of dust and draped couches empurple more than one Baian villa[a] and Thetis yellows with your unguents' oil; though bumpers of Setine burst your clear crystal and Venus sleep in

---

[a] The rich color of the draperies in the dining rooms "dyed" the villas (*SB*[1], citing Pliny *N.H.* 37.63 and Claud. *Prob. et Olybr.* 264f); a fantastic hyperbole, matching the one in the pentameter. For *Baias* = "Baian villa," cf. 10.58.2 and *Stud. F. della Corte* (Urbino, 1987?), IV, 65.

ad nocturna iaces fastosae limina moechae
    et madet heu! lacrimis ianua surda tuis,
urere nec miserum cessant suspiria pectus.
10   vis dicam male sit cur tibi, Cotta? bene est.

15 (14)

Cedere de nostris nulli te dicis amicis.
    sed, sit ut hoc verum, quid, rogo, Crispe, facis?
mutua cum peterem sestertia quinque, negasti,
    non caperet nummos cum gravis arca tuos.
5 quando fabae nobis modium farrisve dedisti,
    cum tua Niliacus rura colonus aret?
quando brevis gelidae missa est toga tempore brumae
    argenti venit quando selibra mihi?
nil aliud video quo te credamus amicum
10   quam quod me coram pedere, Crispe, soles.

16 (15)

Dotatae uxori cor harundine fixit acuta,
    sed dum ludit Aper: ludere novit Aper.

17 (16)

Si donare vocas promittere nec dare, Gai,
    vincam te donis munieribusque meis.
accipe Callaicis quidquid fodit Astur in arvis,
    aurea quidquid habet divitis unda Tagi,

---

[a] Cotta is so well off, he has to invent miseries.

no better down: yet you lie of nights on the threshold
of a haughty adulteress and the deaf door, alack, is
wet with your tears, nor do sighs cease to burn your
unhappy breast. Shall I tell you why it goes badly
with you, Cotta? It goes well.[a]

15 (14)

You say you yield to none of my friends. But I ask
you, what do you do, Crispus, to make this true?
When I requested a loan of five thousand sesterces,
you refused, though your heavy coffer was not large
enough to hold your money. When did you give me a
peck of beans or corn, though a Nile-born tenant
plows your land? When did you send me a short
gown in chill winter time? When did half a pound of
silver come my way? I see nothing else to make me
think you a friend, Crispus, except that you are in
the habit of farting in my presence.

16 (15)

Aper pierced his dowered wife's heart with an
arrow, but it was in a game: Aper knows gamesman-
ship.

17 (16)

If you call it giving to promise and not give, Gaius, I
shall outdo you with my gifts and presents. Accept
whatever the Asturian digs in Galician fields, what-
ever the golden water of rich Tagus possesses, what-

5 quidquid Erythraea niger invenit Indus in alga,
      quidquid et in nidis unica servat avis,
  quidquid Agenoreo Tyros improba cogit aheno:
      quidquid habent omnes, accipe, quomodo das.

18 (17)

Saturnalicio Macrum fraudare tributo
      frustra, Musa, cupis: non licet; ipse petit;
sollemnesque iocos nec tristia carmina poscit
      et queritur nugas obticuisse meas.
5 mensorum longis sed nunc vacat ille libellis.
      Appia, quid facies, si legit ista Macer?

19 (18)

Nec vocat ad cenam Marius, nec munera mittit,
      nec spondet, nec vult credere, sed nec habet.
turba tamen non deest sterilem quae curet amicum
      eheu! quam fatuae sunt tibi, Roma, togae!

ever the black Indian finds in Erythraean seaweed,[a] whatever the one and only bird[b] keeps in her nest, whatever unconscionable[c] Tyre assembles in Agenor's cauldron: whatever all mankind possesses, accept it—as you give it.

18 (17)

In vain, Muse, do you desire to cheat Macer of his Saturnalian tribute. You cannot; he asks for it himself. He demands the customary jests and merry verses, complains that my trifles have fallen silent. But now he has only time for the lengthy reports of surveyors. What will you do, Appia, if Macer reads my poems?[d]

19 (18)

Marius doesn't invite people to dinner or send presents or stand surety, he won't lend money, in fact he doesn't have any. And yet there is not lacking a multitude to cultivate so barren a friend. Ah me, Rome, how foolish are your gowns!

[a] Pearls: cf. 5.37.4.

[b] The phoenix.

[c] As in 10.36.1, *improba* conveys disapproval of the product, purple-dyed fabrics being an article of ostentatious luxury.

[d] The Appian Way will be neglected if its curator Macer takes to reading M.'s verses instead of reports.

20 (19)

Nec doctum satis et parum severum,
sed non rusticulum tamen libellum
facundo mea Plinio Thalia
i perfer: brevis est labor peractae
5 altum vincere tramitem Suburae.
illic Orphea protinus videbis
udi vertice lubricum theatri
mirantisque feras avemque regem,
raptum quae Phryga pertulit Tonanti;
10 illic parva tui domus Pedonis
caelata est aquilae minore pinna.
sed ne tempore non tuo disertam
pulses ebria ianuam videto:
totos dat tetricae dies Mienrvae,
15 dum centum studet auribus virorum
hoc quod saecula posterique possint
Arpinis quoque comparare chartis.
seras tutior ibis ad lucernas:
haec hora est tua, cum furit Lyaeus,
20 cum regnat rosa, cum madent capilli:
tunc me vel rigidi legant Catones.

20.8 regem SB^1 (*cf. SB²*) : regis $\beta\gamma$: regi *Heinsius et Grono-vius*

ᵃ I.e. the ascent up the Esquiline from the Subura.

ᵇ Probably a pool with steps and fountains and a statue
of Orpheus surrounded by animals in the center. Hous-

BOOK X

20 (19)

Go, my Thalia, and take to eloquent Pliny a little
book, not very accomplished and not very serious,
but still not clownish. Once through Subura, the
effort of climbing the uphill path[a] doesn't take long.
There you will immediately see Orpheus standing
slippery at the top of his watery theater,[b] and the
wondering beasts and the royal bird,[c] who bore off
the ravished Phrygian to the Thunderer. There the
small house of your Pedo is chiselled with the wing
of a lesser eagle. But mind you don't knock tipsily
on the eloquent door at the wrong time. He gives all
his days to sour Minerva, at work on compositions
which future ages will be able to compare even with
Arpi's pages,[d] for the ears of the Hundred Men.[e] It
will be safer for you to go when the late lamps are
lit. This is your hour, when Lyaeus runs wild, when
the rose is queen and hair is damp. Then let even
stiff Catos read me.[f]

man, however, takes *theatri* as "audience," the creatures
listening to Orpheus' lute (726).

[c] Jupiter's eagle that carried off Ganymede: cf. 1.6.

[d] Cicero's. *Arpinis* comes from *Arpi* (in Apulia). From
Arpinum the corresponding form would be *Arpinatibus*.
Cf. 4.55.3n.

[e] Cf. 6.38.5.

[f] Pliny quotes the last ten lines of this epigram in *Epist.*
3.21.

21

Scribere te quae vix intellegat ipse Modestus
    et vix Claranus, quid, rogo, Sexte, iuvat?
non lectore tuis opus est, sed Apolline libris:
    iudice te maior Cinna Marone fuit.
5   sic tua laudentur sane: mea carmina, Sexte,
    grammaticis placeant ut sine grammaticis.

22

Cur spleniato saepe prodeam mento
albave pictus sana labra cerussa,
Philine, quaeris? basiare te nolo.

23

Iam numerat placido felix Antonius aevo
    quindecies actas Primus Olympiadas
praeteritosque dies et tutos respicit annos
    nec metuit Lethes iam propioris aquas.
5   nulla recordanti lux est ingrata gravisque;
    nulla fuit cuius non meminisse velit.
ampliat aetatis spatium sibi vir bonus: hoc est
    vivere bis, vita posse priore frui.

21.2 *et* 5 sexte γ : crispe β 6 ut β : et γ : set *Markland*   22.3 philine γ : phil(a)eni β 23.3 tutos $\beta\gamma$: totos T

21

Sextus, why, may I ask, do you like to write stuff that Modestus himself or Claranus would have trouble understanding? Your books need, not a reader, but an Apollo.[a] In your judgment Cinna was greater than Maro. On that basis by all means let your poems be praised; but let mine, Sextus, please commentators so far as, having none, they may.

22

Do you ask, Philaenis, why I often go out with a plaster on my chin or my healthy lips painted with white lead? I don't want to kiss you.

23

Antonius Primus, happy man, now counts fifteen Olympiads[b] gone by in his tranquil life. He looks back in security at past days and years,[c] nor fears the waters of Lethe, now less far away. No day, as he recalls it, is unwelcome and disagreeable; there was none he would rather not remember. A good man enlarges for himself his span of life. To be able to enjoy former life is to live twice over.

[a] They are as obscure as Delphic oracles.
[b] I.e. seventy-five years; cf. 7.40.6n.
[c] Lit. "back at past days and safe years"—nothing can happen to them; cf. Sen. *Ben.* 3.4.2.

24

Natales mihi Martiae Kalendae,
lux formosior omnibus Kalendis,
qua mittunt mihi munus et puellae,
quinquagensima liba septimamque
5   vestris addimus hanc focis acerram.
his vos, si tamen expedit roganti,
annos addite bis, precor, novenos,
ut nondum nimia piger senecta
sed vitae tribus arcubus peractis
10   lucos Elysiae petam puellae.
post hunc Nestora nec diem rogabo.

25

In matutina nuper spectatus harena
   Mucius, imposuit qui sua membra focis,
si patiens durusque tibi fortisque videtur,
   Abderitanae pectora plebis habes.
5   nam cum dicatur tunica praesente molesta
   'ure manum', plus est dicere 'non facio.'

24.9 arcubus *Housman* : auribus L : aureis *cett.* : areis
Aldus   11 Nestora *Heinsius* : nec hora *vel sim.* βγ

---

  [a] Who ordinarily received gifts on that day (cf. 5.84.11).

  [b] The four segments into which the full circle of life (100
years) is divided: cf. Manil. 2.844–55. M., being fifty-
seven, would in eighteen years have completed three arcs,
and have reached the last arc of too protracted age.

  [c] Proserpine.

  [d] I.e. length of days.

24

My natal Kalends of March, day fairer to me than all Kalends, on which even girls send me presents,[a] for the fifty-seventh time I give your altar cakes and this censer. To these years, but only if I ask what is good for me, add, I beg, twice nine, so that not yet slowed by excessive age, but with three arcs of life[b] complete, I may seek the groves of the Elysian girl.[c] Beyond this Nestor[d] I shall not ask for so much as a day.

25

If Mucius,[e] lately seen in the morning arena as he placed his limb on the fire, seems to you enduring and hard and brave, you have the brains of Abdera's populace.[f] For when a man is told in the presence of the Tiresome Tunic[g] "Burn your hand," it's a greater thing to say "I won't."

[e] Cf. 1.21; 8.30.
[f] See Index: Abderitanus.
[g] The *tunica molesta*; cf. 4.86.8.

26

Vare, Paraetonias Latia modo vite per urbes
　　nobilis et centum dux memorande viris,
at nunc Ausonio frustra promisse Quirino,
　　hospita Lagei litoris umbra iaces.
5　spargere non licuit frigentia fletibus ora,
　　pinguia nec maestis addere tura rogis.
sed datur aeterno victurum carmine nomen:
　　numquid et hoc, fallax Nile, negare potes?

27

Natali, Diodore, tuo conviva senatus
　　accubat et rarus non adhibetur eques,
et tua tricenos largitur sportula nummos.
　　nemo tamen natum te, Diodore, putat.

28

Annorum nitidique sator pulcherrime mundi,
　　publica quem primum vota precesque vocant,
pervius exiguos habitabas ante penates,
　　plurima qua medium Roma terebat iter:

26.1 Latia … vite ς : lata … uit(a)e γ : latias … rite β :
latio … uecte T

26

Varus, recently well-known with your Latin vine-rod[a] in Paraetonian cities, a commander of whom your hundred soldiers could be proud, but now promised in vain to Ausonian Quirinus,[b] low you lie, a stranger ghost on the Lagean shore. We could not bedew your cold face with tears or add rich incense to your sad pyre. But an immortal poem gives you a name that will live. Treacherous Nile, this too can you deny?

27

On your birthday, Diodorus, the senate reclines as your dinner guest and few knights are not invited. Your dole lavishes thirty sesterces apiece.[c] Yet nobody thinks you were born, Diodorus.[d]

28

Begetter most fair of the years and the bright universe, first to be invoked by public vows and prayers, formerly you lived on a passage in a tiny dwelling, where Rome in her crowds trod the

---

[a] Carried by centurions.

[b] I.e. whose return to Rome we were expecting.

[c] Between four and five times the usual dole; cf. 9.100.1n.

[d] Cf. 8.64.18n.

nunc tua Caesareis cinguntur limina donis
    et fora tot numeras, Iane, quot ora geris.
at tu, sancte pater, tanto pro munere gratus
    ferrea perpetua claustra tuere sera.

29

Quam mihi mittebas Saturni tempore lancem,
    misisti dominae, Sextiliane, tuae;
et quam donabas dictis a Marte Kalendis,
    de nostra prasina est synthesis empta toga.
5 iam constare tibi gratis coepere puellae:
    muneribus futuis, Sextiliane, meis.

30

O temperatae dulce Formiae litus,
vos, cum severi fugit oppidum Martis
et inquietas fessus exuit curas,
Apollinaris omnibus locis praefert.
5 non ille sanctae dulce Tibur uxoris,
nec Tusculanos Algidosve secessus,
Praeneste nec sic Antiumque miratur;
non blanda Circe Dardanisve Caieta
desiderantur, nec Marica nec Liris,

ᵃ The old temple of Janus was near the Roman Forum, and represented Janus with two faces. Domitian built a new temple, giving Janus four faces, in the Forum Transitorium: cf. 8.2. The other three forums were the Romanum, Iulii, and Augusti.

thoroughfare. Now your threshold is encircled by Caesar's gifts, and you number as many forums, Janus, as you have faces.[a] But do you, holy father, grateful for such munificence, keep your iron doors fast with bolt never drawn.[b]

29

The dish you used to send me at Saturn's time, Sextilianus, you sent to your mistress, and the green dinner suit you gave her on the Kalends that take their name from Mars[c] was bought out of *my* gown. Girls have now started to cost you nothing. You fornicate, Sextilianus, with my presents.

30

Temperate Formiae, sweet shore! When Apollinaris flees stern Mars' town and in weariness puts restless cares aside, he prefers you to all other places. He does not so admire sweet Tibur, home of his virtuous wife, nor Tusculan nor Algid retreats, nor Praeneste nor Antium. Neither does he wish for witching Circe[d] or Dardanian Caieta[e] or Marica[f] or

[b] When the gate of the temple was shut, it was a sign that Rome was not at war.

[c] Cf. 10.24.3n.

[d] Circeii.

[e] See Index.

[f] A Latin nymph, who had a temple and grove at Minturnae at the mouth of the Liris in Campania.

10   nec in Lucrina lota Salmacis vena.
     hic summa leni stringitur Thetis vento;
     nec languet aequor, viva sed quies ponti
     pictam phaselon adiuvante fert aura,
     sicut puellae non amantis aestatem
15   mota salubre purpura venit frigus.
     nec seta longo quaerit in mari praedam,
     sed a cubili lectuloque iactatam
     spectatus alte lineam trahit piscis.
     si quando Nereus sentit Aeoli regnum,
20   ridet procellas tuta de suo mensa:
     piscina rhombum prascit et lupos vernas,
     natat ad magistrum delicata murena,
     nomenculator mugilem citat notum
     et adesse iussi prodeunt senes mulli.
25   frui sed istis quando, Roma, permittis?
     quot Formianos imputat dies annus
     negotiosis rebus urbis haerenti?
     o ianitores vilicique felices!
     dominis parantur ista, serviunt vobis.

31

Addixti servum nummis here mille ducentis,
   ut bene cenares, Calliodore, semel.

30.27 negotiosae *Heinsius*

ª M., no doubt with precedent, has transferred the legend of Hermaphroditus (cf. 6.68.9) from a spring in Caria to one that fell into the Lucrine lake.

ᵇ I.e. not motionless.

Liris or Salmacis, bathed in Lucrine channel.[a] Here
Thetis' surface is brushed by a gentle wind, nor is
the water stagnant; the sea's living[b] calm bears on
the painted boat and the breeze assists; even as with
the movement of a girl's purple fan, one that loves
not summer's heat, comes salutary cool. The line
does not seek its prey in the far-off sea, but the fish,
watched from above, draws the string tossed from
bed or couch. Should Nereus feel the realm of
Aeolus, the table, secure in its own store, laughs at
storms: a fishpond feeds turbot and home-bred bass,
the dainty eel swims to its master, the nomenclator
summons a familiar gurnard, and aged mullets
come forward to order. But when does Rome allow
him to enjoy all this? How many Formian days does
the year chalk up for one involved in the city's busy
affairs? Lucky janitors, lucky bailiffs! These
delights are acquired for their owners, but it is you
they serve.

31

You sold a slave yeseterday for twelve hundred
sesterces, Calliodorus, in order to dine well just
once. But well[c] you did not dine. The chief item of

---

[c] M. plays on two meanings of *bene*, "sumptuously" or
"well" in a moral sense.

nec bene cenasti: mullus tibi quattuor emptus
    librarum cenae pompa caputque fuit.
5 exclamare libet: 'non est hic, improbe, non est
    piscis, homo est; hominem, Calliodore, comes.'

32

Haec mihi quae colitur violis pictura rosisque,
    quos referat vultus, Caediciane, rogas?
talis erat Marcus mediis Antonius annis
    Primus: in hoc iuvenem se videt ore senex.
5 ars utinam mores animumque effingere posset!
    pulchrior in terris nulla tabella foret.

33

Simplicior priscis, Munati Galle, Sabinis,
    Cecropium superas qui bonitate senem,
sic tibi consoceri claros retinere penates
    perpetua natae det face casta Venus,
5 ut tu, si viridi tinctos aerugine versus
    forte malus livor dixerit esse meos,
ut facis, a nobis abigas, nec scribere quemquam
    talia contendas carmina qui legitur.
hunc servare modum nostri novere libelli,
10   parcere personis, dicere de vitiis.

33.6 liuor β : lector γ

---

a See 3.48n.

the dinner, the *pièce de resistance*, was a four-pound mullet you had bought. One feels like crying aloud: "This is no fish, greedy, no, it's a man: Calliodorus, you are a cannibal."[a]

32

This picture which I decorate with violets and roses, do you ask whose face it recalls, Caedicianus? Such was Marcus Antonius Primus in middle life; in this countenance the old man sees his younger self. Would that art could represent his character and soul! No painting in the world would be more beautiful.

33

Munatius Gallus, more guileless than the Sabines of old, you who in goodness of heart surpass the Cecropian ancient,[b] so may chaste Venus grant you by your daughter's undying marriage torch to keep her father-in-law's illustrious household gods:[c] if perchance wicked envy says that verses dipped in green verdigris are mine, drive them away from me, as you do, and maintain that nobody who is read writes such pieces. This rule my little books know how to observe: to spare persons, to speak of vices.

[b] Epicurus (cf. 7.69.3) rather than Socrates. Diogenes Laertius (10.9) writes of Epicurus' "unsurpassed good will to all men" and "unsurpassed qualities of goodness."

[c] I.e. your tie with him. If the marriage broke up, they would no longer be *consoceri* (cf. Cic. *Sest.* 6).

34

Di tibi dent quidquid, Caesar Traiane, mereris
    et rata perpetuo quae tribuere velint:
qui sua restituis spoliato iura patrono
    — libertis exul non erit ille suis —,
5 dignus es ut populum possis servare clientem,
    ut — liceat tantum vera probare — potes.

35

Omnes Sulpiciam legant puellae
uni quae cupiunt viro placere;
omnes Sulpiciam legant mariti
uni qui cupiunt placere nuptae.
5   non haec Colchidos asserit furorem,
diri prandia nec refert Thyestae;
Scyllam, Byblida nec fuisse credit:
sed castos docet et pios amores,
lusus, delicias facetiasque.
10   cuius carmina qui bene aestimarit,
nullam dixerit esse nequiorem,
nullam dixerit esse sanctiorem.
tales Egeriae iocos fuisse
udo crediderim Numae sub antro.
15   hac condiscipula vel hac magistra
esses doctior et pudica, Sappho:
sed tecum pariter simulque visam

34.5 possis populum (*sive* pop- pos-) *Housman* : possis
totum $\beta\gamma$: p- tutum ς 6 ut] et *Scriverius*   35.8
pios β : probos γ 16 esses ς : esse *vel* esset β : esset γ

34

May the gods give you, Caesar Trajan, all you merit
and may they wish their gifts forever valid. You,
who restore his rights to the deprived patron (he
will not be an exile to his own freedmen),[a] deserve to
be able to keep the people as your client, as indeed,
if only truth may be told and believed, able you are.

35

Let all girls who wish to please one man read Sulpi-
cia. Let all husbands who wish to please one bride
read Sulpicia. She does not claim for subject the
madness of the Colchian dame[b] or retail the meal of
dire Thyestes;[c] as for Scylla and Byblis, she doesn't
believe they ever existed. She tells of pure and law-
ful love, playful caprice and merriment. A good
judge of her verses will say there was never a girl
more roguish or more virtuous. Such, I could
believe, were Egeria's jests in Numa's damp grotto.
If she had been your schoolfellow or your teacher,
Sappho, you would have been more accomplished
and you would have been chaste; but unkind Phaon

---

[a] Vitellius had restored to returned exiles their rights
over their freedmen (Tac. *Hist.* 2.92). Trajan's measure
seems to have referred to persons actually in exile.

[b] Medea.

[c] The epithet really belongs to the feast rather than to
Thyestes, who did not know what he was eating.

durus Sulpiciam Phaon amaret.
frustra: namque ea nec Tonantis uxor
20   nec Bacchi nec Apollinis puella
erepto sibi viveret Caleno.

36

Improba Massiliae quidquid fumaria cogunt,
   accipit aetatem quisquis ab igne cadus,
a te, Munna, venit: miseris tu mittis amicis
   per freta, per longas toxica saeva vias;
5 nec facili pretio, sed quo contenta Falerni
   testa sit aut cellis Setia cara suis.
non venias quare tam longo tempore Romam
   haec puto causa tibi est, ne tua vina bibas.

37

Iuris et aequarum cultor sanctissime legum,
   veridico Latium qui regis ore forum,
municipi, Materne, tuo veterique sodali
   Callaicum mandas si quid ad Oceanum —

---

[a] Cf. 10.38.

[b] Cf. 10.17.7n.

[c] M.'s criticisms of smoke-flavored Massilian wines (cf.
3.82.23; 13.123) should perhaps rather have been directed
against other wines of the Narbonensis, which according to
Pliny (*N.H.* 14.68), who commends Massilian, were cor-
rupted in the making by smoke and worse things.

[d] M. does not explain how "Munna" got his friends to
pay a high price for bad wine.

would have loved Sulpicia, if he had seen her and
you side by side—in vain, for she would not live as
the Thunderer's spouse or Bacchus' girl or Apollo's,
should Calenus be taken from her.[a]

36

Whatever the unconscionable[b] smoke rooms of Mas-
silia bring together,[c] whatever jar takes age from
fire, comes from you, Munna. You send your unfor-
tunate friends dire poisons by sea and length of
road, and at no easy price, but one which would con-
tent a flagon of Falernian or Setine, beloved of its
cellars.[d] Methinks the reason why it is so long since
you came to Rome is to avoid drinking your own
wines.

37

Scrupulous devotee of law and just statutes,
Maternus,[e] ruling the Latin Forum[f] with truth-
abiding lips, if you have any message to give your
fellow townsman and old friend for the Galician
ocean—or[g] do you think it better to pull out ugly

[e] A jurisconsult, to whom the Emperor will have given
the *ius respondendi*, the right to publish his opinions on
points of law.

[f] Cf. Cicero's (probably quasi-ironical) reference to the
jurist Aquilius' "monarchy of the law-courts" in *Att.* 1.10.1.

[g] M. anticipates a question: "Why are you off to Spain
then?"

5   an Laurentino turpis in litore ranas
      et satius tenues ducere credis acos
   ad sua captivum quam saxa remittere mullum,
      visus erit libris qui minor esse tribus?
   et fatuam summa cenare pelorida mensa
10   quosque tegit levi cortice concha brevis
   ostrea Baianis quam non liventia testis,
      quae domino pueri non prohibente vorent?
   hic olidam clamosus ages in retia vulpem
      mordebitque tuos sordida praeda canes:
15   illic piscoso modo vix educta profundo
      impedient lepores umida lina meos.
   dum loquor, ecce redit sporta piscator inani,
      venator capta maele superbus adest:
   omnis ab urbano venit ad mare cena macello.
20   Callaicum mandas si quid ad Oceanum —.

38

   O molles tibi quindecim, Calene,
   quos cum Sulpicia tua iugales
   indulsit deus et peregit annos!
   o nox omnis et hora, quae notata est
5   caris litoris Indici lapillis!
   o quae proelia, quas utriumque pugnas
   felix lectulus et lucerna vidit

37.6 acos γ : acus β

---

  [a] Maternus will have had a villa there to which M. seems to be making farewell visit.
  [b] Cf. 6.11.5n.

360

frogs and slender needle fish on the shore of
Laurentum[a] than to throw back on its rocks a cap-
tured mullet that appears to be less than three
pounds; and to dine on insipid peloris[b] as *pièce de
resistance*[c] and the creatures that a small shell cov-
ers with a smooth coating[d] rather than oysters that
do not envy Baian jars, that the slaves devour
unchecked by master. Here you will clamorously
drive a malodorous vixen into your toils and the
ignoble quarry will bite your hounds; there the drip-
ping nets, just drawn laboriously[e] from the fishy
depth, will entrap my hares. Even as I speak, here
comes the fisherman back with an empty creel, and
here is the hunter, proud of his captured badger.
Every seaside dinner comes from the city market. If
you have any message for the Galician ocean—

38

O gentle fifteen years, years of wedlock with your
Sulpicia, Calenus, divinely bestowed and completed!
O each night, each hour, marked by precious peb-
bles of India's shore! What combats, what mutual
bouts were witnessed by the happy bed and the

[c] Such seems to be the force of *summa mensa*, as indi-
cated by Pliny *N.H.* 9.63 *proxima est mensa iecori dum-
taxat mustelarum.*

[d] Perhaps mussels (*mituli*); cf. 3.60.4.

[e] Because of the size of the catch.

nimbis ebria Nicerotianis!
vixisti tribus, o Calene, lustris:
10   aetas haec tibi tota computatur
et solos numeras dies mariti.
ex illis tibi si diu rogatam
lucem redderet Atropos vel unam,
malles quam Pyliam quater senectam.

39

Consule te Bruto quod iuras, Lesbia, natam,
   mentiris. nata es, Lesbia, rege Numa?
sic quoque mentiris. namque, ut tua saecula narrant,
   ficta Prometheo diceris esse luto.

40

Semper cum mihi diceretur esse
secreto mea Polla cum cinaedo,
irrupi, Lupe. non erat cinaedus.

Perfume; cf. 6.55.3.
Fifteen years.
Cf. 8.2.7.

lamp drunk with Nicerotian showers![a] You have lived three lusters,[b] Calenus. This you reckon as your entire span, counting only your married days. If Atropos, long beseeched, gave you back a single one of them, you would rather have it than four times the Pylian's length of days.[c]

39

When you swear, Lesbia, that you were born in Brutus' consulship, you lie. Were you born, Lesbia, in Numa's reign? You lie even so. For, as they recount your centuries, you are said to have been molded from Prometheus' clay.

40

I was always being told that my Polla was closeted with a queen. So I burst in, Lupus. He was no queen.[d]

[d] So what was he? Not, as generally believed, a *cunnilingus* or an *irrumator*, but an honest-to-God adulterer. The best commentary is in the Bodleian fragment of Juvenal, thus paraphrased by Housman, 481: "Wherever a cinaedus is kept he taints the household ... Them do women consult about marriage and divorce ... from them do they learn lascivious motions and whatever else the teacher knows. But beware: that teacher is not always what he seems: true, he darkens his eyes and dresses like a woman, but adultery is his design. Mistrust him the more for his show of effeminacy: he is a valiant mattress-knight. There Triphallus drops the mask of Thais."

41

Mense novo Iani veterem, Proculeia, maritum
    deseris atque iubes res sibi habere suas.
quid, rogo, quid factum est? subiti quae causa doloris?
    nil mihi respondes? dicam ego, praetor erat:
5 constatura fuit Megalensis purpura centum
    milibus, ut nimium munera parca dares,
et populare sacrum bis milia dena tulisset.
    discidium non est hoc, Proculeia: lucrum est.

42

Tam dubia est lanugo tibi, tam mollis ut illam
    halitus et soles et levis aura terat.
celantur simili ventura Cydonea lana,
    pollice virgineo quae spoliata nitent.
5 fortius impressi quotiens tibi basia quinque,
    barbatus labris, Dindyme, fio tuis.

43

Septima iam, Phileros, tibi conditur uxor in agro.
    plus nulli, Phileros, quam tibi reddit ager.

44

Quinte Caledonios Ovidi visure Britannos
    et viridem Tethyn Oceanumque patrem,

41

At the opening of Janus' month, Proculeia, you leave
your husband of long standing and serve him notice
of divorce. What, I ask, *what* has happened? What
is this sudden grievance? Don't you answer me?
Then I'll say it myself: he was praetor. The purple
at the Megalesia was going to cost a hundred
thousand, even if your show erred on the side of
economy, and the plebeian festival would have
carried off twenty thousand. This is not divorce,
Proculeia: it's moneymaking.

42

Your beard is so dubious, so soft that a breath, or
sunshine, or a light breeze wears it away. It is like
the down that hides ripening quinces, which shine
when plucked by a maiden's thumb. Whenever I
give you give rather vigorous kisses, Dindymus, I
get a beard from your lips.

43

You have buried wife number seven on your land,
Phileros. Nobody, Phileros, gets a better return
from his land than you.

44

Quintus Ovidius, you are going to visit the
Caledonian Britons and green Tethys and Father

ergo Numae colles et Nomentana relinquis
    otia nec retinet rusque focusque senem?
5 gaudia tu differs, at non et stamina differt
    Atropos atque omnis scribitur hora tibi.
praestiteris caro — quis non hoc laudet? — amico
    ut potior vita sit tibi sancta fides;
sed reddare tuis tandem mansure Sabinis
10   teque tuas numeres inter amicitias.

45

Si quid lene mei dicunt et dulce libelli,
    si quid honorificum pagina blanda sonat,
hoc tu pingue putas et costam rodere mavis,
    ilia Laurentis cum tibi demus apri.
5 Vaticana bibas, si delectaris aceto:
    non facit ad stomachum nostra lagona tuum.

46

Omnia vis belle, Matho, dicere. dic aliquando
    et bene; dic neutrum; dic aliquando male.

47

Vitam quae faciant beatiorem,
  iucundissime Martialis, haec sunt:
res non parta labore, sed relicta;
  non ingratus ager, focus perennis;

Ocean. So you are leaving Numa's hills and Nomentan leisure, and field and fireside do not hold you in your old age? You postpone your joys; but Atropos does not postpone her spinning and every hour is written down to your account. You will have shown for a dear friend's sake (who but would commend it?) that keeping your word means more to you than life. But do return to your Sabine villa at last to stay, and include yourself among your friendships.

45

If my little books say something smooth and agreeable, if a flattering page has a complimentary sound to it, you think this greasy fare and prefer to gnaw a rib when I give you loin of Laurentine boar. Drink Vatican if you like vinegar; my flagon doesn't suit your stomach.

46

Matho, you want everything you say to be smart. Say something good as well from time to time. Say something neither good nor bad. From time to time say something bad.

47

Most delightful Martialis, the elements of a happy life are as follows: money not worked for but inherited; land not unproductive; a fire all the year round;

5   lis numquam, toga rara, mens quieta;
     vires ingenuae, salubre corpus;
     prudens simplicitas, pares amici;
     convictus facilis, sine arte mensa;
     nox non ebria, sed soluta curis;
10 non tristis torus et tamen pudicus;
     somnus qui faciat breves tenebras:
     quod sis esse velis nihilque malis;
     summum nec metuas diem nec optes.

48

Nuntiat octavam Phariae sua turba iuvencae,
    et pilata redit iamque subitque cohors.
temperat haec thermas, nimios prior hora vapores
    halat, et immodico sexta Nerone calet.
Stella, Nepos, Cani, Cerialis, Flacce, venitis?
    septem sigma capit, sex sumus, adde Lupum.
exoneraturas ventrem mihi vilica malvas
    attulit et varias quas habet hortus opes,
in quibus est lactuca sedens et tonsile porrum,
10 nec deest ructatrix mentha nec herba salax;
secta coronabunt rutatos ova lacertos
    et madidum thynni de sale sumen erit.

48.2 redit iam subiitque *Paley*   3 nimios ... uapores
β : -o . . . -e γ

---

[a] Not over-developed like an athlete's or a laborer's; cf.
3.46.6; 6.11.6.

[b] Io, i.e. Isis, whose temple closed at this hour.

[c] Of the praetorian guard.

lawsuits never, a gown rarely worn, a mind at peace; a gentleman's strength,[a] a healthy body; guilelessness not naive, friends of like degree, easy company, a table without frills; a night not drunken but free of cares; a marriage bed not austere and yet modest; sleep to make the dark hours short; wish to be what you are, wish nothing better; don't fear your last day, nor yet pray for it.

48

Her votaries announce the eighth hour to the Pharian heifer[b] and the pike-carrying cohort[c] returns to camp as another comes on duty. This hour cools the warm baths, the one preceding pants out immoderate heat, the sixth glows with Nero's excess. Stella, Nepos, Canius, Cerialis, Flaccus, are you coming? The sigma[d] takes seven, we are six; add Lupus. The bailiff's wife has brought me mallows to relieve the stomach and the garden's various wealth. There is sessile lettuce and clipped leeks,[e] belching mint is not to seek, nor the salacious herb.[f] Slices of egg will top mackerel flavored with rue and there will be a sow's udder wet from tunny's brine.

[d] A dining couch in the shape of the Greek letter Ϲ.

[e] Leeks were of two kinds (cf. 3.47.8), *capitatum*, where the bulbs were allowed to grow on the top of the stalk, and *sectile, tonsile,* or *sectivum*, where the stalks were cut young: cf. 11.52.6.

[f] *Eruca*, rocket.

gustus in his; una ponetur cenula mensa:
    haedus inhumani raptus ab ore lupi,
15 et quae non egeant ferro structoris ofellae
    et faba fabrorum prototomique rudes;
pullus ad haec cenisque tribus iam perna superste
    addetur. saturis mitia poma dabo,
de Nomentana vinum sine faece lagona,
20   quae bis Frontino consule trima fuit.
accedent sine felle ioci nec mane timenda
    libertas et nil quod tacuisse velis:
de prasino conviva meus Scorpoque loquatur,
    nec faciant quemquam pocula nostra reum.

49

Cum potes amethystinos trientes
et nigro madeas Opimiano,
propinas modo conditum Sabinum
et dicis mihi, Cotta, 'vis in auro?'
5   quisquam plumbea vina vult in auro?

50

Frangat Idumaeas tristis Victoria palmas,
    plange, Favor, saeva pectora nuda manu;

48.20 trima *Heinsius* : pr- T$\beta\gamma$ 23 conviva meus
Scorpoque *SB*[3], *praeeunte Gruter* (S- m- c-) : scutoque m- c-
β : c- m- scipioque γ : c- m- uenetoque T   24 faciant
ed. Rom. : -iunt Tγ : -ient β

---

[a] Cf. 3.47.11n.

[b] See Housman 728f. Frontinus became consul for the

So much for the hors d'oeuvres. The little dinner will be served in one course; a kid, snatched from the jaws of a savage wolf,[a] morsels requiring no carver's knife, workmen's beans and early greens. To these will accrue a chicken and a ham that has already survived three dinners. When my guests are satisfied, I shall offer ripe fruit and leesless wine from a Nomentan flagon twice three years old in Frontinus' consulship.[b] To boot there will be merriment free of malice, frank speech that gives no anxiety the morning after, nothing you would wish you hadn't said. Let my guest talk of Scorpus[c] and the Green; let my cups get no man put on trial.

49

Though you drink amethystine bumpers and get tipsy with black Opimian, you pledge me in Sabine[d] recently laid down and say to me, Cotta, "Would you like it in gold?" Who wants leaden[e] wines in gold?

50

Let sad Victory break the palms of Idumaea.[f] Favor,

second time in 98, but there is no good evidence for *bis* = *iterum* in the classical period.

[c] The charioteer, who doubtless belonged to the Green faction.

[d] A cheap wine: cf. Hor. *Od.* 1.20.1. For the famous Opimian vintage cf. 1.26.7n.

[e] I.e. bad.

[f] Idume, south of Judaea, was celebrated for its palms.

mutet Honor cultus, et iniquis munera flammis
    mitte coronatas, Gloria maesta, comas.
5 heu facinus! prima fraudatus, Scorpe, iuventa
    occidis et nigros tam cito iungis equos.
curribus illa tuis semper properata brevisque
    cur fuit et vitae tam prope meta tuae?

51

Sidera iam Tyrius Phrixei respicit agni
    taurus et alternum Castora fugit hiems;
ridet ager, vestitur humus, vestitur et arbor,
    Ismarium paelex Attica plorat Ityn.
5 quos, Faustine, dies, quales tibi Roma †Ravennam
    abstulit! o soles, o tunicata quies!
o nemus, o fontes solidumque madentis harenae
    litus et aequoreis splendidus Anxur aquis,
et non unius spectator lectulus undae,
10   qui videt hinc puppes fluminis, inde maris!
sed nec Marcelli Pompeianumque nec illic
    sunt triplices thermae nec fora iuncta quater

51.5 quales *unus ex familia* γ : -e sit γ : -em β   raven-
nam β : -nnae γ : recessus *ed. Rom.*

---

[a] Taking *curribus* as ablative and *vitae* as genitive (not
datives). M. means, but does not quite say, "why was your
life's goal (like your chariot's) reached so quickly?"

[b] The Sun is in Gemini, having passed through Aries
and Taurus. May has begun. "Lamb" stands loosely for
the ram with the golden fleece. Was M. thinking of the gol-
den lamb of Mycenae (Apollod. *Epit.* 2.10)?

beat your bare breast with merciless hand. Let
Honor put on mourning. Grieving Glory, cast your
crowned tresses on the unkind flames. Ah villainy!
Scorpus, cheated of your first youth, you die. So
soon you yoke black horses. The goal, ever quickly
gained by your hastening car—your life's goal too,[a]
why was it so close?

51

Now the Tyrian bull looks back at the stars of Phri-
xus' lamb[b] and winter has fled alternate Castor.[c]
The land is smiling, the soil is clothed and clothed
the tree, the Attic adulteress mourns Ismarian
Itys.[d] Faustinus, what days, what[e] * has Rome
taken from you! Ah suns, ah tunic-clad repose! Ah
wood and fountains and the firm shore of moist sand
and Anxur gleaming in her sea waters[f] and the
couch that gazes on double wave, seeing on one side
river[g] craft, on the other marine! But no theater of
Marcellus or Pompey is there, nor the triple baths,
nor the four connecting forums, nor the topmost
sanctuary of the Capitoline Thunderer and the shin-

[c] I.e. Castor or his brother, who took turns to be in
heaven.

[d] Philomela (the nightingale) laments Itys, whom her
sister Procne (the swallow) slew.

[e] Some take "Ravenna" as the name of Faustinus' villa,
but we do not hear of many such names.

[f] Cf. 5.1.6n. M. seems to be thinking of the reflection in
the water.

[g] Actually a canal; see Friedländer's note.

nec Capitolini summum pentrale Tonantis
  quaeque nitent caelo proxima templa suo.
15 dicere te lassum quotiens ego credo Quirino:
  'quae tua sunt, tibi habe: quae mea, redde mihi'

52

Thelyn viderat in toga spadonem.
damnatam Numa dixit esse moecham.

53

Ille ego sum Scorpus, clamosi gloria Circi,
  plausus, Roma, tui deliciaeque breves,
invida quem Lachesis raptum trieteride nona,
  dum numerat palmas, credidit esse senem.

54

Mensas, Ole, bonas ponis, sed ponis opertas,
  ridiculum est: possum sic ego habere bonas.

ing temple close to its own sky.[a] How often I believe
you say in your weariness to Quirinus:[b] "Keep what
is yours; give me back what is mine."

52

Numa saw Thelys the eunuch in a gown and said he
was a convicted adulteress.[c]

53

I am Scorpus, the glory of the clamorous circus, your
applause, Rome, and brief darling. Envious Lache-
sis snatched me away ere my thirtieth year,[d] but,
counting my victories, believed me an old man.

54

You set out good tables, Olus, but set them out
covered. It's absurd. At that rate, *I* can own good
tables.

[a] The temple of the *Gens Flavia*: cf. 9.1.8.

[b] I.e. to Rome. Perhaps Faustinus' house in Rome was
close to the temple of Quirinus, as was M.'s (10.58.10).

[c] Women convicted of adultery had to wear the toga,
like prostitutes; cf. 2.39.2. It may be inferred that
"Numa's" wife had been corrupted by "Thelys" ("Female");
cf. 6.2.6. The eunuch then was an adulterer (*moechus*) but
with his womanish name and appearance he seemed in his
toga like a convicted adulteress. So *SB*[1].

[d] Lit. "in my ninth three-year period."

55

Arrectum quotiens Marulla penem
pensavit digitis diuque mensa est,
libras, scripula sextulasque dicit;
idem post opus et suas palaestras
5 loro cum similis iacet remisso,
quanto sit levior Marulla dicit.
non ergo est manus ista, sed statera.

56

Totis, Galle, iubes tibi me servire diebus
et per Aventinum ter quater ire tuum.
eximit aut reficit dentem Cascellius aegrum,
infestos oculis uris, Hygine, pilos;
5 non secat et tollit stillantem Fannius uvam,
tristia †saxorum† stigmata delet Eros;
enterocelarum fertur Podalirius Hermes:
qui sanet ruptos dic mihi, Galle, quis est?

57

Argenti libram mittebas; facta selibra est,
sed piperis. tanti non emo, Sexte, piper.

56.2 lutum *Heinsius*   6 saxorum β : -onum γ : ser
vorum *Scriverius* : noxarum *Heinsius*

55

When Marulla has weighed an erect penis with her fingers and estimated it at length, she gives the weight in pounds, scruples, and sextules.[a] When the work is done and the same lies like a limp thong after its wrestlings, Marulla tells you how much lighter it has become. That hand of hers isn't a hand, it's a balance.

56

You tell me to be at your service all day, Gallus, and traverse your Aventine three times or four. Cascellius extracts or restores an ailing tooth; you, Hyginus, burn off hairs that trouble the eyes; Fannius doesn't cut but removes a dripping uvula;[b] Eros effaces the repulsive brands of slaves;[c] Hermes is said to be the Podalirius of hernias; tell, me, Gallus, who is it that heals the broken-winded?[d]

57

You used to send a pound of silver plate; it has become half pound, but of pepper. I don't pay that much for pepper, Sextus.

[a] The *scripulum* or *scrupulum* was 1/24 of an ounce (*uncia*), the *sextula* 1/6 of an ounce.

[b] How he would do that without cutting is not clear; hence Alan Ker's proposal *insecat* or *consecat* ("cuts").

[c] Inflicted as a punishment. I translate *servorum*.

[d] Lit. simply "broken"; cf. 12.14.12.

58

Anxuris aequorei placidos, Frontine, recessus
    et propius Baias litoreamque domum,
et quod inhumanae cancro fervente cicadae
    non novere nemus, flumineosque lacus
5 dum colui, doctas tecum celebrare vacabat
    Pieridas; nunc nos maxima Roma terit.
hic mihi quando dies meus est? iactamur in alto
    urbis, et in sterili vita labore perit,
dura suburbani dum iugera pascimus agri
10   vicinosque tibi, sancte Quirine, lares.
sed non solus amat qui nocte dieque frequentat
    limina nec vatem talia damna decent.
per veneranda mihi Musarum sacra, per omnes
    iuro deos: et non officiosus amo.

59

Consumpta est uno si lemmate pagina, transis,
    et breviora tibi, non meliora placent.
dives et ex omni posita est instructa macello
    cena tibi, sed te mattea sola iuvat.
5 non opus est nobis nimium lectore guloso;
    hunc volo, non fiat qui sine pane satur.

---

[a] For *Baias* see 10.14.3n.

[b] *Propius* ("from closer at hand," i.e. closer to Rome
than the real Baiae) belongs grammatically with *colui* in
v. 5.

58

When I dwelt in the calm retreat of Anxur by the sea
and a Baian villa[a] closer to Rome,[b] Faustinus, a
town house on the beach[c] and a wood unknown to
cruel crickets when Cancer blazes, and a river-like
pond, there was time to cultivate with you the poetic
Pierides. Now mightiest Rome wears us out. When
do I have a day to call my own here? I am tossed in
the city's ocean and life goes to waste in fruitless
toil, as I support[d] some acres of suburban land and a
dwelling neighboring yours, holy Quirinus. But he
is not the only loving friend who haunts a threshold
day and night, and such loss of time does not befit a
poet. By the holy things of the Muses that I must
venerate, by all the gods I swear: undutiful as I am,
I love you.

59

If a page is used up with a single title, you pass it by;
you like the shorter items, not the better ones. A
sumptuous dinner furnished from every market is
served you, but you care only for a tidbit. I don't
want a reader with too fine a palate; give me the
man who doesn't feel full without bread.

[c] Meaning either that the villa had the amenities of a
town house (cf. 3.58.51) or that the house was in Anxur
itself.

[d] Lit. "feed"; cf. 10.96.7. The property cost more than it
brought in.

60

Iura trium petiit a Caesare discipulorum
    assuetus semper Munna docere duos.

61

Hic festinata requiescit Erotion umbra,
    crimine quam fati sexta peremit hiems.
quisquis eris nostri post me regnator agelli,
    Manibus exiguis annua iusta dato:
5   sic lare perpetuo, sic turba sospite solus
    flebilis in terra sit lapis iste tua.

62

Ludi magister, parce simplici turbae:
sic te frequentes audiant capillati
et delicatae diligat chorus mensae,
nec calculator nec notarius velox
5   maiore quisquam circulo coronetur.
albae leone flammeo calent luces
tostamque fervens Iulius coquit messem.
cirrata loris horridis Scythae pellis,
qua vapulavit Marsyas Celaenaeus,
10 ferulaeque tristes, sceptra paedagogorum,
cessent et Idus dormiant in Octobres:
aestate pueri si valent, satis discunt.

BOOK X

60

Munna asked Caesar for the Right of Three Pupils, having always been used to teaching two.[a]

61

Here rests Erotion's hastened shade,[b] whom by crime of Fate her sixth winter slew. Make annual offering to her tiny ghost, whoever after me shall be ruler of my plot of land. So may your home continue and your household live on and this stone be the only thing on your property to call for tears.

62

Schoolmaster, spare your innocent flock; so may long-haired boys crowd to hear you and the dainty band around your table hold you in affection, nor any teacher of arithmetic or rapid master of shorthand be surrounded by a larger circle. The bright days glow beneath the flaming Lion and blazing July ripens the roasted harvest. Idle be the Scythian's leather, fringed with horrid lashes, with which Marsyas of Celaenae was scourged, and the sinister rods, scepters of pedagogues; let them sleep till October's Ides. If boys keep well in summertime, they learn enough.

[a] M. parodies the *ius trium liberorum*; cf. 2.91.6; 9.97.6.
[b] Cf. 5.34 and 37.

63

Marmora parva quidem sed non cessura, viator,
    Mausoli saxis pyramidumque legis.
bis mea Romano spectata est vita Tarento
    et nihil extremos perdidit ante rogos:
5 quinque dedit pueros, totidem mihi Iuno puellas,
    cluserunt omnes lumina nostra manus.
contigit et thalami mihi gloria rara fuitque
    una pudicitae mentula nota meae.

64

Contigeris, regina, meos si, Polla, libellos,
    non tetrica nostros excipe fronte iocos.
ille tuus vates, Heliconis gloria nostri,
    Pieria caneret cum fera bella tuba,
5 non tamen erubuit lascivo dicere versu
    'si nec pedicor, Cotta, quid hic facio?'

65

Cum te municipem Corinthiorum
iactes, Charmenion, negante nullo,

---

[a] Cf. 4.1n. Ladies of high rank were chosen to take part
and naturally they would have to be of unblemished char-
acter.
[b] In the conventionally decorous context the word is
explosive.

63

The marble you are reading, traveller, is small indeed, but will not yield to the stones of Mausolus and the pyramids. My life was twice approved at Roman Tarentos[a] and lost nothing down to my dying day. Juno gave me five boys and as many girls; their hands all closed my eyes. Rare glory of wedlock was my lot, and my chastity knew but one cock.[b]

64

Queen Polla, if you handle my little books, receive my jests with unfrowning brow. When your noble bard,[c] the glory of our Helicon, blew fierce warfare on Pierian trumpet, yet he did not blush to say in wanton verse: "If I'm not even sodomized, Cotta, what am I doing here?"

65

Since you boast yourself a fellow townsman[d] of Corinthian bronzes[e] with none to gainsay you,

[c] Lucan (cf. 7.21), whose only surviving work is his epic on the civil war between Caesar and Pompey, sometimes still miscalled the "Pharsalia." The quotation looks as though it came from a collection of epigrams.

[d] Cf. 10.87.10; 14.114.2.

[e] Not "of the Corinthians." *Corinthiorum* (sc. *aerum*) is neuter, as in 9.57.2.

cur frater tibi dicor, ex Hiberis
et Celtis genitus Tagique civis?
5   an vultu similes videmur esse?
tu flexa nitidus coma vagaris,
Hispanis ego contumax capillis;
levis dropace tu cotidiano,
hirsutis ego cruribus genisque;
10   os blaesum tibi debilisque lingua est,
nobis †filia† fortius loquetur:
tam dispar aquilae columba non est
nec dorcas rigido fugax leoni.
quare desine me vocare fratrem,
15   ne te, Charmenion, vocem sororem.

66

Quis, rogo, tam durus, quis tam fuit ille superbus
    qui iussit fieri te, Theopompe, cocum?
hanc aliquis faciem nigra violare culina
    sustinet, has uncto polluit igne comas?
5   quis potius cyathos aut quis crystalla tenebit?
    qua sapient melius mixta Falerna manu?
si tam sidereos manet exitus iste ministros,
    Iuppiter utatur iam Ganymede coco.

67

Pyrrhae filia, Nestoris noverca,
quam vidit Niobe puella canam,
Laertes aviam senex vocavit,
nutricem Priamus, socrum Thyestes,

65.11 Silia *vel* Pilia *SB*^{3} : fi- β (55–72 *om.* γ)

Charmenion, why do you call me "brother," born as I am of Iberians and Celts, a countryman of Tagus? Is it that we look alike? You go around looking smart with your hair in curls, mine is stubborn and Spanish. You are smooth with daily depilatory, my shins and cheeks are hairy. Your mouth lisps and your tongue is feeble; only Silia(?)[a] will speak bolder than I. A dove is not so different from an eagle or a fugitive doe from a stark lion. So stop calling me "brother," Charmenion, in case I call you "sister."

66

Who was so unfeeling, I ask, who was so arrogant as to bid you, Theopompus, become a cook? Does any man have the heart to defile this face with a sooty kitchen or pollute these locks with a greasy flame? Who will more fitly hold the ladles and the crystal cups? By what hand mixed will Falernian taste better? If this is the end that awaits such star-like pages, let Jupiter in future employ Ganymede as a cook.

67

Daughter of Pyrrha, stepdaughter of Nestor, she was grey when Niobe saw her as a girl, old Laertes called her grandmother, Priam nurse, Thyestes

---

[a] Or Pilia; at all events a lady with a loud voice. Cf. *SB*[3] (but see now on 14.143), and 9.29.5–8.

5   iam cornicibus omnibus superstes,
     hoc tandem sita prurit in sepulchro
     calvo Plutia cum Melanthione.

68

Cum tibi non Ephesos nec sit Rhodos aut Mitylene,
      sed domus in vico, Laelia, Patricio,
deque coloratis numquam lita mater Etruscis,
      durus Aricina de regione pater;
5   κύριέ μου, μέλι μου, ψυχή μου congeris usque,
      pro pudor! Hersiliae civis et Egeriae.
lectulus has voces, nec lectulus audiat omnis,
      sed quem lascivo stravit amica viro.
scire cupis quo casta modo matrona loquaris?
10   numquid, quae crisat, blandior esse potest?
tu licet ediscas totam referasque Corinthon,
      non tamen omnino, Laelia, Lais eris.

69

Custodes das, Polla, viro, non accipis ipsa.
      hoc est uxorem ducere, Polla, virum.

67.7 plutia β : Plotia ς   68.10 quae crisat … potest
SB¹ : cum crisas … potes β

ᵃ Crows were said to outlive nine (Hes. *apud* Plut. *De Def. Or.* 11) or at least five (Arist. *Av.* 609) generations of men.
ᵇ Under the Esquiline in the middle of Rome; cf. 7.73.2.
ᶜ "Laelia" talked like a Greek prostitute, but she was still a Roman lady (cf. *SB¹*).

mother-in-law: Plutia, having outlived all crows,[a] was laid at last in this tomb and itches with lust alongside bald Melanthio.

68

Although your home is not Ephesus or Rhodes or Mitylene but in Patrician Row,[b] Laelia, and although your mother, who used no make-up, was a daughter of the sunburnt Etruscans and your dour father came from the district of Aricia, you are always piling on the Greek—"my lord, my honey, my soul"—shame on you, a countrywoman of Hersilia and Egeria! Let the bed hear such expressions, and not every bed at that, but one made for a gamesome gentleman by his lady-friend. Do you wish to know how you talk, you, a respectable married woman? Could a waggle-bottom be more blandishing? You may learn all Corinth by heart and reproduce it, but, Laelia, you will not be altogether Lais.[c]

69

You set men to watch your husband,[d] Polla, but you don't accept them yourself. This, Polla, is taking your husband to wife.[e]

[d] Husbands often set watchers over their wives: cf. Tac. *Ann.* 11.35 with Furneaux's note.
[e] A bridegroom is said *ducere uxorem* as a bride is said *nubere viro* (cf. 8.12).

70

Quod mihi vix unus toto liber exeat anno,
  desidiae tibi sum, docte Potite, reus.
iustius at quanto mirere quod exeat unus,
  labantur toti cum mihi saepe dies.
5 non resalutantis video nocturnus amicos,
  gratulor et multis; nemo, Potite, mihi.
nunc ad luciferam signat mea gemma Dianam,
  nunc me prima sibi, nunc sibi quinta rapit.
nunc consul praetorve tenet reducesque choreae,
10 auditur toto saepe poeta die.
sed nec causidico possis impune negare,
  nec si te rhetor grammaticusve rogent:
balnea post decimam lasso centumque petuntur
  quadrantes. fiet quando, Potite, liber?

71

Quisquis laeta tuis et sera parentibus optas
  fata, brevem titulum marmoris huius ama.
condidit hac caras tellure Rabirius umbras;
  nulli sorte iacent candidiore senes:
5 bis sex lustra tori nox mitis et ultima clusit,
  arserunt uno funera bina rogo.
hos tamen ut primis raptos sibi quaerit in annis.
  improbius nihil his fletibus esse potest.

70.12 roget *duo ex familia* β

ᵃ On the Aventine (cf. 6.64.13), far from M.'s house or
the Quirinal.

70

Because hardly one book of mine comes out in a whole year, you accuse me, lettered Potitus, of laziness. How much more justly you might wonder that *one* comes out, when whole days often slip away from me. Before dawn I see friends who don't return my greetings and I offer congratulations to many; nobody offers any to me, Potitus. Now my signet ring seals a document at the temple of Diana the Light-bringer,[a] now the first hour snatches me for itself, now the fifth. Now a consul or a praetor and the bands that escort him home have hold of me, often I listen all day to a poet. Nor can one say no to a barrister with impunity, nor to a rhetor or a grammarian, if they should ask. After the tenth hour I wearily seek the baths and the hundred farthings.[b] Pollio, when will a book get done?

71

Whoever you are that wish for your parents a happy end and a late, look kindly on this stone's brief legend. In this ground Rabirius buried his dear shades. No old folk in their graves have a fairer lot. A gentle night, their last, closed twelve lusters of wedlock; the two bodies burned on one pyre. And yet he feels their loss as though they had been taken from him in his earliest years. Nothing can be more unconscionable than these tears.

[b] Cf. 3.7.3, where the dole seems to be distributed *before* the bath.

72

Frustra, Blanditiae, venitis ad me
attritis miserabiles labellis:
dicturus dominum deumque non sum.
iam non est locus hac in urbe vobis;
5   ad Parthos procul ite pilleatos
et turpes humilesque supplicesque
pictorum sola basiate regum.
non est hic dominus, sed imperator,
sed iustissimus omnium senator,
10   per quem de Stygia domo reducta est
siccis rustica Veritas capillis.
hoc sub principe, si sapis, caveto
verbis, Roma, prioribus loquaris.

73

Littera facundi gratum mihi pignus amici
    pertulit, Ausoniae dona, Severe, togae,
qua non Fabricius, sed vellet Apicius uti,
    vellet Maecenas, Caesarianus eques.

73.1 pignus β : munus γ 2 Severe ς : seuera β : sera
γ : superba *Heinsius*

---

^a Cf. 5.8.1n; 8.2.6.
^b The Roman *pilleus* was a conical felt cap.
^c Not perfumed.
^d Trajan.

BOOK X

72

Flatteries, you come to me in vain, you poor creatures with your shameless lips. I am not about to speak of "Lord and God."[a] There is no place for you any more in this city. Go far away to turbaned[b] Parthians and kiss the soles of gaudy monarchs—base, abject suppliants. There is no lord here, but a commander-in-chief and the most just of all senators, through whom rustic, dry-haired[c] Truth has been brought back from the house of Styx. Under this ruler,[d] Rome, beware, if you are wise, of talking the language of earlier days.

73

Severus,[e] the letter of an eloquent friend has brought me a welcome pledge, the gift of an Ausonian gown, one which not Fabricius but Apicius would have wished to wear, or Maecenas, Caesar's[f]

---

[e] *Severa* would be a peculiarly unsuitable epithet for a toga which voluptuaries like Maecenas and Apicius would have liked to wear. Severus is the literary friend and critic of 5.80 and 11.57; note *facundi* in v. 1 and *docti* in v. 10. The donor of the gown has generally been identified with M. Antonius Primus, but nothing proves it; the three epigrams about him (9.99; 10.23; 10.32) say nothing of literary accomplishment, though the first makes him an admirer of M.'s verse.

[f] Not that Caesar (Augustus) made him a knight, but because of his faithful service. M. probably had Horace's *care* (or *clare*) *Maecenas eques* (*Od.* 1.20.5) in mind.

5 vilior haec nobis alio mittente fuisset;
     non quacumque manu victima caesa litat:
  a te missa venit: possem nisi munus amare,
     Marce, tuum, poteram nomen amare meum.
  munere sed plus est et nomine gratius ipso
10   officium docti iudiciumque viri.

74

  Iam parce lasso, Roma, gratulatori,
  lasso clienti. quam diu salutator
  anteambulones et togatulos inter
  centum merebor plumbeos die toto,
5 cum Scorpus una quindecim graves hora
  ferventis auri victor auferat saccos?
  non ego meorum praemium libellorum
  — quid enim merentur? — Apulos velim campos;
  non Hybla, non me spicifer capit Nilus,
10 nec quae paludes delicata Pomptinas
  ex arce clivi spectat uva Setini.
  quid concupiscam quaeris ergo? dormire.

75

  Milia viginti quondam me Galla poposcit
     et, fateor, magno non erat illa nimis.
  annus abît: 'bis quina dabis sestertia', dixit.
     poscere plus visa est quam prius illa mihi.

knight. I should have valued it less if another had
sent it. Not slaughtered by every hand does the
sacrifice find acceptance. It comes from you. If I
could not love your gift, Marcus, I could still love my
name.[a] But more welcome than the gift or even the
name is the attention and good opinion of a man of
letters.

74

Spare at length the weary congratulator, Rome, the
weary client. How long shall I be a caller, earning a
hundred coppers in a whole day, among escorts and
petty clients, when Scorpus in a single hour carries
off as winner fifteen heavy bags of gold hot from the
mint? I would not want the plains of Apulia[b] as a
reward for my little books—what do they deserve,
after all? Hybla does not attract me, nor corn-
bearing Nile, nor the dainty grape that surveys the
Pomptine marshes from the top of Setia's slope. Do
you ask what I crave then? Sleep.[c]

75

Once upon a time Galla asked me for twenty
thousand, and I confess she was not overpriced. A
year went by: "You will give ten thousand," she said.
I felt she was asking more than before. Six months

---

[a] The letter may have been headed *Marcus* (or *M.
Severus*) *Marco suo sal.*, a very intimate style (cf. *SB*[1]).

[b] Celebrated for wool; cf. 2.46.6; 8.28.3.

[c] Not to have to rise early; cf. 12.18.13–16.

5   iam duo poscenti post sextum milia mensem
      mille dabam nummos. noluit accipere.
   transierant binae forsan trinaeve Kalendae,
      aureolos ultro quattuor ipsa petît.
   non dedimus. centum iussit me mittere nummos;
10   sed visa est nobis haec quoque summa gravis.
   sportula nos iunxit quadrantibus arida centum;
      hanc voluit: puero diximus esse datam.
   inferius numquid potuit descendere? fecit.
      dat gratis, ultro dat mihi Galla: nego.

76

   Hoc, Fortuna, tibi videtur aequum?
   civis non Syriaeve Parthiaeve,
   nec de Cappadocis eques catastis,
   sed de plebe Remi Numaeque verna,
5   iucundus, probus, innocens amicus,
   lingua doctus utraque, cuius unum est,
   sed magnum vitium, quod est poeta,
   pullo Mevius alget in cucullo,
   cocco mulio fulget Incitatus.

77

Nequius a Caro nihil umquam, Maxime, factum est
   quam quod febre perît: fecit et illa nefas.

---

  [a] 400 sesterces. The *aureolus* was a gold coin worth 25
denarii.
  [b] See SB^1, and for the two meanings of *dat* cf. 7.75.2.

later she asked two thousand sesterces. I offered a
thousand, which she wouldn't accept. Two Kalends
perhaps or three passed, and without waiting for me
herself requested four gold pieces.[a] I didn't give
them. She told me to send a hundred sesterces, but
even this sum seemed to me excessive. A stingy dole
linked me to a hundred farthings. This she wanted;
I said I had given it to my boy. Could she come
down any lower? She did. Galla offers herself for
nothing, she offers *me* money.[b] I decline.

76

Fortune, does this seem fair to you? Mevius, a
citizen, not of Syria or Parthia nor a knight from
Cappadocian platforms,[c] but home-bred, one of
Remus' and Numa's commons, an agreeable, honest,
blameless friend, proficient in both tongues, whose
only fault (a great fault, it's true) is that he is a poet,
shivers in a black cowl; Incitatus the muleteer
blazes in scarlet.

77

Nothing naughtier, Maximus, was ever done by
Carus than his dying of a fever.[d] The fever too did a

[c] I.e. originally a Cappadocian slave; cf. Juv. 7.15; Pliny
N.H. 35.200f.
[d] He deserved worse.

saeva nocens febris, saltem quartana fuisses!
  servari medico debuit ille suo.

78

Ibis litoreas, Macer, Salonas.
ibit rara fides amorque recti
et quae, cum comitem trahit pudorem,
semper pauperior redit potestas.
5　felix auriferae colone terrae,
rectorem vacuo sinu remittes
optabisque moras, et exeuntem
udo Dalmata gaudio sequeris.
nos Celtas, Macer, et truces Hiberos
10　cum desiderio tui petemus.
sed quaecumque tamen feretur illinc
piscosi calamo Tagi notata,
Macrum pagina nostra nominabit;
sic inter veteres legar poetas,
15　nec multos mihi praeferas priores,
uno sed tibi sim minor Catullo.

79

Ad lapidem Torquatus habet praetoria quartum;
  ad quartum breve rus emit Otacilius.
Torquatus nitidas vario de marmore thermas
  extruxit; cucumam fecit Otacilius.

77.3 fuisses β : -sset γ

very bad thing. Cruel, noxious fever, you might at least have been quartan;[a] he ought to have been kept alive for his doctor.[b]

78

Macer, you will go to Salonae[c] by the sea. With you will go rare good faith and love of right, and power, which, when it takes honor for its companion, always comes home the poorer. Happy Dalmatian, farmer of gold-bearing soil, you will send back your governor with empty pockets and pray for delays and escort him with tearful joy. As for me, Macer, I shall make for the Celts and fierce Iberians, missing you sorely. But whatever page of mine, indited by a reed of fishy Tagus, shall thence be conveyed, it shall bear Macer's name. So may I be read among the poets of old, and you not prefer many of my forerunners to me, but rank me below Catullus only.

79

Torquatus has a palace at the fourth milestone: Otacilius bought a small farm at the fourth. Torquatus constructed splendid warm baths of varied marble:

[a] And so not fatal.
[b] Who would have given him a slow, painful death.
[c] The chief town of Dalmatia, where Macer was going as governor. He had been (cf. 10.18) curator of the Appian Way.

5 disposuit daphnona suo Torquatus in agro;
      castaneas centum sevit Otacilius.
  consule Torquato vici fuit ille magister,
      non minor in tanto visus honore sibi.
  grandis ut exiguam bos ranam ruperat olim,
10   sic, puto, Torquatus rumpet Otacilium.

80

Plorat Eros, quotiens maculosae pocula murrae
      inspicit aut pueros nobiliusve citrum,
et gemitus imo ducit de pectore quod non
      tota miser coemat Saepta feratque domum.
5 quam multi faciunt quod Eros, sed lumine sicco!
      pars maior lacrimas ridet et intus habet.

81

Cum duo venissent ad Phyllida mane fututum
      et nudam cuperet sumere uterque prior,
promisit pariter se Phyllis utrique daturam,
      et dedit: ille pedem sustulit, hic tunicam.

Otacilius made a cooking pot. Torquatus laid out a laurel grove on his land; Otacilius planted a hundred chestnuts. When Torquatus was consul, Otacilius was wardmaster,[a] in which high office he felt himself not inferior. As once the bulky ox ruptured the tiny frog, so, methinks, Torquatus will rupture Otacilius.

80

Eros weeps whenever he inspects cups of speckled murrine or boys or a particularly fine citrus tabletop, and groans from the bottom of his chest because he cannot buy the whole Enclosure and carry it home, poor fellow. How many there are who do as Eros does, but do it dry-eyed! Most people laugh at his tears and weep internally.[b]

81

When two had come to Phyllis of a morning to fornicate and each was hoping to take her naked first, Phyllis promised to give to both at once, and kept her word: one lifted her feet, the other her tunic.[c]

[a] Augustus divided Rome into regions and wards (Suet. *Aug.* 30.1), each of the latter being put under four elected *vici magistri*.

[b] See *SB*[3].

[c] Cf. 11.71.8, also Cic. *Att.* 2.1.5 and Ov. *A.A.* 3.775 (*SB*[1]). See Appendix A.

82

Si quid nostra tuis adicit vexatio rebus,
    mane vel a media nocte togatus ero
stridentesque feram flatus Aquilonis iniqui
    et patiar nimbos excipiamque nives.
5   sed si non fias quadrante beatior uno
    per gemitus nostros ingenuasque cruces,
parce, precor, fesso vanosque remitte labores,
    qui tibi non prosunt et mihi, Galle, nocent.

83

Raros colligis hinc et hinc capillos
    et latum nitidae, Marine, calvae
campum temporibus tegis comatis;
    sed moti redeunt iubente vento
5   redunturque sibi caputque nudum
    cirris grandibus hinc et inde cingunt:
inter Spendophorum Telesphorumque
    Cydae stare putabis Hermerotem.
vis tu simplicius senem fateri,
10 ut tandem videaris unus esse?
    calvo turpius est nihil comato.

84

Miraris, quare dormitum non eat Afer?
    accumbat cum qua, Caediciane, vides.

---

[a] The punishment of slaves.
[b] Cf. 9.56; 11.26. On Hermeros see Appendix B.

82

If my hardship is of any benefit to your affairs, I will wear my gown at dawn or from midnight on and bear the howling blasts of cruel Aquila, enduring the rainstorms and receiving the snow. But if you do not get a farthing richer for my groans and crucifixions[a] (and me a free man!), spare my weariness, I beg, and remit useless ordeals, which do no good to you, Gallus, and harm to me.

83

Marinus, you collect your scattered locks from this side and from that, and cover the broad expanse of your shining baldness with hair from your temples. But at the wind's bidding they move and return and are restored to themselves, to surround your bare top with big curls on either side. You would think that Cydas' Hermeros was standing between Spendophorus and Telesphorus.[b] Why not be straightforward and admit to being an old man, so that at last you look like *one* man? Nothing is uglier than a baldhead with a lot of hair.

84

Do you wonder why Afer doesn't go to bed? You see the lady placed next to him, Caedicianus.[c]

[c] To be read two ways: (a) the woman is attractive and he doesn't want to leave. (b) The woman (his wife?) is unattractive and would insist on going to bed with him.

85

Iam senior Ladon Tiberinae nauta carinae
    proxima dilectis rura paravit aquis.
quae cum saepe vagus premeret torrentibus undis
    Thybris et hiberno rumperet arva lacu,
5   emeritam puppem, ripa quae stabat in alta,
    implevit saxis opposuitque vadis.
sic nimias avertit aquas. quis credere posset?
    auxilium domino mersa carina tulit.

86

Nemo nova caluit sic inflammatus amica
    flagravit quanto Laurus amore pilae.
sed qui primus erat lusor dum floruit aetas,
    nunc postquam desît ludere, prima pila est.

87

Octobres age sentiat Kalendas
facundi pia Roma Restituti:
linguis omnibus et favete votis;

85

When Ladon, who was master of a boat on the Tiber, grew old, he bought a country property close to the river he loved. But Tiber often overflowed and covered it with his rushing waters, breaking up the fields with a winter lake. So Ladon filled his boat, which stood in retirement on the high bank, with stones and opposed it to the waters. Thus he turned the flood aside. Who could have believed it? A sunken boat came to its owner's rescue.

86

Nobody was ever so aflame with passion for a new mistress as Laurus was fired with love for the ball. While youth lasted, he was first player; but now that he has stopped playing, he is first ball.[a]

87

Come, let Rome in duty notice the October Kalends[b] of eloquent Restitutus.[c] Honor the occasion with all

[a] I.e. broken and decrepit. There is an untranslatable play on two meanings of *pila*, "ball" and "dummy (as thrown to a bull)." The "first dummy," i.e. the first to be thrown to the bull (cf. 2.43.6), would naturally take the most punishment.
[b] Cf. 8.64.4n.
[c] No doubt Claudius Restitutus, an able advocate mentioned by Pliny (*Epist.* 3.9.16).

natalem colimus, tacete lites.
5   absit cereus aridi clientis,
et vani triplices brevesque mappae
expectent gelidi iocos Decembris.
certent muneribus beatiores:
Agrippae tumidus negotiator
10 Cadmi municipes ferat lacernas;
pugnorum reus ebriaeque noctis
cenatoria mittat advocato;
infamata virum puella vicit,
veros sardonychas, sed ipsa tradat;
15 mirator veterum senex avorum
donet Phidiaci toreuma caeli;
venator leporem, colonus haedum,
piscator ferat aequorum rapinas.
si mittit sua quisque, quid poetam
20 missurum tibi, Restitute, credis?

88

Omnes persequeris praetorum, Cotta, libellos;
  accipis et ceras. officiosus homo es.

---

^a Repeated from 7.72.2.

^b I.e. Tyrian.

^c I.e. the collector of antiques. *Laborum* (Gronovius for
avorum), "works of art," may well be right, but cf. 7.72.4.
Veteres . . . avos occurs in 3.63.12.

your tongues and vows. We are celebrating a birth-
day; lawsuits, be silent. No shrivelled client's wax
taper, if you please; let idle three-leaved tablets and
exiguous napkins[a] await the jollities of chill
December. Let the richer sort vie with their gifts.
Let Agrippa's puffed-up tradesman bring cloaks, fel-
low townspeople of Cadmus.[b] Let one arraigned for
fisticuffs and a drunken night send dinner suits to
his advocate. Has a defamed young woman won her
case against her husband? Let her hand over
genuine sardonyxes, and in person too. Let the aged
admirer of our antique forefathers[c] present
embossed work of Phidias' chisel. Let the hunter
bring a hare, the farmer a kid, the fisherman the
plunder of the seas. If each one sends his special
gifts, what do you think a poet will send you, Resti-
tutus?

88

You take down all the praetors' documents, Cotta,
and you accept wax tablets. You are a conscientious
fellow.[d]

[d] Cotta was a *pragmaticus* (cf. 12.72). "Take down at
dictation" seems in this context the most appropriate
meaning for *persequeris* (see *OLD* s.v.). The joke is that
after filling many rolls of papyrus with these screeds, all he
gets in return is *cerae*—wax tablets, as we should say,
notebooks; cf. 14.3–9 (*SB*[1]).

89

Iuno labor, Polyclite, tuus et gloria felix,
    Phidiacae cuperent quam meruisse manus,
ore nitet tanto quanto superasset in Ide
    iudice coniunctas non dubitante deas.
5 Iunonem, Polyclite, suam nisi frater amaret,
    Iunonem poterat frater amare tuam.

90

Quid vellis vetulum, Ligeia, cunnum?
quid busti cineres tui lacessis?
tales munditiae decent puellas;
at tu iam nec anus potes videri.
5 istud, crede mihi, Ligeia, belle
non mater facit Hectoris, sed uxor.
erras si tibi cunnus hic videtur,
ad quem mentula pertinere desît.
quare, si pudor est, Ligeia, noli
10 barbam vellere mortuo leoni.

91

Omnes eunuchos habet Almo nec arrigit ipse:
    et queritur pariat quod sua Polla nihil.

89.1 tuus, Polyclite, labos *Heinsius*   4 coniunctas ς :
conuinc- *unus e familia* β : conuic- β (*deest* γ)   90.4 at
SB[1] : iam T : nam β (*deest* γ)

89

Your work and happy glory, Polyclitus, glory that
Phidias' hands would have been fain to earn, Juno
shines with a countenance that would have over-
come her fellow-goddesses on Ida—the judge[a] would
not have hesitated. If her brother[b] did not love his
own Juno, Polyclitus, her brother[c] might have loved
yours.

90

Why do you pluck your aged cunt, Ligeia? Why stir
up the ashes in your tomb? Such elegances befit
girls; but you cannot even be reckoned an old
woman any more. Believe me, Ligeia, that is a
pretty thing for Hector's wife to do, not his mother.
You are mistaken if you think this a cunt when it no
longer has anything to do with a cock. So, Ligeia,
for very shame don't pluck the beard of a dead lion.

91

Almo's household consists of eunuchs and he doesn't
rise himself; and he grumbles because his Polla
gives birth to nothing.

[a] Paris.
[b] Jupiter.
[c] As if there were two Juno's, each Jupiter's sister.

92

Marri, quietae cultor et comes vitae,
quo cive prisca gloriatur Atina,
has tibi gemellas barbari decus luci
commendo pinus ilicesque Faunorum
5   et semidocta vilici manu structas
Tonantis aras horridique Silvani,
quas pinxit agni saepe sanguis aut haedi,
dominamque sancti virginem deam templi,
et quem sororis hospitem vides castae
10 Martem, mearum principem Kalendarum,
et delicatae laureum nemus Florae,
in quod Priapo persequente confugit.
hoc omne agelli mite parvuli numen
seu tu cruore sive ture placabis;
15 'ubicumque vester Martialis est', dices,
'hac ecce mecum dextera litat vobis
absens sacerdos; vos putate praesentem
et date duobus quidquid alter optabit.'

93

Si prior Euganeas, Clemens, Helicaonis oras
    pictaque pampineis videris arva iugis,
perfer Atestinae nondum vulgata Sabinae
    carmina, purpurea sed modo culta toga.

---

[a] Martial, being about to return to Spain, commends to
Marrius the Nomentan farm, and the duty of keeping up
its sacred observances.

92

Marrius,[a] cultivator and companion of the quiet life, vaunted citizen of ancient Atina, to you I commend these twin pines, ornament of a rough copse, and the holm oaks of the Fauns, and the altars of Jupiter and bristly Silvanus constructed by my bailiff's half-skilled hand, which the blood of a lamb or kid has often bedewed, and the virgin goddess,[b] mistress of her holy shrine, and Mars, whom you see, his chaste sister's guest, ruler of my Kalends,[c] and the laurel grove of dainty Flora, into which she fled from Priapus' pursuit. All this gentle godhead of my little plot you will propitiate with blood or with incense, and say: "Wherever your Martial is now, see, by my hand he along with me makes you acceptable offering, an absent priest. Think of him as present, and give to both whatever either shall pray for."

93

Clemens, if before me you shall see Helicaon's Euganian land and the fields decked with vine-hung trellises,[d] bring to Sabina of Atesta poems not yet published, only lately embellished with their purple

[b] Diana.
[c] Of March, M.'s natal month.
[d] "*Iugum* is here the crosspiece along which vines were trained in a *vinea iugata*" (Housman, 730, with parallels).

5   ut rosa delectat metitur quae pollice primo,
      sic nova nec mento sordida charta iuvat.

94

Non mea Massylus servat pomaria serpens,
   regius Alcinoi nec mihi servit ager,
sed Nomentana securus germinat hortus
   arbore, nec furem plumbea mala timent.
5 haec igitur media quae sunt modo nata Subura
    mittimus autumni cerea poma mei.

95

Infantem tibi vir, tibi, Galla, remisit adulter.
   hi, puto, non dubie se futuisse negant.

96

Saepe loquar nimium gentes quod, Avite, remotas
   miraris, Latia factus in urbe senex,
auriferumque Tagum sitiam patriumque Salonem
   et repetam saturae sordida rura casae.
5 illa placet tellus in qua res parva beatum
    me facit et tenues luxuriantur opes:
pascitur hic, ibi pascit ager; tepet igne maligno
   hic focus, ingenti lumine lucet ibi;

---

[a] Lit. "plucked by the first thumb," apparently a careless expression.

[b] Cf. 1.66.8.

410

gown. As a rose delights us freshly plucked[a] so pleases a new sheet unsoiled by the chin.[b]

94

No Massylian snake guards my orchard,[c] nor does Alcinous' royal domain serve me; my garden with its Nomentan trees germinates in security, and its low-grade apples fear no thief. Therefore I send you these yellow fruits of my autumn, born recently in the middle of Subura.

95

Your husband, Galla, and your lover sent your baby back to you. In no uncertain manner, methinks, they deny having fucked you.[d]

96

Does it surprise you, Avitus, that I, who have grown old in Latium's city, often speak of very far-off peoples, that I thirst for gold-bearing Tagus and my native Salo, that I am going back to the rough fields of a well-stocked cottage? Give me a land where a small competence makes me wealthy and narrow means are luxury. Here the soil is supported,[e] there it supports. Here the hearth warms with a grudging fire, there it is bright with a huge blaze. Here

---

[c] I.e. unlike the garden of the Hesperides mine contains nothing of value.

[d] They had done something else; cf. 12.26 and 3.96.1.

[e] Cf. 10.58.9.

hic pretiosa fames conturbatorque macellus,
10   mensa ibi divitiis ruris operta sui;
    quattuor hic aestate togae pluresve teruntur,
      autumnis ibi me quattuor una tegit.
    i, cole nunc reges, quidquid non praestat amicus
      cum praestare tibi possit, Avite, locus.

97

Dum levis arsura struitur Libitina papyro,
    dum murram et casias flebilis uxor emit,
iam scrobe, iam lecto, iam pollinctore parato,
    heredem scripsit me Numa: convaluit.

98

Addat cum mihi Caecubum minister
Idaeo resolutior cinaedo,
quo nec filia cultior nec uxor
nec mater tua nec soror recumbit,
5   vis spectem potius tuas lucernas
aut citrum vetus Indicosque dentes?
suspectus tibi ne tamen recumbam,
praesta de grege sordidaque villa
tonsos, horridulos, rudes, pusillos
10   hircosi mihi filios subulci.
perdet te dolor hic: habere, Publi,
mores non potes hos et hos ministros.

98.11 dolor β : pudor γ

hunger is costly and the market makes men bankrupt, there the board is spread with the riches of its own countryside. Here four or more gowns wear out in a summer, there one covers me through four autumns. Go now, pay court to patrons, Avitus, when a place can provide you with all that a friend does not provide.

97

As the light pyre was a-building with soon-to-burn papyrus and his tearful wife was buying myrrh and casia,[a] when the grave and the bier and the undertaker were all in readiness, Numa wrote me down his heir. He recovered.

98

When a page more willowy than Ida's catamite[b] pours me Caecuban, groomed as smart as your daughter or your wife or your mother or your sister reclining at the table, do you want me to gaze instead at your lamps or your antique citrus wood or your Indian tusks? However, so that I am not suspect at your board, provide me with pages from the crew on your squalid farm, the close-cropped, frowzy, clownish, undersized sons of a goat-scented swineherd. This jealousy of yours will be your undoing, Publius. You cannot have such a disposition and such a staff.

[a] For embalming, according to *OLD*. Rather, to be cast on the pyre; cf. 11.54.1.

[b] Ganymede.

413

99

Si Romana forent haec Socratis ora, fuissent
    Iulius in Satyris qualia Rufus habet.

100

Quid, stulte, nostris versibus tuos misces?
cum litigante quid tibi, miser, libro?
quid congregare cum leonibus vulpes
aquilisque similes facere noctuas quaeris?
5   habeas licebit alterum pedem Ladae,
inepte, frustra crure ligneo curres.

101

Elysio redeat si forte remissus ab agro
    ille suo felix Caesare Gabba vetus,
qui Capitolinum pariter Gabbamque iocantes
    audierit, dicet: 'rustice Gabba, tace.'

102

Qua factus ratione sit requiris,
qui numquam futuit, pater Philinus?
Gaditanus, Avite, dicat istud,
qui scribit nihil et tamen poeta est.

---

[a] On a statue or bust of Socrates, who, as everyone
knew from Plato, had the face of a Satyr. If Socrates had
been a Roman, says M., his face would have figured among

99

If these features of Socrates had been Roman, they
would have been among the Satyrs, like those of
Julius Rufus.[a]

100

Fool, why do you mix your verses with mine? What
do you want, wretch, with a book at odds with itself?
Why seek to herd foxes with lions and to make owls
resemble eagles? Though you have one foot like
Ladas, it's no use, you silly man, trying to run with
a wooden leg.

101

If Gabba of old, happy in his own Caesar, were per-
chance to return, sent back from the Elysian Fields,
anybody who heard Capitolinus and Gabba jesting
together would say: "Clownish Gabba, hold your
tongue."

102

You want to know how Philinus, who never fucks,
became a father? Let Gaditanus answer that,
Avitus, who writes nothing and yet is a poet.[b]

the Satyr statues in the Portico of Octavia (Pliny *N.H.*
36.29), one of which resembled a certain Julius Rufus: *in
Satyris fuissent, qualia in Satyris habet Iulius Rufus* (cf.
SB[1]).

[b] His verses are by other people; cf. 1.72.

103

Municipes Augusta mihi quos Bilbilis acri
    monte creat, rapidis quem Salo cingit aquis,
ecquid laeta iuvat vestri vos gloria vatis?
    nam decus et nomen famaque vestra sumus,
5 nec sua plus debet tenui Verona Catullo
    meque velit dici non minus illa suum.
quattuor accessit tricesima messibus aestas,
    ut sine me Cereri rustica liba datis,
moenia dum colimus dominae pulcherrima Romae:
10   mutavere meas Itala regna comas.
excipitis placida reducem si mente, venimus;
    aspera si geritis corda, redire licet.

104

I nostro comes, i, libelle, Flavo
longum per mare, sed faventis undae,
et cursu facili tuisque ventis
Hispanae pete Tarraconis arces:
5 illinc te rota tollet et citatus
altam Bilbilin et tuum Salonem
quinto forsitan essedo videbis.
quid mandem tibi quaeris? ut sodales
paucos, sed veteres et ante brumas
10 triginta mihi quattuorque visos
ipsa protinus a via salutes,
et nostrum admoneas subinde Flavum

103.5 tenero *Heinsius*   104.9 sed ς : et βγ

103

You whom Augustan Bilbilis on her steep hill, that Salo girdles with his rapid waters, created my fellow townsmen, do you rejoice in the flourishing fame of your poet? For I am your ornament and renown and glory, nor does his Verona owe more to spare Catullus, or would wish me less to be called hers. A thirtieth summer has joined four harvests since you first gave Ceres your rustic cakes without me, while I have lived among the fair structures of imperial Rome. The realms of Italy have changed my hair. If you receive me back in kindly mood, I come; if the hearts within you are ungentle, I can return.

104

Go, little book, with my Flavus over the far-flung sea; but be the waters kind, and in an easy voyage with favoring winds make for the heights of Spanish Tarraco. Wheels will take you from there, and with rapid travel you will perhaps see lofty Bilbilis and your Salo at the fifth stage. Do you ask my commissions? Please to greet some friends fresh from the road, not many but long-standing, not seen for four and thirty winters; and remind my good Flavus

iucundos mihi nec laboriosos
secessus pretio paret salubri,
15   qui pigrum faciant tuum parentem.
haec sunt. iam tumidus vocat magister
castigatque moras, et aura portum
laxavit melior. vale, libelle:
navem, scis, puto, non moratur unus.

from time to time to find me a pleasant retreat not needing much work at a reasonable price, to make your father lazy. That's all. Now the pompous skipper is calling and berating delays and a fairer breeze has opened the harbor. Good-bye little book. You know, I think, that a ship does not wait for one passenger.